TESTAMENT
OF WAR

The purple testament of bleeding war
   Shakespeare, *Richard II*, Act III, Scene 3, l. 93

TESTAMENT OF WAR

LITERATURE, ART AND THE FIRST WORLD WAR

A. D. HARVEY

AMBERLEY

First published 2018

Amberley Publishing
The Hill, Stroud
Gloucestershire, GL5 4EP

www.amberley-books.com

Copyright © A. D. Harvey, 2018

The right of A. D. Harvey to be identified as
the Author of this work has been asserted in
accordance with the Copyrights, Designs and
Patents Act 1988.

ISBN 978 1 4456 7827 6 (paperback)
ISBN 978 1 4456 7828 3 (ebook)

British Library Cataloguing in Publication Data.
A catalogue record for this book is available
from the British Library.

Typesetting and Origination by Amberley
Publishing.
Printed in the UK.

CONTENTS

AUTHOR'S NOTE

Much of the material in this book appeared in an earlier work, *A Muse of Fire* (London, 1998), which not only discussed the development of writing about the war before 1914 in more detail but also gave an account of the literature of the Second World War. What I published two decades ago about the Second World War more or less accords with what I still think today, but the sections of *A Muse of Fire* dealing with the First World War are here presented in an extensively revised, reconsidered, amplified and updated form, with a number of factual errors belatedly corrected.

INTRODUCTION

One of my grandfathers was deaf and therefore exempted from military service when it became compulsory in Britain in 1916; the other was in the *Honvéd*, the Hungarian territorials, serving I think on the Italian front, though all that my mother remembered him saying about it was that he was now and then commanded to point his rifle over a parapet and pull the trigger. Both grandfathers died in their forties two decades before I was born, but during the summer before I started university I worked in the geriatric wards of the local psychiatric hospital with men who had lost limbs in the First World War or, in one case, had eight scars like long sunken rips in the soft parts of his flesh as a result of a shell or grenade exploding close to him; this man, already nearly thirty back in 1914, surly but normally unobtrusive, would never co-operate with being undressed for bed in the evening and it was often my job to shut myself into his room with him and forcibly remove his day clothes. Hence my acquaintance with his scars. He and the other geriatrics, fellow survivors of the war, were the ones whom, to adopt the phrasing of Laurence Binyon's poem 'To The Fallen', age had wearied and the years condemned. The most distinctive part of what now remains of the consciousness and vitality of their generation, the testimony of an ordeal that supposedly helped shape the twentieth century, is the subject of the following pages.[1]

This book is not a summary of existing scholarly literature or a bibliography, let alone an English man's riposte to American studies like Paul Fussell's *The Great War and Modern Memory* (1975), Samuel Hynes's *A War Imagined: The First World War and English Culture* (1990), or Vincent Sherry's *The Great War and The Language of Modernism* (2004). Nor is it the attempt of someone with a Ph.D in history to expropriate a subject hitherto allocated to professors of English Literature. It is merely one individual's attempt to see patterns and cross-connections in the responses of writers and artists to events that he himself had the good fortune not to have to live through.

Birth, prejudice and limited opportunities for carrying out research in libraries abroad have caused this survey to take on a predominantly British perspective but the account I have tried to give would have been meaningless without reference to the literature and art of other countries, and if at times I use foreign examples simply to back up my British material in other instances I have had to emphasize the independent trajectory of developments beyond the English Channel. Similarly I have tried to present developments in art as providing parallels with developments in literature, but more often than not have found them apparently moving in different directions.

I have generally made use of published translations of prose works originally written in other languages, when available, though a number of important texts have never been rendered into English, including F.T. Marinetti's gimmicky war sketches and Werner Beumelburg's *Die Gruppe Bosemüller* ('Bosemüller's Squad'), which sold a million copies in Germany during the Nazi period. The translations offered of poetry are my own, but as Robert Frost said, 'Poetry is what is lost in translation', and a number of passages have been printed in the original, in the belief that some readers will want to pause and read them out aloud.[2]

A much-admired article by James Campbell published in the American quarterly *New Literary History* in 1999 entitled 'Combat Gnosticism: The Ideology of First World War Criticism', complained of the equation of war with combat and 'the canonization of male war writers who not only have combat experience but represent such experience in their texts'. Both in the following pages and in the original version, published as part of my book *A Muse of Fire* the year before James Campbell's article appeared, I was quite clear about the distinction between writing about war and writing about combat, and also the distinction between writing about combat when one has not participated in it and writing about combat when one has; but it is perfectly true that I contribute to 'the canonization of male war writers who not only have combat experience but represent such experience in their texts' (though I am not sure that my treatment of, for example, Ernst Jünger is what one would normally understand by 'canonization'). I even quote combat veterans who pour scorn on writers who don't know what they are talking about. As it happens none of the authors discussed in this book wrote quite as much about the war as David Lloyd George or Winston Churchill, and from a historian's point of view none of them wrote anything to compare in importance with what Lloyd George wrote, and not all of them wrote with Churchill's literary distinction: he was the only frontline combatant from the 1914–18 war to win the Nobel Prize for Literature. But it is stretching any normal understanding of the concept of war literature as *literature* to include the memoirs of cabinet ministers alongside those of ordinary people who tried with average success to put their personal impressions into words. As for 'privileging' the experience of frontline combatants, for a critic to do anything else is to deny the validity of experience that the critic himself has not shared.[3]

Of course people far away from the fighting line in war time also have lives invaded and dominated by war: separation from loved ones, heart-ending bereavements, perhaps following one after another in stunning succession, diversion and distraction or even thwarting of career prospects, bankruptcy in the case of small businessmen, challenges to big businessmen that sometimes they fail to measure up to, physical upheaval, shortages of food and clothing, new levels of bureaucratic interference. Yet privations and hardships of this sort are of a nature belonging to civilian life, even if intensified by the economic and social conditions of wartime. It is only during the last one hundred and thirty years, with the reduction in the mortality of infectious diseases, that families in Europe have been spared the horror of family members dying in rapid successions when infectious fever invaded a household, and of course one recalls the Brontë sisters succumbing one after the other, at a more protracted but still awful rhythm, to tuberculosis. Small businessmen go bankrupt and big businessmen are supplanted in the control of their business empires also in peacetime. Wartime controls might actually help the diet of the poor, and the mass-evacuation of children from the inner-city involves much the same anguish for children of primary-school age and working-class mothers as the upper-class custom of dispatching eight-year-old boys to prep schools does for the families of the rich. The intolerable interference of incompetent officialdom does not end with the coming of peace, it merely focuses more exclusively on the vulnerable and those too poor and ill-educated to defend themselves by legal action. There are air raids of course: a Battle of Britain-era Heinkel He 111 could carry eight 550 lb bombs, each one containing at least eight times the weight of explosive of a 21 cm howitzer shell – what British soldiers of the previous generation called a Jack Johnson – and certain nights in certain parts of London in the last four months of 1940 may have been as bad as some parts of the Western Front in 1917: but nothing in civilian life corresponds to having a man holding a revolver urging one to trot or walk or crawl towards enemy machine guns and to kill anybody one meets with a bayonet or hand grenade, and the sudden elimination, day after day after day, of the co-workers and fellow-sufferers one lives amongst has had no peacetime equivalent in Britain since the great cholera epidemics of 1832, 1849 and 1853. The general apprehensiveness, the pervasive background sense of malaise, that civilians experience in wartime is of the same character but surely not of the same order of magnitude, as that felt by soldiers living in moment-by-moment expectation of annihilation, though some soldiers are so stimulated by the atmosphere of the battlefield that they come to take it as natural, and some civilians, in no personal danger, find the stress unbearable.

Quite apart from such considerations, it is the quality of the expression not the quality of the experience that makes literature. Nearly a quarter of the poets listed in Catherine Reilly's *English Poetry of the First World War: A Bibliography* (1978) were women, but who among these women wrote poetry that demands to be quoted alongside Wilfred Owen's or Isaac Rosenberg's? Perhaps the finest poet to be caught up in the Second World War was Miklós Radnóti (1909–44), who was a non-combatant: I have not found his counterpart amongst the poets of the First World War, and particularly not amongst the 532 women poets of the First World War in Catherine Reilly's bibliography. Let's face it, war is not politically correct. Other than to state that it is a bad thing it is not possible to say anything of much relevance or illumination about war that *is* politically correct. That at least is my view. I don't expect other people to share it. Despite the solipsistic artifices of latter-day Post-modernism, professional historians and critics still mostly seem to pretend that they speak not for or about themselves but on behalf of some great entity called History, or Eng. Lit., that exists outside and independent of themselves, but what they are really saying is, 'Look, I've followed the rules and the protocols, so I am not personally responsible for the results.' This is not an alibi that this particular historian/literary historian would wish to claim. I have tried to do my best with my material, but it has obviously always been a case of *me* trying and *my* angle on the literature of the 1914–18 war.[4]

All books cited were published in London unless otherwise indicated.

I

BEFORE 1914

The Renaissance is sometimes described as representing the birth of the modern, but by no means all modern ways of perceiving and doing things can be traced back to the fifteenth and sixteenth centuries. For example, neither the poets nor the artists of the time seem to have had much interest in a topic which from about 1500 onwards was both a key preoccupation of governments and an immediate concern of growing numbers of individuals. Improvements in technology and communications meant that the scale, expense and destructiveness of war grew exponentially during this period – as Albrecht Dürer said in 1527 'the necessities of war weigh more heavily and in a new manner upon our age' – yet they seem to have had little impact on the imaginations of those not directly involved.[1]

In England, Elizabethan and Jacobean playwrights and poets steered clear of contemporary themes. The most up to date Shakespeare ever got was the reign of Henry VIII, which closed seventeen years before his birth, and though George Chapman, in his tragedy *Bussy D'Amboise*, ventured down to the 1580s, not much more than twenty years earlier than the time of writing, his subject was from the history of a foreign country, and he was in any case probably much more interested in his translations of Homer. It was not that writers were totally unresponsive to contemporary

events: during the 1590s soldiers were frequently to be encountered
in the streets and taverns of London, and in *Henry V* Shakespeare
showed a convincing familiarity with their manners and habits:

> *Gower:* Why, 'tis a gull, a fool, a rogue, that now and then
> goes to the wars, to grace himself, at his return into London,
> under the form of a soldier. And such fellows are perfect in
> the great commanders' names: and they will learn you by rote
> where services are done – at such and such a sconce, at such
> a breach, at such a convoy; who came off bravely, who was
> shot, who disgraced, what terms the enemy stood on.

But apart from some coolly impersonal passages in the memoirs
of Robert Carey, Earl of Monmouth no first-hand accounts of
the campaigns against successive rebellions in Ireland or the
expeditionary forces sent to France and the Netherlands have
come down to us.[2]

Even civil war, in which entire societies were mobilized to a far
greater extent than in wars fought by professional armies deployed
by rival monarchs, only occasionally seems to have provoked the
kind of existential shock that was later almost commonplace.
George Wither, a Parliamentarian officer in the English Civil War
of the 1640s as well as a poet, wrote of

> Walks and Fields, which I have visited
> With peacefull Mates, and free from fear of harmes;
> Yea, there, where oft *Fair-Ladies* I have led,
> I now lead on, a *Troupe* of men in Armes.
> In Medowes, where our sports were wont to be,
> (And, where we playing wantonly have laine)
> Men sprawling in their blood, we now doe see,
> Grim postures, of the dying, and the slaine.

More typical of the era was Edmund Waller's poem 'Of a War
with Spain, and a Fight at Sea', published as a broadsheet

in 1658, and the passages dealing with the Second Dutch War in John Dryden's *Annus Mirabilis; the Year of Wonders, MDCLXVI*, which appeared nine years later; Dryden may have come close enough to a naval battle to perceive 'the air to break about them like the noise of distant thunders, or of swallows in a chimney: these little ululations of sound, though almost vanishing before they reached them, yet still seeming to retain somewhat of their first horrour, which they had betwixt the fleets', but his evocation of sea warfare in *Annus Mirabilis* is merely a compilation of bookish irrelevancies –

> And now, where *Patroclus* body lay,
> Here *Trojan* Chiefs advanc'd, & there the *Greeks* –

and hackneyed similes pretending real-life observation but actually entirely redolent of the library:

> So I have seen some fearful Hare maintain
> A course, till tired before the Dog she lay.[3]

Waller and Dryden became models for stay-at-home imitators. The next generation's best-known contribution to the genre was Addison's 'The Campaign' of 1704:

> With floods of gore that from the vanquished fell
> The marshes stagnate and the rivers swell
> Mountains of slain lie heaped upon the ground
> Or 'midst the roarings of the Danube drowned ...

Yet by 1780 Samuel Johnson could claim:

> Everything has its day. Through the reigns of William and Anne no prosperous event passed undignified by poetry. In the last war [1756–63], when France was disgraced and overpowered in every quarter of the globe, when Spain,

coming to her assistance, only shared her calamities, and the name of an Englishman was reverenced through Europe, no poet was heard amidst the general acclamation; the fame or our counsellors and heroes was intrusted to the Gazetteer.[4]

The celebration of warfare in eighteenth-century English literature most read today, Laurence Sterne's satirical treatment of the rambling military reminiscences of Uncle Toby in Volume One of *The Life and Opinions of Tristram Shandy* (1760), may even have served to deter veterans from setting forth their recollections:

> I must remind the reader, in case he has read the history of King William's wars, – but if he has not, – I then inform him, that one of the most memorable attacks in that siege, was that which was made by the English and Dutch upon the point of the advanced counterscarp, between the gate of St Nicolas, which inclosed the great sluice or water-stop, where the English were terribly exposed to the shot of the counter-guard and demi-bastion of St Roch ...
>
> As this was the principal attack of which my uncle Toby was an eye-witness at Namur, – the army of the besiegers being cut off, by the confluence of the Maes and Sambre, from seeing much of each other's operation, – my uncle Toby was generally more eloquent and particular in his account of it; and the many perplexities he was in, arose out of the almost insurmountable difficulties he found in telling his story intelligibly, and giving such clear ideas of the differences and distinctions between the scarp and counterscarp, – the glacis and covered-way, – the half-moon and ravelin, – as to make his company fully comprehend where and what he was about ...[5]

There was however an increasing interest – encouraged by the patronage of monarchs as different as George III and later Napoleon – in *paintings* depicting battles, and after 1800 artists frequently accompanied armies on campaign, through usually in the capacity of combatant officers. Yet the truest war artist of the period was one who never witnessed or painted a battle as such, and, as a middle-aged (almost elderly) court painter at the fuddy-duddiest court in Europe, was very far from regarding war as an attractive professional opportunity. Goya's *The Disasters of War* etchings are amongst the most striking depictions ever executed of the awfulness of war, and leave no doubt at all that he knew what it *felt* like to be a citizen of a country overrun by invaders, though the fact that the preliminary drawings for these etchings were done two years or more after the events shown raises questions about his emotional state and motivation: perhaps, after all, they were as much propaganda, though for a different type of audience, as the work of officially sponsored painters of battle like Antoine-Jean Gros or Benjamin West.[6]

Some time before Goya began preparing his war etchings Major Charles Napier of the British army's 50th Regiment of Foot was experiencing the sharp edge of war at the Battle of La Coruña. Later in life he wrote an account of his experiences which, in its patient transcription of sensations and responses, its occasional striking images and its deft sketching in of the horrors inseparable from violent death, gives as powerful a sense of the author's individuality as anything produced by the First World War more than a century later:

> about a dozen of us lodged ourselves behind this breastwork, and then it appeared to me that by a rush forward we could carry the battery above; and it was evident we must go on or go back, we could not last long where we were. Three or four men were killed at my side, for the breastwork was but a slender protection, and two were killed by the fire of our own men from the village behind. The poor fellows kept crying out as they died, Oh God! Major, our own men are killing us! Oh Christ God I'm shot in the back of the head! The last man was so, for he fell against me, and the ball had entered just above the poll. Remembering then that my father had told me he saved a man's life, at the siege

of Charleston, by pulling a ball out with his finger before inflammation swelled the parts, I thought to do the same, but could not find it, and feared to do harm by putting my finger far in. It made me feel sick, and the poor fellow being laid down, continued crying out that our men had killed him, and there he soon died.

The war (or series of wars) in which Napier fought lasted from 1792 till 1815 and Napier was yet to join the British army as an eleven-year-old subaltern when someone – not in fact a soldier but a Member of Parliament visiting the front line in Flanders – became perhaps the first person to write about war as something that one experienced *subjectively* and that might enable one to learn some sort of fundamental truth about oneself:

July 17th [1793] – Though I had thus seen the plan of the trenches, and the manner of their formation, more effectually than I could in any other way, yet I had not seen, or rather had not experienced, what was most the object of my curiosity, the situation of persons employed in doing duty there. I therefore accepted readily the offer of Major Crawford to accompany me thither the next morning. It was not without anxiety that I ventured into a situation so new and untried, as that in which I was about to enter. It was impossible to tell the effect of circumstances, which have been found occasionally to operate so strangely on minds not distinguishable beforehand from the rest of the world. How could I be certain, that the same might not happen to me, as happened to certain person, that one knows of? The result of the trial answered, I am happy to say, to my most sanguine expectations. I think, with confidence, that during any part of the time, I could have multiplied, if necessary, a sum in my head.[7]

A number of impecunious would-be poets attempted to write up the war but despite claiming first-hand experience in the armed forces they made little impact: two of the most notable, Thomas Dermody and George Woodley, were almost certainly never in a battle as such. War was still not regarded as an eligible literary theme: even contemporaries remarked on how little interest writers showed in the war:

> There is no point in which our age differs from those which preceded it, than in the apparent apathy of our poets and rhymers to the events which are passing over them ... some of them roam back to distant and dark ages: others wander to remote countries, instead of seeking a theme in the exploits of a Nelson, an Abercromby, or a Wellesley; others amuse themselves with luscious sonnets to Bessies and Jessies; and all seem so little to regard the crisis in which we are placed, that we cannot help thinking they would keep fiddling their allegros and adagios, even if London was on fire, or Buonaparte landed at Dover.

As a later commentator was to point out, 'it does not seem to have occurred to any young lady of that time to ask Scott, Wordsworth or Jane Austen what they were doing during the war.'[8]

The recollections of the few enthusiasts for the war probably exaggerate the degree to which opportunities for military adventure were welcomed. Someone who was a schoolboy in 1808 later recorded:

> Every boy at school was ardently looking forward to the time when he should be old enough to join either the Army or the Navy. The patriotic enthusiasm which had been excited throughout Great Britain by the threatened invasion of the French, under Bonaparte, was scarcely subsided, and was kept alive by the accounts which were constantly reaching England of fresh triumphs of our arms both by sea and land. In short, the profession of arms, both Naval and Military, was highly popular; and the sons of the noblemen and gentlemen of Great Britain were eagerly entering both services.

Yet other sources provide little confirmation of this. There do not seem to have been many men like George Robert Gleig, later famous as author of that dull novel *The Subaltern*, who at the age of fifteen interrupted his studies at Balliol to join the 85th Foot. It is noteworthy that, in contrast to the dreadful slaughter of graduates in the twentieth-century world wars commemorated on memorial plaques in every Oxford and Cambridge college, only two Oxbridge men died in battle during the entire 1792–1815 period: the Hon. Edward Meade of Wadham, who was killed at the head of the flank company of the 40th Foot at the Aboukir landing on 8 March 1801, and Charles Taylor of Christ Church, lieutenant colonel in the 20th Light Dragoons, killed at Vimeiro: another Oxford man, W.G. Browne, and the Rev. Joseph Richard Turner of Gonville and Caius College, Cambridge, were murdered by brigands on the Continent during the war years, in separate incidents, which suggests that a certain class of Briton found the war no more dangerous than foreign holidays.[9]

We unfortunately have no record of the private opinions of the man who may well be the period's unique instance of someone sacrificing a successful career in order to take part in the war. In 1804 the Rev. George Grigby, Dean of Chapel at Caius and formerly headmaster of the Perse School, bought a commission in the 1st Dragoons, despite the prejudice against clergymen bearing arms. Later he transferred to the 11th Foot as a captain, and was drowned with 233 others off Falmouth when a Royal Navy frigate rammed the transport vessel carrying him and his troops towards the theatre of war in Spain.[10]

The problem with explaining writers' relative indifference to the war simply in terms of their membership of a social class that was able to avoid having anything to do with the fighting is that, though there was no conscription in Britain other than to the militia, which did not serve abroad, military service was obligatory for men of all social classes in France and parts of Italy and Germany, and substitutes willing to take one's place in the ranks were much harder to find and thus relatively much more expensive than militia substitutes in Britain: yet apart from a passage describing the Battle of Waterloo in Stendhal's novel *La Chartreuse de Parme* one looks in vain for prose and poetry in French, Italian and German that has anything to say about the war that is not being said, and more frequently, in English. Stendhal, who was in action as a cavalry officer in Italy in 1800 and 1801, recalled thirty-six years later that coming under fire for the first time was 'the *sublime*, yet a little too close to danger. Instead of pure enjoyment, the soul was still a little bit concerned with holding itself steady', but he hastened to point out 'all the fine reflections of this sort belong to 1836; I would have been greatly astonished by them in 1800.' The battle he chose to describe in *La Chartreuse de Parme* was in any case one that had taken place when he was hundreds of miles away; nevertheless his account of his youthful protagonist's baptism of fire was one that was to influence even Tolstoy:

Suddenly they all moved off at full gallop. A few minutes later Fabrizio saw, twenty paces ahead of him, a ploughed field the surface of which was moving in a singular fashion. The furrows were full of water and the soil, very damp, which formed the ridges between these furrows kept flying off in little black lumps three or four feet into the air. Fabrizio noticed as he passed this curious effect; then his thoughts turned to dreaming of the Marshal and his glory. He heard a sharp cry close to him; two hussars fell struck by shot; and, when he looked back at them, they were already twenty paces behind the escort. What seems to him horrible was a horse streaming with blood that was struggling on the ploughed land, its hooves caught in its own entrails; it was trying to follow the others: its blood ran down into the mire.

'Ah! So I am under fire at last!' he said to himself. 'I have seen shots fired!' he repeated with a sense of satisfaction. 'Now I am a real soldier.' At that moment, the escort began to go hell for leather, and our hero realised that it was shot from the guns that was making the earth fly up all round him. He looked vainly in the direction from which the balls were coming, he saw the white smoke of the battery at an enormous distance, and, in the thick of the steady and continuous rumble produced by the artillery fire, he seemed to hear shots discharged much closer at hand: he could not understand in the least what was happening.

One notes however that this was not published till 1839, nearly four decades after Stendhal's own combat experience.[11]

After Napoleon's defeat at Waterloo, at a not inconvenient distance for tourists from England, several poets rushed to the scene with the object of producing remunerative literary masterpieces. (One may see in this a belated revival of the original emergence in Britain, back in Addison's day, of the idea that war was at least a *marketable* literary subject.) Foremost amongst the poets who travelled to Belgium was Walter Scott, whose *The Field of Waterloo* was a reversion to his earlier *Marmion* style:

In one dark torrent broad and strong,
The advancing onset roll'd along,
Forth harbinger'd by fierce acclaim,
That from the shroud of smoke and flame,
Peal'd wildly the imperial name.

Another poet who visited the site of the battle was Robert Southey, who in his earlier, francophile years had published an anti-war poem that is still anthologized today:

It was a summer evening,
Old Kaspar's work was done,
And he before his cottage door
Was sitting in the sun;
And by him sported on the green
His little grandchild Wilhelmine.

She saw her brother Peterkin
Roll something large and round
Which he beside the rivulet
In playing there had found;
He came to ask what he had found
That was so large and smooth and round.

Old Kaspar took it from the boy
Who stood expectant by;
And then the old man shook his head,
And with a natural sigh
'Tis some poor fellow's skull,' said he,
Who fell in the great victory.'

'I find them in the garden,
For there's many here about;
And often when I go to plough
The ploughshare turns them out.
For many thousand men', said he,
'Were slain in that great victory.'[12]

When, seventeen years after publishing these verses, Southey had his first experience of a recent battlefield, he must have been surprised by how reminiscent it was of the picture he had suggested:

The ground is ploughed and sown, and grain and flowers and seeds already growing over the field of battle, which is still strewn with vestiges of the slaughter, caps, cartridges, boxes, hats, &c. We picked up some French cards and some bullets, and we purchased a French pistol and two of the eagles which the infantry wear upon their caps. What I felt upon this ground, it would be difficult to say; what I saw, and still more what I heard, there is no time at present for saying. In prose and in verse you shall some day hear the whole. At Les Quatre Bras, I saw two graves, which probably the dogs or

the swine had opened. In the one were the ribs of a human
body, projecting through the mould; in the other, the whole
skeleton exposed. Some of our party told me of a third, on
which the worms were at work, but I shrank from the sight.

In his *The Poet's Pilgrimage to Waterloo* it was the rubbish left
behind by battle which inspired perhaps his most memorable stanza:

> Some marks of wreck were scattered all around,
>   As shoe, and belt, and broken bandoleer,
> And hats which bore the mark of mortal wound;
>   Gun-flints and balls for those who closelier peer;
> And sometimes did the breeze upon its breath
> Bear from ill covered graves a taint of death.

Viewing the scene three months after the battle, he found only one
trace of blood, in a farm building, but that one trace was striking
enough:

> One streak of blood upon the wall was traced,
>   In length a man's just stature from the head;
> There where it gushed you saw it uneffaced:
>   Of all the blood which on that day was shed
> This mortal stain alone remained impressed...
> The all-devouring earth had drunk the rest.

One almost wishes Wordsworth, who attended the same victory
celebration as Southey on the summit of Skiddaw, could have seen
it, and written about it: he did not visit the battlefield till 1820 and
his principal poetic achievement in 1815 was 'Artegal and Elidure',
a poem based on a story in Geoffrey of Monmouth and composed
'as a token of affectionate respect for the memory of Milton'.
Perhaps it was not entirely an accident that at the festivities on
Skiddaw he knocked over the boiling water needed for the punch
'and thought to slink off undiscovered'.[13]

The uninterrupted years of peace in Europe that followed Waterloo made the idea of a really big war seem more interesting than it had appeared at the time. One symptom of this was the stream of memoirs and reminiscences that began to issue from the presses, and continued, sons publishing their fathers' manuscripts, right up until the breakout of the First World War, and beyond. William Matthews's *British Autobiographies* (Berkeley, 1955), under the index entry for the Napoleonic and Peninsular Wars, lists eighty-seven journals and memoirs by army personnel alone, including one by James Hope, *The Military Memoirs of an Infantry Officer*, that anticipates the title of Siegfried Sassoon's First World War classic. More have been published since the 1950s. There are also a number of unpublished items in the National Army Museum and other archive depositories which appear to have been written with eventual publication in mind. Although the population of Britain in 1810 was perhaps twice what it was in 1640 (though not proportionately much more literate), a larger percentage of the population saw action in the Civil War than in the campaigns against Napoleon, it being in the nature of civil war that the same society provides both armies: more Britons fought at Marston Moor that at Waterloo. The fact that the later conflict produced at least five times more personal memoirs reflects a change in sensibility, not in population statistics. This memoir-writing by other than generals, incidentally, was mainly a British phenomenon: eight of Napoleon's marshals died by violence, six wrote memoirs; of Britain's senior commanders only Sir John Moore even left a diary; but the French have little more than the *Mémoires de Robert Guillemard, sergent en retraite* (Paris, 1826) and Sergeant Bourgogne's *Mémoires de la campagne de Russie en 1812* (Valenciennes, 1856) to match the scores of memoirs written by men who served in the lower ranks of the British army.[14]

Charles Napier's account of the Battle of La Coruña quoted above was a one-off of a few pages, and none of the book length memoirs of the war are of a quality to be compared with the best personal accounts of the 1914–18 war. Occasionally one comes across a bizarre or horrific detail that sticks in the memory:

> A tall athletic soldier of the 52d lay amongst the dead at the foot of the breach, on his back; his arms and legs being at their full extent. The top of his head, from the forehead to the back part of his skull, was split in twain, and the cavity of the head entirely emptied of brains, as if a hand-grenade had exploded within, and expanded the skull, till it had forced it into a separation with the parts ragged like a saw, leaving a gaping aperture nine inches in length, and four in breadth. For a considerable time I looked on his horrible fracture, to define, if possible, by what missile or instrument so wonderful a wound could have been made; but without being able to come to any conclusion as to the probable cause.

Or, a little less gruesome, an artillery officer's account of his efforts to persuade his men to hold their fire while being shot at by French cavalry skirmishers riding forty yards away:

> Seeing some exertion beyond words necessary for this purpose, I leaped my horse up the little bank, and began a promenade (by no means agreeable) up and down our front, without even drawing my sword, though these fellows were within speaking distance of me. This quieted my men; but the tall blue gentlemen, seeing me thus dare them, immediately made a target of me, and commenced a very deliberate practice, to show us what very bad shots they were and verify the old artillery proverb, 'The nearer the target, the safer you are'. One fellow certainly made me flinch, but it was a miss; so I shook my finger at him, and called him *coquin*, etc. The rogue grinned as he reloaded, and again took aim. I certainly felt rather foolish at that moment, but was ashamed, after such bravado, to let him see it, and therefore continued my promenade. As if to prolong my torment, he was a terrible

time about it. To me it seemed an age. Whenever I turned, the muzzle of his infernal carbine still followed me. At length bang it went, and whiz came the ball close to the back of my neck, and at the same instant down dropped the leading driver of one of my guns (Miller), into whose forehead the cursed missile had penetrated.

At their best such accounts are examples of the painstaking fidelity to detail which became part of the nineteenth century's literary and artistic ideal: but fidelity to detail in itself does not constitute literature.[15]

The only known instance of a participant in the wars trying, long afterwards, to write a great work of art on the subject was an unfortunate Waterloo veteran who, out of admiration for Tennyson's ode on the death of Wellington, brought him 'twelve large cantos' on the Battle of Waterloo. 'The veteran had actually taught himself in his old age to read and write that he might thus commemorate Wellington's great victory', recorded the laureate's son. 'The epic lay for some time under the sofa in my father's study, and was a source of much anxiety to him.' Tennyson finally told the old soldier, when he called to collect his manuscript, 'Though great images loom here and there, your poem could not be published as a whole.'[16]

Perhaps the most popular – certainly the most widely disseminated – branch of writing to come out of the Napoleonic War was the swashbuckling tale of derring-do in the Royal Navy, in which authors like Frederick Chamier, Edward Howard and above all Frederick Marryat had served, in accordance with the conventions of the day, when little more than children. Judging by the results, spending one's teens on active service as probably not the best means of fostering a literary sensibility, especially when Smollett's *Roderick Random* and John Davis's *The Post-Captain* (a best-selling novel published in 1806 which chiefly deals with the flirtations of socially inept naval officers) provided the most obvious literary models. It may be no coincidence that Edward John Trelawny, the most talented of the striplings who served in the Royal Navy after Trafalgar and lived to write about it, took an early opportunity to desert and, according to his own account, become a pirate: amongst his later exploits were supervising the cremation of Shelley's body on an Italian beach and, two years later, arriving at Missolonghi too late to see Lord Byron die, but in time to sneak a look at the feet of his corpse to check out the precise nature of their much-canvassed deformity. And one of the most popular of the naval adventure yarns, Michael Scott's *Tom Cringle's Log* (1834) was written by a man whose only experience of seafaring was the several Atlantic crossings he made between 1806 and 1822 in the course of pursuing his business interests in Jamaica.[17]

At least Michael Scott had been on the high seas during the war. Charles Lever, who wrote the nineteenth century's most popular novel of the army side of the struggle against Napoleon, *Charles O'Malley*, was aged nine at the time of Waterloo, and James Grant, author of *the Romance of War: or The Highlanders in Spain*, though able to draw on the reminiscences of his father, who had served in the Peninsula as an officer in a Scottish regiment, was not born till a year after Napoleon's death, as was Emile Erckmann, the elder of the two co-authors of the most popular French novel about the Napoleonic War, *Histoire d'un conscrit de 1813* (1864).

Marryat's *Frank Mildmay* (1829), *Peter Simple* (1834) and *Mr Midshipman Easy* (1836), Frederick Chamier's *The Arethusa* (1837) and *Tom Bowling* (1841), and Edward Howard's *Rattlin the Reefer* (1836) present a curious literary irony. The post-war years coincided with the growing fame of Goethe's *Wilhelm Meister*, the archetypal *Bildungsroman*, that is to say a novel dealing (at a significantly more reflective level than, for example, works like *Tom Jones*) with the developing self-awareness and individuation of a young man at the outset of his career. From the time of Stephen Crane's *The Red Badge of Courage* onward the *Bildungsroman* was to be one of the most enduring influences on novels and memoirs dealing with war service. One can already see

elements of the *Wilhelm Meister* tradition in an insipid novel of
army life, *The Youth and Manhood of Cyril Thornton* by Thomas
Hamilton, a Peninsular veteran, published in 1827, four years after
the appearance of what is generally considered the first British
Bildungsroman, John Gibson Lockhart's *Reginald Dalton*, which,
not untypically, deals with the completely civilian preoccupations
of an undergraduate at Oxford about the time of the Battle of
Salamanca. But the war novels of Marryat, Chamier and Howard,
in which young boys are sent to sea and in the course of a brutal
introduction to the most horrific aspects of real life achieve such
personal maturity as they are capable of, represent a kind of
Bildungsroman without Goethe's intellectual and psychological
pretensions, and without much sign of his influence. The following
was written, more than a quarter of a century after the event, by a
man who, as a fourteen-year-old midshipman, commanded more
than forty men operating a battery of 32-pounders on the lower
deck of HMS *Defence*, at the Battle of the First of June:

> After the two or three first broadsides, I became anxious
> to have a good view of the ship we were engaging. To
> effect this object, I requested the man at the foremost gun
> to allow me a few seconds, when the port was hauled up,
> to look out from it. They complied with my wishes. The
> gun being loaded, I took my station in the centre of the
> port; which being held up, I beheld our antagonist firing
> away at us in quick succession. The ship was painted a
> dark red, as most of the enemy's Fleet were, to denote (as
> previously mentioned) their sanguinary feelings against
> their adversaries. I had not enjoyed the sight long – only a
> few seconds – when a rolling sea came in and completely
> covered me. The tars, noticing this, instantly let down the
> port, but I got a regular soaking for my curiosity. The men
> cheered me, and laughingly said, 'We hope, Sir, you will not
> receive further injury. It is rather warm work here below:
> the salt water will keep you cool.'

One of these, John Polly, of very short stature, remarked that he was so small the shot would all pass over him. The words had not been long out of his mouth when a shot cut his head right in two, leaving the tip of each ear remaining on the lower part of the cheek. His sudden death created a sensation among his comrades, but the excitement of the moment soon changed those impressions to others of exertion. There was no withdrawing from our situation, and the only alternative was to face the danger with becoming firmness. The head of this unfortunate seaman was cut so horizontally that anyone looking at it would have supposed it had been done by the blow of an axe. His body was committed to the deep.

'The only alternative was to face the danger with becoming firmness.' Indeed: and the midshipman, as the officer in charge of men twice or three times his age, had to lead by example. He may even have given the order for committing John Polly's body to the deep, which presumably consisted of bundling his corpse out through the gun port prior to running out the gun for another salvo: he was certainly standing there when it was done. The reason why he says nothing of his own feelings, other than his curiosity, was at least partly that he had had to learn not to have any: and Marryat and Chamier had been trained in the same school.[18]

Novels by British writers were immensely popular in the U.S.A. and may have helped prepare the way for contemporary warfare emerging as a key literary theme during the American Civil War of 1861–5. The War between the States produced the first mass-selling (not merely best-selling) war book and the first anthology of war poetry but turned out to have little appeal to the best writers of the war generation. Herman Melville remained silent during the war, and his 1866 collection of poems, *Battle Pieces and Aspects of the War*, lacked both originality and conviction. Walt Whitman's war poems were later to be extravagantly admired by Isaac Rosenberg, one of the greatest of First World War poets – he told a friend,

'Walt Whitman in "Beat, drums, beat", has said the noblest thing on war':

Beat, beat! Drums – blow! Bugles! blow!
Through the window – through the doors – burst like a
   ruthless force
Into the solemn church, and scatter the congregation.

But it is arguable that this poem and its companion pieces were not up to the standard of Whitman's original *Leaves of Grass* collection of 1855. Bret Harte stayed in California, well away from the war, and Mark Twain, having joined a volunteer company that almost immediately fell apart, beat a hasty retreat to Nevada. Ambrose Bierce was an officer in the Federal Army and eventually published a number of stories derived from his experiences, but the authentic voice of the young Bierce – still a teenager when the war began – seems to have become quite lost under what he felt proper to add in the years that intervened between soldiering and writing, as if the incidents of the war itself had been insufficiently striking.[19]

It was an author now comparatively little known, Joshua Chamberlain, who wrote of the American Civil War in a way that most closely adumbrates the preoccupations of authors who fought in and wrote about the 1914–18 War, though his account of 'battles, horrible scenes, shocking to the senses, burrowing in memory, to live again in dreams and haunting visions', did not in fact appear in print till the second year of the Great War. Chamberlain, a former professor of Modern Languages at Bowdoin College who as Colonel of the 20th Maine Infantry at Gettysburg won the Congressional Medal of Honor and was said to be the last Civil War veteran to die as a result of wartime injuries was also probably the first veteran to reflect in what one might have thought a twentieth-century way, on an issue that was to be frequently canvassed in connection with the twentieth-century world wars:

Curious people often ask the question whether in battle we are not affected by fear, so that our actions are influenced by it: and some are prompt to answer, 'Yes, surely we are, and anybody who denies it is a braggart or a liar.' I say to such, 'Speak for yourself.' A soldier has something else to think about. Most men at the first, or at some tragic moment, are aware of the present peril, and perhaps flinch a little by an instinct of nature and sometimes accept the foregoing confession, – as when I have seen men pin their names to their breasts that they may not be buried unknown. But any action following the motive of fear is rare, – for sometimes I have seen men rushing to the front in a terrific fire, 'to have it over with.'

But, as a rule, men stand up from one motive or another – simple manhood, force of discipline, pride, love, or bond of comradeship – 'Here is Bill; I will go or stay where he does.' And an officer is so absorbed by the sense of responsibility for his men, for his cause, or for the fight that the thought of personal peril has no place whatever in governing his actions. The instinct to seek safety is overcome by the instinct of honor.[20]

More typical of the period was a poem which later suggested the title of the English translation of Erich Maria Remarque's First World War classic *Im Westen Nichts Neues*; and which though written by a woman from New York state was otherwise chiefly notable for the number of men – especially Southerners – who claimed to be its author:

All quiet along the Potomac, they say,
    Except here and there a stray picket
Is shot, as he walks on his beat to and fro,
    By a rifleman hid in the thicket.
'Tis nothing, a private or two now and then,
    Will not count in the news of the battle.

Not an officer lost, only one of the men
   Moaning out all alone the death-rattle.[21]

The Franco-German War of 1870 produced nothing of much more interest though Paul Derouléde, who had been captured by the Prussians but escaped, and was later wounded fighting against the Commune, enjoyed a huge popular success – forty-nine editions 1872–8 – with his *Chants du soldat*. The best of the writers to deal with the war either had been on the sidelines or else, like Maupassant (who had been in the fighting) took an onlooker's point of view, as in his short story 'Boule de Suif', which deals with the aftermath of defeat. Zola's *Débâcle*, and *La bête humaine* with its unforgettable final image of the driverless troop train – 'a blind, deaf beast, unleashed amidst death, it rolled on and on, loaded with cannon fodder, with soldiers dazed with exhaustion, drink and singing' – dealt with the war as only a single part of the huge canvas of his twenty-volume Rougon-Macquart series. The best-known German novels about the war, published not long before the First World War, were by Walter Bloem, who was a toddler at the time of the events he described in *Das eiserne Jahr* and *Volk wider Volk*: in 1914 he served as a frontline officer in the invasion of Belgium and finally discovered what it was like to be shot at, noting ruefully: 'How many times had I not experienced all this in my imagination during the writing of those war-novels, and yet now, just this one time, I was asked to believe it to be solid fact.'[22]

In Britain the incessant warfare on the frontiers of the expanding Empire and the increasing circulation of daily and weekly newspapers fostered the growth of public interest in military affairs. During the 1850s rifle clubs began to be formed on a semi-military basis and in 1859, when war broke out between France and Austria, the British middle classes' new enthusiasm for military training expressed itself in the formation of training corps at the universities and public schools, and the establishment of Volunteer units in cities and towns up and down the country: by

1861 there were 140,100 volunteers classed as militarily efficient, and by 1901 the figure had risen to 281,000. Nevertheless the outbreak of the Boer War – actually the *second* Boer War – in 1899 produced no real counterpart of the mad rush to enlist that was to be seen in 1914, and the best book about war by a participant, Deneys Reitz's *Commando*, was actually written by a Boer, and was not published till 1929.[23]

At least the Boer War helped prepare little boys in Britain for what lay ahead of them in 1914: 'I had played at "fighting the Boers" in the nursery,' recalled Charles Carrington in his First World War memoirs. But there was also a growing assumption that sooner or later there would be a great European war, and the sheer vigour of the organizational effort put into the conscription system abroad, and the Volunteer movement in Britain after 1859, must have encouraged some people to see war as something to hope for, or to dread: in 1871, shortly after France's defeat by the German states, an Indian Army officer named G.T. Chesney published a story about a successful German invasion of England entitled 'The Battle of Dorking' in *Blackwood's Magazine*. As a sixpenny pamphlet it sold 80,000 copies in a month and set a fashion for novels like the anonymous *The Invasion of 1883* (1876), *The Invasion of 1910* (1906), by William Le Queux, and *The Invasion That Did Not Come Off* (1909), by Napier Hawke. P.G. Wodehouse parodied the genre in *The Swoop! or How Clarence Saved England: A Tale of the Great Invasion* (1909). Military themes also found favour in the growing market for juvenile literature. George Alfred Henty, who had served in the hospital commissariat of the British army in the Crimea, and of the Sardinian army in the war against Austria in 1859, became almost a household name and made a better income than the Chief Paymaster and the Chief Accountants at the War Office with his adventure stories about the wars of previous centuries. He occasionally treated some comparatively recent British imperial triumph and as the years passed his novels followed ever closer on the heels of the mayhem they romanticized: *For Name and Fame: or Through the Afghan Passes* (1885) and

The Dash for Khartoum: A Tale of the Nile Expedition (1891) both appeared half-a-dozen years after the events that inspired them, whereas *With Buller in Natal; or, A Born Leader* (1900) and *With Roberts to Pretoria: A Tale of the South African War* (1901) were almost as up to date as the newspapers.[24]

Henty himself had seen a fair amount of action as a young man: following his official employment in the Crimea and in Italy, he had been with the Austrian fleet at the Battle of Lissa in 1866 as a newspaper correspondent and in the same capacity accompanied Sir Robert Napier's invasion of Abyssinia in 1867. (This, incidentally, was the first British campaign to be commemorated by a systematic Official History.) As the titles of so many of his books imply, he regarded it as a worthwhile object in a war simply to be there and see it for oneself. From the Crimean War onward newspapers began employing people like Henty to be on the spot to write up what they saw for the benefit of their steadily expanding readership. The idea of war as a unique personal experience was also to be found, in a more self-conscious form, in *The Red Badge of Courage* (1895) by the American novelist Stephen Crane (who did not himself experience action till more than two years after his book was written). The notion that personal sensations were something inexpressibly important, the very essence of the uniqueness of one's individuality, derived of course from Romantic poetry, but the assumption that the more intense the sensations, the more inexpressibly precious they would be took on a particular colouring from the Romantics' fascination with the exotic and the historically remote. As early as the 1850s Tennyson had hailed the outbreak of the Crimean War as an escape from the narrowness and moral abdications of a hum-drum present:

> many a darkness into the light shall leap
> And shine in the sudden making of splendid names,
> And noble thought be freer under the sun,
> And the heart of a people beat with one desire.

The growth of the Volunteer movement in Britain coincided with an extraordinary revival of interest in what was perhaps the most insubstantial and tantalizing aspect of medieval culture: chivalry. Knights in armour, whether or not tended by glamorous Burne-Jones maidens or bearing the tokens of latter-day Guineveres, provided much of the Volunteer movement's iconography. Military training was not merely fresh air and fun, it was fellowship with King Arthur and the Knights of the Round Table; both the militarism and the medieval trappings were a symptom of a revolt against being born in what William Morris called 'a dull time oppressed with bourgeoisdom and philistinism'. The Romance of War was to a large extent a late nineteenth-century discovery: which was to carry almost a whole generation through Gallipoli and the Battle of Loos, before withering under the machine guns of the Somme:

> Here lies a clerk who half his life had spent
> Toiling at ledgers in a city grey,
> Thinking that so his days would drift away
> With no lance broken in life's tournament:
> Yet ever 'twixt the books and his bright eyes
> The gleaming eagles of the legions came,
> And horsemen, charging under phantom skies,
> Went thundering past beneath the oriflamme.
>
> And now those waiting dreams are satisfied;
> From twilight to the halls of dawn he went;
> His lance is broken; but he lies content
> With that high hour, in which he lived and died.
> And falling thus, he wants no recompense,
> Who found his battle in the last resort;
> Nor needs he any hearse to bear him hence,
> Who goes to join the men of Agincourt.[25]

Not everyone was taken in by these fantasies of course. The Russo-Japanese War of 1904–5, with its battles 'engaging half a million men on fronts of sixty miles, struggles lasting for weeks, flaming up fierily and dying away from sheer exhaustion, to flame up again in desperate persistence and end – as we have seen them end more than once – not from the victor obtaining a crushing advantage, but through the mortal weariness of the combatants', had provided a warning of what was to come.[26]

Wilhelm Lamszus's *Der Menschenschlachthaus: Bilder vom kommenden Krieg* published in 1912 – the English edition of 1913 was entitled *The Human Slaughterhouse (Scenes from the War that is to Come)* – became an international best-seller. Though reminiscent of Crane's *The Red Badge of Courage*, with its naïve youth goggle-eyed at his first experience of battle, it gave more emphasis to the confusion and, especially, the horrors of modern warfare. It is in fact the first programmatic anti-war novel. The author, born in 1881, had no personal experience of warfare but his evocation of its darker side was so convincing that his book sold even better in Germany after the outbreak of war in 1914 than before it: 23,000 copies sold by 1913, 75,000 by 1923. (The British Library's 1913 paperback edition of the English translation announces on the cover '100,000 copies sold' but this seems to refer to world sales.) There seems to have been no French translation, the French apparently preferring a work in a quite contrary vein, Ernest Psichari's novel *L'appel des armes* (1913) in which a teacher's son revolts against the values of his anti-militarist father, joins a colonial regiment, and learns that the army is the incarnation of the eternal France, and that war is the most divine of the divine things left to us, the most clearly marked with the hallmark of the divine (*'du sceau divin'*). Psichari, a professional officer in the artillery, was killed in the first month of the world war, before he had a chance to reconsider his ideas.

The works of Stephen Crane, Wilhelm Lamszus and Ernest Psichari are part of the reason why literary young men had different expectations of war in 1914 from those detectable amongst writers in 1793, but an even greater influence – one that in fact dated from the decade of the American Civil War, though it was still in the process of being assimilated by western literary culture at the end of the century – was that of Leo Tolstoy's 587,000-word novel *War and Peace*.[27]

As a young man Tolstoy had been an officer in the Russian army and during the Crimean War had been part of the garrison of Sevastopol during its siege by the French and British. The Crimean War gave the Charge of the Light Brigade, Florence Nightingale and 'the thin red line' to British folklore but seems to have had little significant impact on the literary imagination of anyone in the invading armies. For Tolstoy however the war was a major factor in his development as a writer. Though a lover of books – he claimed Homer's poetry and Goethe's *Hermann und Dorothea* had had 'very great influence on him' – he also thoroughly enjoyed military life in wartime, noting in his diary during the twenty-seventh week of the siege of Sevastopol, 'The constant charm of danger and my observations of the soldiers I am living with, the sailors and the very methods of war are so pleasant that I don't want to leave here, especially as I would like to be present at the assault, if there is one.' One of his earliest stories, 'The Raid', describing a volunteer's first experience of war in the Caucasus, had also been one of the earliest *Bildungsroman*-type treatments of war. The sketches he wrote during the siege of Sevastopol show that he already had an eye for the disconcerting, and possibly symbolic, contrasts that war throws up, as in the conclusion of the first of these sketches: 'The sound of an old waltz played by a military band on the boulevard is borne along the water and seems, in some strange way, answered by the firing from the bastions.' This corresponds with a passage in his diary: 'The sun was already setting behind the English batteries, puffs of smoke were rising here and there and shots could be heard ... on the Grafskaya pier music was playing and the sounds of trumpets and a familiar tune drifted across.' Some of the incidental details in *War and Peace* also seem to be transcriptions of actual experience: the 'strange acid smell of saltpetre and blood' on the battlefield, for example, or the army surgeon 'holding a cigar between thumb and little finger of one of his bloodstained hands so as not to smear it'.[28]

Tolstoy also learnt from others – notably Stendhal. In 1901 he told a French visitor:

> I am more indebted to him than to anyone else: I owe it to him that I have understood war. Reread the account of the Battle of Waterloo in *The Charterhouse of Parma*. Who before him had described war like that, that is to say, like it really it is? ... Later, in the Caucasus my brother, an officer before I was, confirmed the accuracy of Stendhal's descriptions ... A little later, in the Crimea, I had only to look to see it with my own eyes. But, I repeat, in everything I know of war, Stendhal was my first teacher.

Yet in spite of this compliment to Stendhal, *War and Peace* was an avowedly chauvinistic work, full of jibes at the French and the Germans. Tolstoy's western European readers overlooked this aspect, or took it in their stride as splashings of Russian local colour. A case can be made for arguing that wars directed and managed by political systems dominated by the upper class, as before 1815, produced far less literature than wars directed and managed by political systems dominated by the middle class, as after 1914. The career of the aristocratic Tolstoy, as the greatest individual influence on war literature in the period of apparent transition between upper-class and middle-class dominated political systems, suggests the limitations of this kind of sociology; perhaps what was developing was not so much a new class system but, out of the old class system, a new idea of classlessness, of citizens equal in their obligation to serve and to risk their all for the collective. Tolstoy would fit in better with that view of what was happening. On the other hand, his nationalism suggests some sort of common ground with Deroulède and Henty, and the enthusiasts who founded the University Rifle Volunteers in Oxford. The rise of European nationalism was so strongly involved with the rise of the middle class that it is easy to assume that the processes were identical, or organically connected; but the social and ideological roots of nationalism in Russia do not seem to have been at all the same as in Britain and France: the fact is we are still a very long way from possessing a unified field theory of historical change that will enable us to make a neat expository package of such relationships.[29]

What one can see in the later nineteenth century is the accumulation of materials for a tradition of writing about war such as did not exist a century earlier. It may be that the real input did not relate primarily to war at all. The increasingly egalitarian and democratic nature of western society in the later nineteenth century sponsored the evolution both of a more realistic, naturalistic literature dealing with the real lives of real people and, by a complex reflex, also of a tradition of romantic evasion and chivalrous fantasy. Opposing tendencies reinforced one another. Romanticism had legitimized subjectivism in literature but had not made it compulsory to go off into odd corners of the world in order to experience the unique: but exploration of odd corners was precisely what was encouraged by the nineteenth century's growing list of true-life adventure stories. What one sees in the nineteenth century is not so much the growth of war literature as a kind of traditional discourse, but the maturing of all its potential ingredients. By 1914 one could have said that all that was needed to carry the tradition forward was a really big war for people to write about.

And at the beginning of August 1914 just such a war broke out.

2

POETS

First some facts and figures. No other commonly shared but essentially objective and external experience has generated anything like the quantity of poetry, fiction and reminiscences inspired by the two world wars of the twentieth century. Léon Riegel notes that the New York Public Library's *Subject Catalog of the World War I Collection*, dating from 1961, lists 1,350 novels 'mainly in English'. First-hand nonfiction accounts of the war are probably equally numerous: Jean Norton Cru's *Témoins*, an analysis of eye-witness accounts of the First World War published in French, which appeared in 1929 at a time when many such testimonies were still to appear, deals with the work of forty-nine novelists and 202 authors of memoirs, journals, letters and reflections. In 1919 Edmund Gosse estimated that 500 volumes of war poetry had been published in Britain between August 1914 and November 1918: the British Museum's *Subject Index of the Books Relating to the European War, 1914–1918 Acquired by the British Museum, 1914–1920* only lists a few more than 200, but it is evident that a large number of volumes printed for private circulation or issued by small provincial publishers never reached the British Museum. Gosse's figure may even be an underestimate: *Whitaker's Almanack* states that the number of volumes in the poetry and drama category published in 1911 alone was 538, and the war seems to have affected the subject-matter of poetry rather than altered the quantity being produced. In 1917 William Hudson thought for some reason that not enough verse was being written and produced some doggerel entitled 'Why Are the Poets Silent?':

Why is the harp untouched, the singer dumb...?
Bards hear not poesy in German hate,
Or Belgian massacre, or French death-pain,
Or British anguish, or aught of the fate
Endured in battle-trenches.

But in the following year William S. Murphy expressed what was probably a juster view of wartime poetry when he stated, 'Measured by quantity alone, it is unique; at no time has so great a volume of verse been produced in as short a period.' Although scholars accord First World War poetry an importance in English Literature that it does not have in the literary annals of other countries, Britain was far from having a monopoly of war poets. 'From the bloody earth of the trenches sprouted a magnificent literary flowering,' wrote a Frenchman in 1916. Jean Vic's five-volume *La littérature de la guerre: manuel méthodique et critique des publications de langue française*, which only goes up to the Armistice, has eighteen pages of listings of poetry books, including such forgotten treasures as Emmanuel Soy's *Des palmes sur les tombes* (1916), Gilles Normand's *La voix de la fournaise* (1916), *Sous-lieutenant* André Dollé's *Pages de gloire, d'amour et de mort* (1916), *La muse et les ailes* by J.M. Renaitour, *Pilote aviateur* (1917) and Jean Fontaine-Vive's *Jeunesse ardente* (1918). At least forty war poets writing in Flemish made themselves known during the first seventeen months following the invasion of Belgium, though the most interesting of the younger Flemish poets of the time, Paul van Ostaijen, spent the war in Antwerp working with the German occupation authorities. Nearly 350 authors who published volumes of war poems are listed in Julius Bab's *Die deutsche Kriegslyrik* of 1920, but according to a professor at

Munich University writing in 1915 the total number of war poems produced by German authors in the first six months of hostilities was three million. That's approximately 17,000 a day, but a later expert raised the possibility that the figure might be higher. The Italians versified on a less heroic scale, though their finest twentieth-century poet, Giuseppe Ungaretti, produced some of his best work while *soldato semplice della 19ª Fanteria*, an ordinary soldier of the 19th Infantry Regiment.[1]

One of the most persistent images of the First World War – one that had first been formulated in the Crimean War but was hardly applicable to earlier conflicts – is of young men being herded to their deaths at the behest of bloodthirsty older men who were making a good thing of the war at a safe distance from the guns:

> If I were fierce, and bald, and short of breath,
> I'd live with scarlet Majors at the Base,
> And speed glum heroes up the line to death.
> You'd see me with my puffy petulant face,
> Guzzling and gulping in the best hotel,
> Reading the Roll of Honour. 'Poor young chap,'
> I'd say – 'I used to know his father well … '

There is an element of truth in this. As early as December 1914 *The Egoist* jeered:

> At the sound of the drum,
> Out of their dens they come, they come,
> The little poets we thought were dead.
> The poets who certainly haven't been read...

One of the people the author of these verses had in mind was probably would-be Poet Laureate William Watson who, at the age of fifty-six, decided that he wanted his war poems to be 'so much in evidence that people [would] be saying that W.W. is the real national poet in this crisis'; he managed to have sixteen war poems printed in different newspapers within the first six weeks. Even those present found something grotesque in the meeting of prominent British writers who assembled at government request to discuss efforts to counter German propaganda:

> It was an extraordinary gathering. Galsworthy, cool, bald and solemn; Conan Doyle, strong, solid and good-humoured: R. Bridges a glorious sight, wavy hair, black coat, huge red tie, light trousers, white socks, patent leather shoes; he sat in a tilted chair, looking at his ease, calmly indifferent, every now and then craning his head backwards out of an open window ... Wells – fat, brown and perky, very smart; Chesterton enormous, streaming with sweat, his hair dripping ... Hugh [Benson] next him looking hot; Hardy very old and faded ... Barrie small and insignificant. Arnold Bennett very pert and looking every inch a cad. Newbolt cool and anxious.

Catherine W. Reilly's *English Poetry of the First World War: A Bibliography* (1978) lists 2,225 British First World War poets, only 417 of whom actually wore uniform. But it would be unjust to pretend that the folks back home had no feeling (other than *Schadenfreude)* for the ordeal of their sons and brothers in the trenches. One recalls Kipling's little poem on his son, killed in action while serving with the Irish Guards:

> My son was killed while laughing at some jest, I would I knew
> What it was, and it might serve me in a time when jests are few.[2]

In any case soldiers at the front often had to deal with the fact that their families back home were themselves in physical danger. It was not just Flemish troops from parts of Belgium over-run by the Germans –

> Een dagblad kwam mij 't melden,
> ons dorpje lief was nêergebrand,

een moordkreet klonk door heel het land,
er waren vrienden die 't vertelden.

('A newpaper came to tell me our dear little village was burnt
down, a murder cry rang through the land, it was friends who
told it.') – British and German troops too found that their homes
were in range of enemy incursions. On 16 December 1914 German
battlecruisers shelled Scarborough, Whitby and Hartlepool; in
Hartlepool ninety-three people were killed and 436 injured. On
31 May 1915 a German airship bombed London:

From a blur of female faces
Distraught eyes stand out,
And a woman's voice cries:
'The Zeppelins – they are attacking us;
Kingsland Road is alight,
Stoke Newington is burning.
Did you not hear the guns?
Oh, what shall we do!'

By 11 November 1918 the Germans had carried out fifty-one raids
on English towns with airships, and fifty-two with aeroplanes.
Though it was England's centres of population that experienced
the heaviest air-raids of the war, there were also thirty-four
attacks on Venice, and by the time of the Armistice the Royal
Air Force, hitherto unable to reach targets east of Stuttgart, was
finalizing plans for raiding Berlin with four-engined bombers.
The scale of destruction in the pioneer raids of the First World
War was far from negligible: on 22 June 1916 nearly a hundred
children were killed in a French raid on Karlsruhe when a
direct hit was scored on a circus, and on 11 November of the
same year ninety-three people attempting to find shelter in
the old fortifications at Padua were killed by a single bomb
from an Austrian aeroplane. On 16 February 1918 a German
four-engined Zeppelin-Staaken R.VI dropped a bomb weighing

one metric ton on London, destroying a wing of the Royal Hospital at Chelsea (the wing was rebuilt and again demolished by a German rocket on 31 January 1945).[3]

Scarce resources had to be held back from the battle zone to meet these attacks:

We wandered through the chill autumnal Park.
And spoke of courage and the youthful dead,
And how the boldest spirit may be cowed
By indiscriminate terror. Overhead,
The moon rode high on her predestined arc,
Steadfast through tidal waves of sombre cloud.
Like vast antennae, search-lights swept the sky,
When, suddenly, as if in swift reply,
Out of the south, with jets of luminous smoke.
And coughing clatter, hidden guns awoke.

But counter-measures might be almost as dangerous as the attacks themselves: on 7 July 1917 a daylight raid on London by twenty-one Gotha twin-engined bombers resulted in the death of ten people, and the injury of fifty-five, from cascading fragments of anti-aircraft shells, in addition to the forty-four killed and 125 injured by German bombs. The Germans also employed long-range guns. At first it was only the Scarlet Majors at the Base who were at risk: on 27 June 1917 the Casino Hotel at Dunkirk, housing the HQ of the British 15th Corps, was hit by a 38 cm. shell fired from an emplacement at Leugenboom near Ostend, twenty-four miles away, though fortunately no staff officers were in the building at the time: 'Casualties among clerks and orderlies – ten killed, fifteen wounded. Corps Commanders', BGGS', CE's, DA & QMG's, G, Q and several other offices were all destroyed.' Nine months later, on 23 March 1918, the German army began shelling Paris with specially designed 21 cm. guns positioned in railway sidings sixty-seven miles away near Laon: one of the shells brought down the roof of a crowded church, killing eighty-eight worshippers. And even without being directly involved in such incidents, people were at once enormously energized and enormously worried by the war: not least those, like Bertrand Russell and D.H. Lawrence, who bitterly opposed the war on principle but were exempted, by age or medical condition, from active participation.[4]

Though one might be somewhat irritated by civilians writing things like 'We ate our breakfast lying on our backs/Because the shells were screeching overhead', at its best the work of those who experienced the sharp edge of war only at second hand achieved genuine pathos. The following is by the Marquess of Crewe, who was a cabinet minister at the outbreak of the war:

Here in the marshland, past the battered bridge,
One of a hundred grains untimely sown,
Here with his comrades of the hard-won ridge,
He rests, unknown.

His horoscope had seemed so plainly drawn:
School triumphs, earned apace in work and play:
Friendships at will; then love's delightful dawn
And mellowing day;

Home fostering hope; some service to the State;
Benignant age; then the long tryst to keep
Where in the yew-tree shadow congregate
His fathers sleep.

Was here the one thing needful to distil
From life's alembic, through this holier fate,
The man's essential soul, the hero will?
We ask; and wait.

Writing at a distance, authors on the Home Front were sometimes betrayed by the recalcitrance of facts of which they were uninformed. When W.B. Yeats was inspired by the death of 'my dear friend's dear son', Major Robert Gregory, to write his poem 'An Irish Airman Foresees His Death' –

> I know that I shall meet my fate
> Somewhere among the clouds above

– he did not know that Gregory had crashed into the side of a hill obscured by low cloud, during a test flight. On the other hand no one nowadays asks how much Laurence Binyon of the British Museum knew about the reality of war when he wrote:

> They shall grow not old as we that are left grow old.
> Age shall not weary them, nor the years condemn.
> At the going down of the sun and in the morning
> We will remember them.[5]

In fact the most famous verses of the war years (though their fame came only in another war a generation later) were written during basic training, before the author had heard a shot fired in anger:

> Vor der Kaserne
> vor dem grossen Tor
> stand eine Laterne
> und steht sie noch davor,
> so wollen wir uns da wiedersehn
> bei der Laterne wolln wir stehn
> wie einst, Lili Marleen

('In front of the barracks, in front of the great gate, there stood a wicket entrance, and it's still standing there, we still want to see each other again, we want to stand at the wicket, like we used to, Lili Marleen.') A version of this was recorded by the singer Lale Andersen in 1938. In 1941, the German army broadcasting station in Belgrade, for want of other suitable records, transmitted it frequently and it quickly became popular all over the Mediterranean war zone, being eventually translated into twenty-six languages and providing the subject for a British feature film of 1944 misleadingly entitled *The True Story of Lili Marleen.*[6]

A certain physical remoteness from the worst horrors might even have been of assistance to someone trying to describe the realities of war. In August 1914 John Masefield was in his mid-thirties. He greeted the outbreak of war with a fine elegiac poem –

And silence broods like spirit on the brae,
A glimmering moon begins, the moonlight runs
Over the grasses of the ancient way
Rutted this morning by the passing guns.

and in 1915, having worked for a period in a French military hospital sixty miles behind the lines, was sent to the Dardanelles to help organize the evacuation by motor boat of soldiers wounded in Gallipoli fighting. He saw a great deal of suffering and – from a reasonably safe distance – the places where the suffering had been incurred, but was never in much danger of sharing it personally. After a successful propaganda tour in the United States, he was commissioned to write a popular history of the Gallipoli campaign. Not surprisingly, considering the time when it was written and the nature of the information made available to him, the resulting book was something of a whitewash as far as the military aspects were concerned. A later generation, more accustomed to anti-war than to pro-war propaganda, may give a double meaning to the judgement of one of Masefield's contemporaries that 'It is on a level with Tennyson's "Charge of the Light Brigade", only it is in prose', but it remains perhaps the finest book of its type ever written:

Those who wish to imagine the scene must think of twenty miles of any rough and steep sea coast known to them, picturing it as roadless, waterless, much broken with gullies, covered with scrub, sandy, loose, and difficult to walk on, and without more than two miles of accessible landing throughout its length ... Then let them imagine the hills entrenched, the landing mined, the beaches tangled with barbed wire, ranged by howitzers and swept by machine guns, and themselves three thousand miles from home, going out before dawn, with rifles, packs, and water-bottles, to pass the mines under shell fire, cut through the wire under machine-gun fire, clamber up the hills under the fire of all arms, by the glare of shell-bursts, in the withering and crashing tumult of modern war, and then to dig themselves in in a waterless and burning hill while a more numerous enemy charge them with the bayonet ... Let them imagine themselves driven mad by heat and toil and thirst by day, shaken by frost at midnight, weakened by disease and broken by pestilence, yet rising on the word with a shout and going forward to die in exultation in a cause foredoomed and almost hopeless ... But as they moved out these things were but the end they asked, the reward they had come for, the unseen cross upon the breast ... They went like kings in a pageant to the imminent death. As they passed from moorings to the man-of-war anchorage on their way to the sea, their feeling that they had done with life and were going out to something new welled up in those battalions; they cheered and cheered till the harbour rang with cheering. As each ship crammed with soldiers drew near the battleships, the men swung their caps and cheered again, and the sailors answered, and the noise of cheering swelled, and the men in the ships not yet moving joined in, and the men ashore, till all the life in the harbour was giving thanks that it could go to death rejoicing...[7]

Masefield's *Gallipoli* was published in September 1916. At that stage one of the chief problems for writers who had seen the reality of war from an even closer viewpoint was that they were mostly still in the thick of it. A battlefield, even a static one, was not the best environment for the production of literature. Roland Dorgelès explained that he did not write on the front line 'not only for want of spare time, but also and above all for lack of liberty of mind … As far as I'm concerned I knew nothing more incompatible with the duties of a novelist than those of a machine-gun corporal.' René Hugues felt obliged to apologize to Apollo, the Greek god of music and poetry:

> Si ne te plaisent mes sonnets
> Qu'en spontanéite tristement relative,
> Excuse: heure etait incontemplative

('If you only like my sonnets for their sadly relative spontaneity, forgive me; the time was not right for contemplation.') Patrick MacGill, by then wounded and unfit for further service, claimed in the preface to his wartime novel *The Great Push* (1916) that 'the chapter dealing with our last night at Les Brebis, prior to the Big Push, was written in the trench between midnight and dawn of September the 25th' – i.e. during the hours immediately prior to the commencement of the Battle of Loos – but one is not quite sure whether to believe him:

> I poked my head through the upper window of our billet and looked down the street. An ominous calm brooded over the village, the trees which lined the streets stood immovable in the darkness, with lone shadows clinging to the trunks … My mind was suddenly permeated by a feeling of proximity to the enemy. He whom we were going to attack at dawn seemed to be very close to me. I could almost feel his presence in the room. At dawn I might deprive him of life and he might deprive me of mine. Two beings give life to a man, but one can deprive him of it. Which is the greater mystery? Birth or death? They who are responsible for the first may take pleasure, but who can glory in the second? … To kill a man … To feel for ever after the deed that you have deprived a fellow being of life!

'We're beginning to strafe again,' said Pryor, coming to my side as a second reverberation shook the house.

It certainly seems remarkable that MacGill managed to write so much while taking part in the dialogue he recorded:

'And who will I write to for you, Bill?' I asked.
Bill scratched his little white potato of a nose, puckered his lips, and became thoughtful. I suddenly realised that Bill was very dear to me.
'Not afraid, matey?' I asked.
'Naw', he answered in a thoughtful voice.
'A man has only to die once, anyhow,' said Felan.
'Greedy! 'Ow many times d'yer want ter die?' asked Bill.[8]

This chapter which MacGill says was written during the night before the battle is a little less than 4,000 words long; Trollope, who at least had his own desk to sit at, used to average 10,000 words a week. Other frontline writers were more sparing in their use of ink and paper. Another writer who claimed to have written a novel 'at the front while the things described in it were occurring' was Hugh Walpole, who was serving as a medical orderly on the Russian front while writing *The Dark Forest* (1916). He claimed later, 'It is a diary, of actual events,' though the only parts in diary format are supposedly by one of the characters (not the narrator): three of the entries run to 2,500 words each. Richard Aldington on the other hand wrote of composing haiku:

One frosty night when the guns were still
I leaned against the trench
Making for myself *hokku*
Of the moon and flowers and of the snow.
But the ghostly scurrying of huge rats
Swollen with feeding upon men's flesh
Filled me with shrinking dread.

One wonders too if the most distinctively novel feature of Giuseppe Ungaretti's frontline poems, their short disjointed lines, does not owe something to their having been written on scraps of paper resting on the author's knee – rather thin boney knees too – with frequent glances up to check if anything stirred in No Man's Land:

Una intera nottata
buttato vicino
a un compagno
massacrato
con la sua bocca
digrignata
volta al plenilunio
con la congestione
delle sue mani
penetrata
nel mio silenzio
ho scritto
lettere piene d'amore

Non sono mai stato
tanto attaccato
alla vita

('For one entire night thrown next to a comrade butchered with his mouth gnashing in the direction of the full moon with the swelling of his hands sticking into my silence I wrote letters full of love. I have never been so attached to life.') Quite independently a reserve lieutenant in the German army, August Stramm, had been experimenting with a similar technique in his own language:

Die Erde blutet unterm Helmkopf
Sterne fallen
Der Weltraum tastet
Schauder brausen

Wirbeln
Einsamkeiten.
Nebel
Weinen
Ferne
Deinen Blick.

('The earth bleeds under its helmeted head – stars fall – space fumbles – shudders heave – lonelinesses whirl. Fogs weep distance from your look.') By the time Ungaretti was writing at the front however, Stramm had already been killed in action, sixty kilometres beyond Brest-Litovsk.[9]

In fact, a great deal was written in the trenches, and not only letters to wives and parents, and the occasional prohibited diary. The relatively small Belgian army, operating in the last unoccupied corner of its homeland and to a large extent cut off from all family contact, gave birth to no less than 290 trench newspapers, and the French army had perhaps 400, of which 170 published by the French land forces in France itself have survived in libraries. The editors were in some cases subaltern officers; there was one uncommissioned soldier amongst the eleven editors of *Le diable au cor*, 1915–18, whereas *L'argonnaute* was edited by five privates and three corporals. These men were actually at the front, and in many cases died in action: units of the French army which operated in the rear and had access to better facilities produced magazines relatively rarely. In the British army 107 frontline magazines have been identified, the first being the *Fifth Gloucester Gazette*, produced under the direction of a chaplain attached to the 5th Battalion Gloucestershire Regiment in April 1915. They were usually printed in England by commercial printers (as were the numerous magazines produced by home-based units) but the famous *Wipers Times* (later the *BEF Times*), produced by the 12th Battalion Sherwood Foresters, was printed with Belgian presses found in the Ypres Salient. At least one rear-areas magazine, *The Strafer*, edited by Army

Service Corps captains at '3 GHQ A.M. Park' was partly roneod, no doubt on government-issue roneo machines. Many of these magazines were short-lived but those that survived were likely to increase their circulation: *The 7th Manchester Sentry* in England claimed a print-run of 26,000 in May 1916 and on the Western Front *The Listening Post* (7th Battalion Canadian Expeditionary Force) claimed 20,000 in October of the same year (this may be compared to the 47,000 circulation of *The Times* before the war, or the 20,000 claimed by *The Cambridge Magazine*, which could be described as the trench journal of the war's opponents back in England). In the Italian and Austro-Hungarian armies frontline journals were usually official initiatives by HQ staff (as was later the case with the British army in the 1939–45 war): the novelist Robert Musil, as a *Landsturmoberleutnant*, edited one such, the *Soldaten-Zeitung*, in the Bolzano sector from July 1916 till April 1917. The Germans also had a number of army newspapers organized by HQs of larger formations (the largest circulation of any soldiers' newspaper in the 1914–18 – 52,000 copies – was achieved by the *Zeitung der 10. Armee oder Armee-Zeitung Scholz* on the Eastern Front late in 1916), but there were also fifty-five frontline journals issued by units of the German army below divisional level, including *Hohnacker neueste Nachrichten*, which was first produced in a run of eighty hectographed copies on a quiet stretch of the Vosges front by men of the 4. *Kompagnie* of the 2. *Bayerische Landwehr Regiment* as early as 14 September 1914: this, the very first such small-unit paper in any army, was later extended to cover the entire brigade, with a circulation of 2,000.[10]

Frontline soldiers read as well as wrote: 'It is really remarkable how you learn to read at the front', Otto Braun told a family friend: 'only a few books up till now, Faust, Hölderlin, and Zarathustra, but, as should be, learning them almost by heart'. Ernst Jünger later claimed that during the British offensive of August 1918 he occupied what spare moments he had with *Tristram Shandy*, 'which imprinted itself on my memory more deeply than all the events of combat'. He finished it in hospital after being wounded for the fourteenth time. Edmund Blunden found comfort in a text of the same vintage: 'At every spare moment I read in Young's *Night Thoughts on Life, Death and Immortality* and I felt the benefit of this grave and intellectual voice, speaking out of a profound eighteenth-century calm.' (A review of Blunden's *Pastorals* in *The Times Literary Supplement* led to his being summoned to battalion HQ and appointed Field Works Officer, his colonel being 'overjoyed at having an actual author in his battalion'). Osbert Sitwell sought not calm in his reading but a kind of commentary on what he was living through:

> As a pessimist, and in an effort to make this existence seem more tolerable, in general I avoided works of a cheerful tendency, and once more abandoned myself to the genius of Dostoievsky ... When after reading *The Brothers Karamazov*, *Crime and Punishment* and *The Idiot*, *King Lear* or *Othello*, I needed a change of feeling, I turned to the novels of Dickens again ... With what certainty he would have comprehended and rendered a night of duty: rats and mud, and the particular horror they hold for human beings, he already understood (think of the opening of *Our Mutual Friend* on the waters of the Pool of London!), and he would at once have captured the feeling of these coffin-like ditches, where death brooded in the air after the same manner that some fatal disease, such as malaria, hangs suspended, but ever-present, over the deserted marshlands of Italy and Greece.

Harold Duke Collison-Morley, a career officer – in September 1915 he was commanding the 19th Battalion London Regiment (the St Pancras Battalion) – wrote home, 'There is no hardship or terror or doubt that happens out here that Shakespeare does not touch on or give advice for.' A few days later the British army launched the second of its major offensives, at Loos, and Collison-Morley was 'killed at the head of his men, after being twice wounded, just before reaching the German trenches'; a copy of *Henry V* was found on his body. The continuing relevance of *Henry V* was also acknowledged by David Jones, when he recalled years later, 'Trench life brought that work pretty constantly to mind.' Siegfried Sassoon recorded 'reading *Tess of the D'Urbervilles* and trying to forget about the shells which were humping and hurrooshing overhead', and later, when waiting to be sent into action, found 'A sort of numb funkiness invaded me. I didn't want to die – not before I'd finished reading *The Return of the Native* anyhow.' Another Thomas Hardy novel, *Far From the Madding Crowd*, provided Wilfrid Ewart with distraction at Ypres in 1916. Edgell Rickword wrote a cruel little poem about reading Donne and Tennyson aloud to the 'gaping, mackerel-eyed' corpse of a dead friend:

I tried the Elegies one day,
But he, because he heard me say
'What needst thou have more covering than a man?'
Grinned nastily, and so I knew
The worms had got his brains at last ...
There was one thing that I might do
To starve the worms; I racked my head
For healthy things and quoted 'Maud'.
His grin got worse and I could see
He laughed at passion's purity.
He stank so badly, though we were great chums
I had to leave him; then rats ate his thumbs.[11]

Rickword himself later recalled picking up a copy of Siegfried Sassoon's *Counter-Attack* when returning to France from leave and finding it 'devastating because he was the first poet I knew of who dealt with the war in the vocabulary of war'. Blunden also mentioned on one occasion having to 'thrust aside my *Cambridge Magazine* with Siegfried Sassoon's splendid war on the war in it'. Indeed the soldiers in the front line had the unprecedented experience of being able to read substantial literary treatments of a war they were still engaged in. Franz Marc read the poems of August Stramm printed in the issue of

Sturm that announced his death in action, noting, 'For him language was neither a form nor a vessel in which you offer ideas ... instead it was material from which he struck fire, marble which he wanted to awaken to life, like a true sculptor.' Jean Norton Cru remembered that, 'During our attack of late June 1916 at Verdun on the eastern slope of the Vignes ravine I had in my haversack Genevoix's *Sous Verdun* and Paul Lintier's *Ma pièce*.' Henri Barbusse's *Le feu* sold 200,000 copies by the time of the Armistice and many of these found their way into the hands of soldiers. Sassoon recalled of Wilfred Owen, 'And didn't I lend him Barbusse's *Le feu* which set him alight as no other war book had done?' Cru regarded Barbusse's novel as a tissue of inaccuracies and implausibilities, but noted that even frontline soldiers who admitted its inaccuracy found it a refreshing change from the romantic picture of war that was being circulated on the home front: he quoted a captain, *un vrai poilu*, as saying 'Of course its inaccurate, but look how long they've been stuffing the heads of the people in the rear with rubbish about our life here, and Barbusse now says the exact opposite.'[12]

André Bridoux wrote in 1930 of *Le feu* passing from hand to hand in the trenches of Champagne:

> The men sought to take stock of themselves; they were eager to find a precise rendering of the confused but stirring picture they had formed of themselves and their new destiny; they counted on the writer to help them achieve a clearer awareness of what they saw around them and what they felt within themselves.

At the same time a great deal of both reading and writing was expressive of an urge to escape from the awfulness of the present. One of the earliest soldier poets, F.W. Harvey, wrote mainly about the Gloucestershire countryside and in introducing a volume of his poems the colonel of his battalion explained, 'Mud, blood and Khaki are rather conspicuously absent. They are, in fact, the last things a soldier wishes to think or talk about.' Siegfried Sassoon agreed:

Soldiers are dreamers; when the guns begin
They think of firelit homes, clean beds, and wives.

I see them in foul dug-outs, gnawed by rats,
And in the ruined trenches, lashed with rain,
Dreaming of things they did with balls and bats,
And mocked by hopeless longing to regain
Bank-holidays, and picture shows, and spats,
And going to the office in the train.

Partly perhaps it was a matter of fixing one's thoughts on beauty,
fresh air and calm when surrounded by ugliness, cordite fumes and
man-made racket. 'If only this fear would leave me I could dream
of Crickley Hill', wrote Ivor Gurney; and Ford Madox Hueffer
elaborated much the same idea in his poem 'The Iron Music':

The French guns roll continuously
And our guns, heavy, slow;
Along the Ancre, sinuously,
The transport wagons go,
And the dust is on the thistles
And the larks sing up on high ...
But I see the Golden Valley
Down by Tintern on the Wye ...

Dust and corpses in the thistles
Where the gas-shells burst like snow,
And the shrapnel screams and whistles
On the Bécourt road below,
And the High Wood bursts and bristles
Where the mine-clouds foul the sky ...
But I'm with you up at Wyndcroft,
Over Tintern on the Wye.[13]

Yet even the ability to day-dream, let alone to read books or compose poems, represented something of a triumph of the human spirit over material reality. In a letter to his mother Wilfred Owen wrote: 'I can't tell you any more Facts. I have no Fancies and no Feelings. Positively they went numb with my feet.' T.E. Hulme told a friend: 'My mind is a corridor. The minds about me are corridors. Nothing suggests itself. There is nothing to do but keep on.' Robert Graves confessed, 'I feel exactly like a man who has watched the "Movies" for a long evening and then suddenly found himself thrown on the screen in the middle of scalp-hunting Sioux and runaway motor cars.' Rupert Brooke, recalling his baptism of fire at Antwerp, confessed, 'Most of the time I was thinking of food, or marching straight, or what to say to the men, or, mostly, not thinking at all.' While in the trenches Siegfried Sassoon confided to his diary, 'I wonder what Thomas Hardy would think of the life out here. How the Pre-Raphaelites would have loathed it.' Later he wrote of 'the veritable gloom and disaster of the thing called Armageddon ... a place of horror and desolation which no imagination could have invented ... a place where a man of strong spirit might know himself utterly powerless against death and destruction'.[14]

There were of course moments when even men like Wilfred Owen who hated the war passionately found themselves caught up and energized by the vast drama of an advance under fire:

There was an extraordinary exultation in the act of slowly walking forward, showing ourselves openly. There was no bugle and no drum for which I was very sorry. I kept up a kind of chanting sing-song:
  Keep the Line straight!
  Not so fast on the left!
  Steady on the Left!
  Not so fast!
Then we were caught in a Tornado of Shells. The various 'waves' were all broken up and we carried on like a crowd moving off a cricket-field. When I looked back and saw the

ground all crawling and wormy with wounded bodies I felt no horror at all but only an immense exultation at having got through the Barrage.

R.H. Tawney, a pillar of the Fabian Society and later a Professor of Economic History, also no lover of war, found exhilaration merely in the discovery that he was not at all frightened at being shot at:

we went forward, not doubling, but at a walk ... I hadn't gone ten yards before I felt a load fall from me. There's a sentence at the end of *The Pilgrim's Progress* which has always struck me as one of the most awful things imagined by man: 'Then I saw that there was a way to Hell, even from the Gates of Heaven, as well as from the City of Destruction.' To have gone so far and be rejected at last! Yet undoubtedly man walks between precipices, and no one knows the rottenness in him till he cracks, and then it's too late. I had been worried by the thought: 'Suppose one should lose one's head and get other men cut up! Suppose one's legs should take fright and refuse to move!' Now I knew it was all right. I shouldn't be frightened and I shouldn't lose my head. Imagine the joy of that discovery! I felt quite happy and self-possessed.

But such moments were few and far between: neither Richard Aldington nor Ford Madox Hueffer, for example, ever took part in a set-piece attack, though they served for months at the front.[15]

No flame we saw, the noise and the dread
Was battle to us...

wrote Ivor Gurney. According to Max Deauville, the 'heaps of corpses, the terrible hand-to-hand combats' never existed:

The face of war is more sober, more dull, more formed out of boredom, fear, moral constraint, cafard, slavery and melancholy. It is ugly and uninteresting, it never satisfied the instinct for struggle and combat which sleeps in men's hearts. Heroes were killed without glory, without knowing how or by whom, without seeing anything, in an unleashing of hidden forces amidst which only chance ruled.

Recollecting his first days on the Western Front, Vivian Gilbert wrote:

Who has not experienced or read of the trenches in France? The mud, the flies and the stench, and death forever waiting round the next traverse! And, worst of all, the dreary monotony of inaction, the crushing out of individualism and the fatalistic anticipation of conflict! I had come out from England prepared to fight, eager to do my share, but somehow this did not seem like real fighting; never to see one's opponent; to stand for hours with liquid mud up to one's thighs – for the heavy shelling brought constant rain; to fire machine guns at unseen targets for pre-arranged periods throughout the night on elevations worked out with map, compass and clinometer; and then if one *did* have any time to oneself, to spend it like a rat in a deep, damp dugout. It was so unlike all my pre-conceived notions of warfare.

It was also unlike most people's idea of what a writer would want to write about. Adding to the general sense of monotony and malaise was the numbing effect of the sheer physical degradation of frontline conditions:

They talk about the glory of war, but they should see this place; the stench of it is too terrible, bodies and bits of bodies everywhere, covered with enormous maggots and awful big green flies which leave the piece of putrefaction as you pass and swarm all around your face ...

Pervading everything was the 'carrion reek of putrefaction'; Raymond Asquith, the prime minister's son, wrote home of 'bodies and bits of bodies, masses of derelict rifles and equipment, woods turned into a wilderness of short, stubby blackened stumps and a stink of death and corruption which is quite supernaturally beastly'. And again and again it was the sheer repulsiveness of it all that obsessed the men who had to live with it:

> I suppose I can endure cold, and fatigue, and the face-to-face death, as well as another; but extra for me there is the universal pervasion of *Ugliness*. Hideous landscapes, vile noises, foul language and nothing but foul, even from one's own mouth (for all are devil ridden), everything unnatural, broken, blasted; the distortion of the dead, whose unburiable bodies sit outside the dug-outs all day, all night, the most execrable sights on earth. In poetry we call them the most glorious. But to sit with them all day, all night ... and a week later to come back and find them still sitting there, in motionless groups. *THAT* is what saps the 'soldierly spirit' ...

One man succeeded in making art out of that ugliness: Paul Nash, the greatest painter of the war, but also amongst the greatest of English letter writers:

> The ground for miles around furrowed into trenches, pitted with yawning holes in which the water lies still and cold or heaped with mounds of earth, tangles of rusty wire, tin plates, stakes, sandbags and all the refuse of war. In the distance runs a stream where the stringy poplars and alders lean about dejectedly, while farther a slope rises to a scarred bluff the foot of which is scattered with headless trees standing white and withered, hopeless, without any leaves, done, dead. As shells fall in the bluff, huge sprouts of black, brown and orange mould burst into the air amid a volume of white smoke, flinging wide incredible debris, while the crack and roar of

the explosion reverberates in the valley. In the midst of this strange country, where such things happen, men are living in their narrow ditches, hidden from view by every cunning device, waiting and always on the watch, yet at the same time, easy, careless, well fed, wrapped up in warm clothes, talking, perpetually smoking, and indifferent to anything that occurs ... As night falls the monstrous land takes on a strange aspect ... the horizon brightens and again vanishes as the Very lights rise and fall, shedding their weird greenish glare over the land, and [in] acute contrast to their lazy silent flight breaks out the agitated knocking of the machine guns as they sweep the parapets ...[16]

The number who simply could not bear it was perhaps fewer than one would expect. The Austrian poet Georg Trakl had a breakdown after only a month as pharmacist in a field hospital on the Galician Front; and after a month under medical care managed to kill himself with an overdose of cocaine. Robert Nichols lasted just over five weeks in France as a second-lieutenant in the Royal Field Artillery, including a month behind the lines and ten days at the front though 'not actually under fire', before collapsing with 'Nervous lack of control' and 'emotional instability.' Ivor Gurney, who wrote 'War brings greater self-control – or breakdown', was gassed in September 1917, rehospitalized in February 1918 because of the recurrence of symptoms of gas-poisoning and transferred to a hospital specializing in neurasthenia cases in May 1918. He spent most of the rest of his life in asylums. But the ideal age for military service is also the age at which people are most likely to begin showing the symptoms of mental illness: Ivor Gurney seems to have been a classic case of schizophrenia; Trakl had been a drug addict for at least a year before the war broke out; the nature of Nichols's breakdown is not clear but he too had had psychiatric problems before the war. The official verdict in the British army was that 80 per cent of war psychosis cases had a family history of nervous or mental disease. At the beginning of the war army medics had known nothing about 'shell shock' but by the second half of 1916 it was being diagnosed comparatively freely. Later, when it was discovered that the symptoms often disappeared after a period of rest, the reported incidence of battle neurosis went down. During the period 1 August to 31 October 1917, 55 per cent of shell shock cases returned to their units after two or three weeks rest in an advance hospital, 16 per cent were sent to base hospitals, where a quarter of them were reassessed as not having a neurological problem, and 29 per cent were temporarily put to agricultural work: just over 1 per cent were sent home. In the American Expeditionary Force in 1918 sixty-five out of every 100 soldiers who complained of symptoms of neurasthenia were returned to duty from Field Hospitals, and a further twenty from the specialist neurological hospitals attached to each of the two armies composing the American Expeditionary Force: and of the 15 per cent who ended up at Base Hospital 117, where longer-term battle neurosis cases were dealt with, only one in fifteen was sent back to America for further treatment: the others eventually returned to duty. As the criteria for diagnosis and the stage at which statistics were collected varied at different stages of the war, it is difficult to assess the actual incidence of battle neurosis: the British Army's statistics for the second half of 1916 suggest a ratio of one battle neurosis case for every thirteen men killed, whereas the AEF statistics for October 1918 show one battle neurosis case reporting to Field Hospitals for every five men killed, and one case admitted to Base Hospital 117 for every thirty killed. The total of battle neurosis cases in the British army in France and Belgium was estimated at 80,000 (as compared to 1,937,364 killed and wounded). In 1922 50,000 British ex-soldiers were receiving government pensions for neurasthenic disablement, which seems a very poor recovery rate: possibly the majority of these cases were men whose psychiatric problems, though first manifesting themselves in the army, would have occurred in any case. On the other hand, it was perfectly normal for ex-soldiers who suffered no obvious psychiatric disablement to have nightmares about the war for the rest of their lives: if they slept. William Linton Andrews claimed in 1930:

For many years after the War, like many, many others who had been there a long time, I woke almost every night in terror from a nightmare of suffocation by gas, or of being trapped by a bombardment from which I ran this way and that, or of fighting a bayonet duel with a gigantic Prussian Guardsman.

And Ugo Dell'Aringa of the Italian army claimed to have had precisely one hour's sleep in thirty-nine years after his return home from the war.[17]

Soldiers suffering from battle trauma were not necessarily lacking in enthusiasm. One doctor recorded the case of a former student of University College, Aberystwyth, twice wounded in action on previous occasions, who was struck deaf and dumb – a not infrequent phenomenon – by a shell exploding close beside him. By means of scribbled notes he requested and obtained permission to stay and participate in the next attack instead of going to the rear. In the attack he operated a Lewis Gun with his usual competence, was wounded a third time and sent to hospital. 'I've been too long up there to look on it with any fear', he wrote in another note. He recovered his power of speech under ether eleven days later, and was eventually returned to duty.[18]

After the war it was claimed that some men had only been able to keep themselves going by heavy drinking. Mark Plowman wrote of his company commander,

He is just a good-natured fellow, with any amount of pluck, whose morals have been damaged by the war and its whisky. The amount of whisky he and Mallow, the bombing-officer, can drink is astonishing. Every time Mallow reaches for the bottle he repeats the parrot phrase, 'This war will be won on whisky or it won't be won at all', apparently intending to float home on whisky himself.

A school-boy hero transmogrified into whisky-toping company commander featured in R.C. Sherriff's hit play *Journey's End*, first staged in January 1929. It may have been the furore provoked by *Journey's End* that encouraged Robert Graves to state in his memoir *Good-Bye to All That*, published in November of the same year, that officers who stayed too long in the trenches often became dipsomaniacs:

> I knew three or four who had worked up to the point of two bottles of whiskey a day before being lucky enough to get wounded or sent home in some other way. A two-bottle company commander of one of our line battalions is still alive who, in three shows running, got his company needlessly destroyed because he was no longer capable of taking clear decisions.

One has only to think of how many units were needlessly destroyed as a result of clear decisions made when stone-cold sober to find something suspicious in this, and a writer in *The Times Literary Supplement* remarked 'One of the chief impressions that many of us took away from *Journey's End* was that Stanhope and his friends were very lucky to have such lavish supplies of whiskey at their disposal.' Nevertheless official statistics show that, of officers court-martialled while serving abroad, the percentage who were charged with drunkenness fell by more than a quarter after the Armistice.[19]

Not everyone was adversely affected by the atmosphere of the battle zone however: some men found it positively bracing. According to Wyndham Lewis,

> Arrival at 'the Front' for us was not unlike arrival at a big Boxing Match, or at a Blackshirt Rally at Olympia. The same sinister expectancy, but more sinister and more electric, the same restless taciturnity of stern-faced persons assembling for a sensational and bloody event, their hearts set on a knockout. Somebody else's, of course.

Charles Carrington recalled of joining a battalion in the line: 'It was far more like stepping out from the pavilion to bat for the first time in a match, than like waiting with horrid anticipation at the dentist's door.' Later he reflected:

As for the danger, it must be remembered that most men like adventures. Anyone who has ever been through a street accident, anyone who has climbed a mountain, knows that. It is one of the strange attributes of the mind that we enjoy what makes our flesh creep, and no one was very long at the front without sometimes feeling a thrill of excitement which quite banished the dragging fears of anticipation.

A.W. Smith wrote:

As a whole, in between the moments of intensity I remember great arid stretches of drabness and mild boredom. They are overshadowed by the dark cloud of an immense tiredness. Sleep seemed the only thing that mattered – to be let alone to sleep.

Being at the front flattered my conceit. I was on the stage – if only in the chorus. I was one of the initiated. I was the centre of interest of my relations and friends.

I did not dislike being at the front.[20]

Some people even attempted to make a joke of it:

Except for the banal booming and flashing of the guns one might be at one of those old-fashioned balls in Arthur Grenfell's garden at Roehampton – the same tiresome noise of electricity being generated in the too near foreground, the same scraggy oaks, the same scramble for sandwiches, the same crowd ... the same band playing the same tunes, the same moon in the same sky.

In the same vein perhaps was the suggestion of an officer in the Grenadier Guards that the trenches were not as bad as prep school:

At least there were no masters, matrons, or compulsory games. The discomfort was, at times, perhaps a little greater, the food, though tinned, perhaps a little more palatable ... Through the long course of Samurai-like discipline to which they were, with few exceptions, obliged to submit in their most impressionable years, the children of the former British governing classes had been taught to bear with composure a high degree of physical hardship and spiritual misery, while enclosed in an atmosphere of utmost frustration ... certainly the young of this class could bear bodily suffering and exhaustion, and a sense of the cruellest isolation, with a stoical equanimity unknown among those who came from good working-class homes and had been brought up, right from their earliest years to manhood, in an unaltering atmosphere of domestic affection.

There may have been something in that: after having been caught in No Man's Land by a German bombardment an Old Etonian wrote home, 'it was good fun while it lasted', and another remarked:

You never exist long in this battalion, so I expect it will be my turn next. Still we're very cheerful. It does seem funny to be playing a gramophone and roaring with laughter at everything, when you're only about half a mile from the German trenches.

Similarly a former pupil at Radley told a correspondent, 'It really is great fun out here, and awfully exciting at times.' Even Siegfried Sassoon (educated at Malborough) initially responded with enthusiasm: 'the excitement of things bursting is positively splendid. I had no idea I would enjoy it so much.' The poet Edward Thomas – who had also been at Public School but as a day boy – was another who saw little essential difference between life at the front and peacetime existence:

Physical discomfort is sometimes so great that it seems a new thing, but of course it is not. ... Of course, one seems very little one's own master, but then one seldom does seem so ... An alternation of comfort and discomfort is always a man's lot. So is an alternation of pleasure or happiness or intense interest with tedium or dissatisfaction or misery. I have suffered more from January to March in other years than in this.[21]

Cyril McNeile, who rose from captain to lieutenant colonel during the war, thought people tended to forget the worst moments in any case:

What are the moments that stick out like landmarks in my mind as I look back? Those of palsied fright, when, cowering behind a blade of grass, ears numbed with the inferno of noise around, it seemed merely a question of seconds before the inevitable end? Honestly – I don't think so. Those of intense physical discomfort, when, wet to the skin and well nigh frozen to the bone, teeth chattering, eyes full of mud, nostrils full of stench, it seemed as if the limit of human endurance had been reached? Honestly – I don't think so. Those when one heard suddenly that the fellow whose leg you had pulled two hours before had stopped an odd one in the brain? No: not even those ...

What he remembered was 'the spirit of camaraderie' and the epicurean pleasure of a decent dinner and a decent bed when one came out of the line. Similarly Charles Carrington wrote:

If no man now under thirty can guess the meaning of twenty-four hours' bombardment, nor has he any notion of the joy of ninety-six hours' rest. Who has never been drenched and frozen in Flanders mud, has never dreamed of the pleasure derivable from dry blankets on a stone floor.

Even during the war itself Siegfried Sassoon admitted to a newspaper editor, 'One soon forgets the bad times, it's probably something to do with being in the open air so much and getting a lot of exercise.'[22]

Some people positively thrived in the line:

> The horrors of the Great War and the miseries of those who were called upon to take part in it have been described by innumerable writers. For my own part I have to confess that I look back on the years 1914–1918 as among the happiest I have ever spent. That they contained moments of boredom and depression, of sorrow for the loss of friends and of alarm for my personal safety is indeed true enough. But to be perfectly fit, to live among pleasant companions, to have responsibility and a clearly defined job – these are great compensations when one is very young.

That was written seventeen years after the end of the war but was by no means an instance of viewing the past through a romantic haze: the same officer wrote to his mother six and a half weeks after the Armistice (and after the best part of four years at the front as a subaltern in the 4th Battalion Oxfordshire and Buckinghamshire Light Infantry), 'it will be very hard to leave the regiment after so many years ... Could you ever have guessed how much I should enjoy the war?'[23]

It would not be difficult in fact to compile a thick anthology of first-hand accounts of the war that testify to its having been a positive, even life-enhancing experience. The retrospective view we have of the horrors of the First World War is a social construct, composed not merely from the most successful – that is, *commercially* the most successful – literary accounts of the Western Front, but also from the attitudes which became prevalent after the 1939–45 war, especially during the 1960s when military technology finally reached a *reductio ad absurdum* and the world seemed poised on the brink of total annihilation by thermo-nuclear weapons. Yet the testimony of those who fought in the First World War, as it has come down to us, is not only refracted and distorted to our gaze by the events of the intervening years, but is also, in its very origins, subject to bizarre anomalies and asymmetries. It may for example be simply one of those meaningless agglomerations of coincidence which one now and again encounters when studying human groups that, with more than a hundred infantry regiments in the British army in 1914, the authors of three of the best memoirs of the war, Siegfried Sassoon, Robert Graves and Bernard Adams, should have served together as officers in the same battalion, the 1st Royal Welch Fusiliers, in December 1915, and that Frank Richards, J.C. Dunn (as attached medical officer) and Wyn Griffith, who also wrote notable accounts of the war, the poet David Jones, and Vivian de Sola Pinto, the critic who in middle age launched the post-Second World War revival of interest in the 'trench poets', should have been in other battalions of the same regiment. Similarly the authors of two of the best novels about the war, Henry Williamson and Victor Yeates, had been contemporaries in the same house at the same obscure south London grammar school. Perhaps less of a coincidence was that Nicolae Vulovici, the leading Romanian poet of patriotic militarism, was killed in action within a fortnight of Romania's entry into the war, and the two other leading Romanian poets of military age were killed within the next few weeks, whereas the two most interesting younger Portuguese poets kept out of the war altogether, Mário de Sá-Carneiro committing suicide in Paris, apparently before the authorities got round to calling him up, and Fernando Pessoa having already drunk himself into physical unfitness. Meanwhile all but one of the most notable Russian poets of the earlier part of this century managed to avoid frontline service in the war with Germany which helped bring down the Tsarist regime, though they were mostly caught up in the Revolution that followed. Gumilev, the husband of the now better-known Anna Akhmatova, volunteered and became a hero, winning two St George's Crosses and a commission, but Pasternak failed his medical, and it is probable that Mandelshtam was not conscripted for the same reason; Mayakovsky, initially turned down for military service for political reasons – something only possible in Russia – was, when finally inducted into the army, assigned to the Petrograd Automobile School because he was a qualified draughtsman; Blok served as an artillery officer at Pinsk; Yesenin, initially exempted because of poor eye-sight, eventually became a clerk on an ambulance train based at Tsarskoe Selo; Khlebnikov, sent to hospital with a skin disease soon after being called up, was still begging his commanding officer to assign him to active service when the Revolution came. This is part of the reason why most of the best soldier poets of the First World War were British: apart from Gumilev, the Russian poets simply never got close enough to see it.[24]

British war poets also had another advantage. The conditions in which, in every army, the rank and file lived in the frontline were appreciably worse than those experienced by their officers; in the French and German and Russian armies the officers were mostly either pre-war professional soldiers, all three armies having much larger officer cadres in 1914 than the British, and conserving this resource better by having fewer officers in frontline units, or else 'reserve' officers promoted from the ranks on account of their demonstrated competence. The British officers who wrote poetry were predominantly 'temporary gentlemen' who had been commissioned mainly because of their class and education, rather than their military bearing. It is difficult to believe Ford Madox Hueffer (later Ford Madox Ford) or Richard Aldington would ever have become officers in the French or German armies; and Wilfred Owen and Robert Graves would certainly not have been commissioned as quickly as they were. Osbert Sitwell had already been a Special Reserve officer in the Grenadier Guards when war broke out, but it was precisely the fact that they had officers like Osbert Sitwell which made the Brigade of Guards different from the elite formations of other countries' armies:

We are the greatest sheep in the world;
There are no sheep like us.
We come of an imperial bleat;
Our voices,

Trembling with music,
Call to our lambs oversea.
With us they crash across continents.

We will not heed the herdsmen,
For they warned us,
'Do not stampede';
Yet we were forced to do so.
Never will we trust a herdsman again ...

We are stampeding to end stampedes.
We are fighting for lambs
Who are never likely to be born.

When once a sheep gets its blood up
The goats will remember ...

Censorship conditions were also more favourable in Britain: in Germany and France *The Cambridge Magazine*, which published several of Siegfried Sassoon's anti-war poems, would almost certainly have been suppressed, whereas in Britain it merely had to put up with surveillance by the Special Branch and a rather pointless dirty tricks campaign conducted by the Foreign Office. The importance of *The Cambridge Magazine* cannot be overstated: in publishing Sassoon's work it provided a platform for the man whose anti-war poems encouraged Wilfred Owen and Osbert Sitwell to write their own.[25]

Such factors may have had more influence in determining the distinctive quality of the war literature of the various belligerent nations than more substantial institutional differences such as conscription. Till 1916 the British armed forces were composed entirely of volunteers: before the war France, Germany and Russia had maintained large peacetime armies by means of a system of compulsory military service, and those who had already completed their military service obligation were available for call-up as reservists once a general mobilization had been ordered. The

British contribution to the literature of the First World War is unique in that it was written almost entirely by volunteers. One hundred and twenty years earlier, Coleridge and Wordsworth had kept out of the war at least in part because they saw themselves as poets: for the writers of the 1914 generation it was precisely *because* they were writers that they felt they had to join in. Though unlike other writers he waited till he was conscripted, Richard Aldington thought the war was 'the biggest thing that ever happened'; Arnold Toynbee, hearing of the death of one of his friends at the front, wondered, 'when there is all this going on, why am I not in it?' Such a question had never occurred to the intellectuals of the 1800s. Yet the uniqueness of Britain's volunteer army was an institutional rather than a psychological phenomenon: that peculiar quality of outrage which one detects in the poetry of Sassoon and Owen, as if they had volunteered for service in the belief that the war would be much less terrible than it turned out to be, is to be found also in the writings of draftees in the German and French armies, like Remarque or Giono. Nor can there be any doubt that if France and Germany had *not* had conscription, they too would have been able to raise armies on a volunteer basis. Before the war, in fact, the Germans had needed to call up only part of each age-group to man the army, and many of those who went to the front in 1914 were men who had enlisted voluntarily, including thousands of teenagers like the Gymnasium-students in Erich Maria Remarque's *Im Westen Nichts Neues* who volunteered for service months ahead of becoming old enough to be called up in the routine way. (In real life Remarque was drafted, but, for example, Ernst Jünger and Gorch Fock were volunteers.) There were also volunteers in the French army, including the pioneer Surrealists Guillaume Apollinaire and Blaise Cendrars, neither of whom were French citizens. Joseph Roth and Józef Wittlin volunteered together in Austria, and even in Bulgaria, which mobilized a higher percentage of the country's adult male population than any other belligerent, Dimcho Debelyanov, the most notable Bulgarian writer to be killed in the war, enlisted of his own free will despite being exempted because of his technical qualifications. And once one had volunteered, of course, one was faced with the same assault on one's values, intellect and sensibilities as any conscript.[26]

One also ran the same risk of sudden death. Ernest Psichari and Nicolae Vulovici have already been mentioned: amongst other authors snuffed out by the war before they had any real chance to write about it were the poet and essayist Charles Péguy, killed on 5 September 1914 during the Battle of the Marne, Henri Alain-Fournier, author of *Le Grand Meaulnes*, killed on 22 September 1914, and Hermann Löns, killed 26 September 1914, whose 'Blood and Soil' poetry was later esteemed by the Nazis and whose novel *Der Wehrwolf* (1910), about peasants defending themselves against marauding foreign troops during the Thirty Years' War, provided the name adopted for the underground resistance groups organized when Allied forces began encroaching on German territory at the end of 1944. Péguy, Alain-Fournier, Löns and Vulovici may be regarded as belonging amongst the Lost Voices of First World War literature: had they lived the course of the war would not have been perceptibly altered, but the way we remember it might have been different.[27]

3

ARTISTS

Amongst those who survived long enough to make any sort of artistic statement about the war, it seems to have been painters rather than writers who were most immediately influenced by the vagaries of the military machine, though in painting as much as in literature the effect of institutional arrangements was balanced by more recondite factors.

It may be argued that the hundred years of material progress in Europe after Waterloo, the development of factories, of railways, of international money markets, made a conflict on the scale of the First World War inevitable, but the premise that sooner or later neighbouring states will find occasion to go to war is in fact no truer for the industrial era than for the pre-industrial – indeed experience since 1945 suggests it may be less true. In any case events as such are only part of the historical process: even more important is the sequence and timing of events. Though the outcome of the First World War might have been much the same if it had broken out before the aeroplane had been invented, and though Britain might still have gone to war with Germany for the sake of Belgium even if there had not been an eight-year build up of Anglo-German tension over Germany's desire to have a stronger battle fleet, all the details of what actually happened are inextricably bound up with the fact that they happened when and in the order they did. And one of the things that happened was that the war came just as artists, at least pictorial artists, were becoming, artistically speaking, ready for it.

In suggesting that artists were ready for the war in August 1914 one inevitably brings to mind Italian Futurism. The Futurist leader F.T. Marinetti had already declared that war was the only hygiene of the world in 1912, and Italy's war in what is now Libya in 1911–12, and the Balkan Wars of 1912–13, which took place in a zone where the Italians counted on increasing their influence, provided plenty of warlike images. Marinetti wrote an evocation of the Battle of Tripoli in relatively decorous French, and of the siege of Adrianople in demented Italian. But the Futurists did not have a monopoly of warlike special effects. The German Expressionist Ludwig Meidner's *Apocalyptic Landscape* paintings, his *Revolution*, and his ink, pencil and gouache composition *Bombing a City*, all dating from 1913, seem to have been inspired by his perception of the violent energies mobilized by contemporary urban life rather than by any prescience regarding the outbreak of war, while the military scenes painted by French Cubists such as Roger de La Fresnaye and Jacques Villon seem to have had less to do with bellicosity than with the way the angularity and regularity of peacetime military parades, their merging of individuals into masses, lent themselves to the compositional preoccupations of the Cubist movement. Such paintings can be seen as making only the tiniest contribution to the general assumption that war was a natural and, sooner or later, inevitable phenomenon. When the politicians (admirers of Landseer and Winterhalter almost to a man) decided on war, Marinetti was prominent amongst those in Italy who campaigned for Italian participation, but even if it is pretended that the Futurists had an important role in bringing Italy into the war in May 1915, it was after all a war that had started without them ten months earlier. The timeliness of Futurism, Expressionism, Cubism is not that they facilitated the outbreak of war, but that they provided the ideal expressive medium for depicting it.[1]

Surprisingly enough, the best of this depicting did not occur in the heartlands of the pre-war *avant garde*. William Rothenstein was too cautious when he wrote, 'the work produced by English painters during the war remains a significant contribution to the European art of our times.' In fact the British produced the most important paintings of the war, just as they produced the most important poetry. As suggested in the last chapter, poets in the British army had certain advantages compared to poets in other armies, but institutional advantages and opportunities do not automatically generate poetry. They may however make all the difference to a painter's ability to get on with his painting. In 1914 most European countries had conscription. Young artists were enrolled in the army, went to the front, and were buried there – often literally. In this way Germany lost Franz Marc (1886–1916), August Macke (1887–1914), Wilhelm Morgner (1891–1917), Hermann Stenner (1891–1914) and the more academically-inclined Hans Fuglsang (1889–1917) and Albert Weisgerber (1878–1915). With regard to August Macke, his friend Max Ernst later wrote:

> The attitude of Macke baffled us. Influenced by Futurism he accepted the war not merely as the most grandiose expression of contemporary madness but also as a philosophical necessity (war necessary for achieving the concept of humanity!) His bellicosity was however in no way coloured by patriotism, as was that of Apollinaire who – we later learnt – also allowed himself to be thrown off course by events. For those who have come to believe in the black irony of fate it is worth remembering that these two men who knew and loved each other, and who were haunted by the same ideas, perished as 'enemies', the one just after the declaration of war, the other on the eve of the Armistice.

France lost the sculptor Henri Gaudier-Brzeska (1891–1915); Georges Braque, like the poet Guillaume Apollinaire, was wounded in the head and underwent brain surgery. In the Italian army Umberto Boccioni met a fate by no means appropriate for a Futurist – he died as a result of falling from a horse, though admittedly it was an artillery horse.[2]

Once they were in the army many artists continued to make sketches, but the conditions in which they had to live were even less encouraging for art than for literature. Max Ernst, who managed to spend the war at HQs and base depots, and even found time to continue with his writing and painting, nevertheless wrote later, 'Max Ernst died on the 1st of August 1914', and on another occasion, '*1914–1915 Black Out*'. His final verdict was:

> In the shit for four years. 'Victorious, we are going to beat France, die as brave heroes!' we had to sing, with raging hearts, during the long night marches.
>
> What can one do against military life – its stupidity, its ugliness, its cruelty? To yell, swear, throw up in anger is no use. The temptation to abandon oneself to the therapeutic virtues of the contemplative life doesn't get one very far.

Ludwig Meidner was so depressed by the war that even though not called up till 1916 he painted relatively little during the first eighteen months of hostilities: once in the army, unable to paint or draw, he began to write and for a while even 'dreamt of becoming a second Byron, Heine or Victor Hugo'. Otto Dix became a sergeant in a machine-gun unit but found his comrades in arms contemptible, telling a visiting fellow-artist, 'You know, they think I'm mad, anything they can't eat they can't understand.' Oskar Schlemmer, an infantryman on the Russian Front, was pleased by the colours he saw, noting down 'the tents from inside, the greys transparent and grey-green, the browns rust-red – the colour of my pictures', but even as he amused himself with the way natural and unnatural shades combined, his depression and weariness with the army leaked through: 'I am seeing my fill of the splendour of colours, the differently green ground, the grey soldiers, and I eat and smoke and seek calm, the buddhist calm which I now only manage on the march.' Ernst Ludwig Kirchner did not even reach the front; he had a nervous collapse during preliminary training. Paul Klee, assigned to the German army air department to guard aircraft in transit, varnish fuselages and paint on registration numbers with a template, eventually became a paymaster's clerk at a flying school; about the nearest he ever came to the frontline was at Cambrai, where he was shocked by the sight of troops coming out of the line:

> ... an overwhelming sight. Everything yellow with mud. The unmilitary, matter-of-fact appearance, the steel helmets, the equipment. The trotting step. Nothing heroic, just like beasts of burden, like slaves. Against a background of circus music.

But rather than give him new ideas, the war merely consolidated old ones:

> The more horrible the world (as today, for instance), the more abstract our art, whereas a happy world brings forth an art of the here and now.
>   I have long had this war inside me. This is why, interiorly, it means nothing to me.[3]

The sheer uninterestingness of the war, in artistic terms, was also insisted upon by Gaudier-Brzeska in a kind of manifesto 'written from the Trenches' and published in Wyndham Lewis's magazine *Blast*:

> THE BURSTING SHELLS, the volleys, wire entanglements, projectors, motors, the chaos of battle DO NOT ALTER IN THE LEAST the outlines of the hills we are besieging. A company of PARTRIDGES scuttle along before our very trench.
>   IT WOULD BE FOLLY TO SEEK ARTISTIC EMOTIONS AMID THESE LITTLE WORKS OF OURS.
>   THIS PALTRY MECHANISM, WHICH SERVES AS A PURGE TO OVERNUMEROUS HUMANITY ...

<u>MY VIEWS ON SCULPTURE</u> REMAIN ABSOLUTELY <u>THE SAME</u> ...

I have made an experiment. Two days ago I pinched from an enemy a Mauser rifle. Its heavy unwieldy shape swamped me with a powerful IMAGE of brutality

I was in doubt for a long time whether it pleased or displeased me.

I found that I did not like it.

I broke the butt off and with my knife I carved in it a design, through which I tried to express a gentler order of feeling, which I preferred.

BUT I WILL EMPHASIZE that MY DESIGN <u>got its effect</u> (just as the gun had) FROM A VERY SIMPLE COMPOSITION OF LINES AND PLANES

GAUDIER-BRZESKA

(This text was followed by an announcement of Gaudier-Brzeska's death in action at Neuville St-Vaast on 5 June 1915.)[4]

In France wartime chauvinism encouraged an anti-modernist, anti-*avant-garde* tone in much art criticism, and the turning away from innovation detectable in the work of Dufy, Picasso and Matisse may perhaps be related to this, yet the objective conditions of the war zone encouraged some Cubist experimentation by artists like André Mare, who had been on the fringes of Cubism before 1914 but kept well away from it after 1918, and André Fraye, who was not involved with Cubism either before or after the war. Fernand Léger, a sapper during the war, even experienced a minor epiphany: 'I was dazzled by the open breach of a 75-millimetre gun in the sunlight, by the magic of the light on the white metal ...That open breach of a 75 in the full sunlight has taught me more for my plastic development than all the museums of the world.' Derain, in an infantry regiment, seems however to have turned against Cubism because of its emphasis on form at the expense of meaning:

On leave I saw plenty of things that didn't fill me with enthusiasm from the painting angle. It's the mess too ...

Cubism is a really idiotic thing which revolts me more and more …

I had some ideas about what should concern painters: simply the unknown. No more mechanics, that's to say no more means of expression, colours, line etc. – but just the unexplainable.

But the main burden of his wartime letters was the awfulness, ugliness and uninterestingness of the war:

The artillery! The artillery – always artillery. The mud – the rain or the dust – Nothing to tuck into, nothing to lie on and always like that, with never any letting up.

And the shells, and the aeroplanes, the night …

It's less picturesque than one could ever have believed and yet full of continual surprises …

If you knew the dumbness of the soldiers, it's beyond imagining. They don't understand a thing, nothing at all. You really couldn't have believed the generality of men were so stupid.

At least three *avant-garde* painters who served in the French army, Jacques Villon, André Dunoyer de Segonzac and Roger de La Fresnaye, were assigned to painting camouflage. This line of work resulted in some notable woodcuts and a striking canvas, now in the National Gallery of Canada, by the English Vorticist Edward Wadsworth, who had worked on camouflage in the Royal Navy, and it made Jacques Villon interested in colour theory, but it seems to have contributed little to the artistic development of Dunoyer de Segonzac, though he published a number of sketches of French soldiers in the trench newspaper *Le Crapouillot*: as for Roger de La Fresnaye, he contracted tuberculosis in 1918 and, having produced a few last paintings in an agreeably derivative style, died in November 1925. The French artist who had perhaps the best opportunities to draw what he liked at the front was

Paul Maze, who was attached to the British army as an interpreter and was able to make frequent use of his sketchbook. In his memoirs he quotes a British colonel at Mametz saying, 'I am afraid you won't find the landscape very inspiring', and judging by the bright, cheerful Impressionist style of his work from other periods, this was probably true: some of his sketches were passed on to the British staff for their topographical value but he seems to have destroyed most of the rest of his wartime work. One feels on the whole that the French *avant garde* failed to come to grips with the war; and perhaps the most eloquent depictions of the war to be painted in France were by conservative, eclectic artists, the Swiss-born Félix Vallotton, already forty-nine in 1914, and George Leroux, aged thirty-seven in 1914, who had won the Prix de Rome, accolade of academic respectability, back in 1906. Leroux's *L'enfer*, now in the Imperial War Museum, says as much about the sheer mind-boggling awfulness of the war as Otto Dix's *War Tryptich* of 1932 and *Flanders* of 1934–6, for all Dix's bitter unsmiling humour and stylish reminiscences of Breughel and Altdorfer and Hans Baldung Grien. It seems to have required the defeat of his country to make Dix see the war in terms of unendurable horror and degradation, for only a short while before Leroux, serving in the *302ᵉ Régiment d'Infanterie*, was making the sketches for what was to become *L'enfer*, Dix (possibly by way of distracting himself from the awful company he had to keep in the trenches) was producing crayons such as *Going Over the Top*, *Dying Warrior*, *Hand to Hand Fighting*, *Direct Hit* which were charged, almost supercharged, with brightness and energy.[5]

In Britain conditions were substantially different from those in France and Germany. There was no conscription till 1916: Christopher Nevinson, who was to emerge as one of the two outstanding painters of the war, first encountered its horrors as a volunteer medical orderly behind the French lines. In 1916 the British government decided to send official war artists to the front (as the Germans, Austro-Hungarians and even the Turks had done virtually since the beginning), and in March 1917 approved a scheme for a National War Museum (now the Imperial War Museum) which would exhibit the work of war artists. And whereas the more prominent German and Austrian war artists like Theodor Rocholl, Wilhelm Schreuer, Albin Egger-Lienz and Rudolf Konopa were men too old for combatant service, and were perhaps for that reason more inclined to recycle their pre-war work, the British employed a number of younger painters who had been serving as soldiers at the front and might thus be counted on to see things from the point of view of participants rather than onlookers: notably Wyndham Lewis and Paul Nash.[6]

One of the organizers of the war artists' scheme, Campbell Dodgson, Keeper of Prints and Drawings at the British Museum, thought that 'Nash is decidedly post-impressionist, not cubist, but "decorative", and his art is certainly not what the British public will generally like.' Few Keepers of Prints and Drawings have been more mistaken. The spokesmen of public opinion were ready for novelty, quickly recognizing that the new fashion of warfare could not be depicted in an old-fashioned way. Even *The Illustrated London News* did not hesitate to condemn paintings which were accurate enough in matters of detail but which seemed too nineteenth-century in spirit:

The general character of this work reminds us too closely of the battle-pieces of thirty years ago: there is nothing save in detail, to identify it with the New War. And there, in a nutshell, is the weakness of three-fourths of the year's war pictures – they do not belong to the year.

A contributor to another weekly wrote:

These scenes are freshly observed, but what are we to say of the battle-charges and turbulent horses, executed in the dear old manner, and familiar to us for a hundred years, and which at best were good enough for the old-fashioned papers – in which, I hasten to add, such 'fancy' subjects no longer appear! The impression we gather is that it is difficult to paint, realistically, the din and horror of a modern battle; and that War must be treated synthetically, and its various aspects suggested to the mind rather than, brutally, to the eye.[7]

One of the out-of-date middle-aged establishment artists complained of in this last quotation was John Lavery who later fully admitted the error of his ways:

Instead of the grim harshness and horror of the scenes I had given charming colour versions, as if painting a bank holiday on Hampstead Heath ... I felt nothing of the stark reality, losing sight of my fellow-men being blown to pieces in submarines or slowly choking to death in mud. I saw only new beauties of colour and design.

The efforts of some established artists to use conventional representational techniques in combination with a disconcerting irony and an element of hyper-realism that came near to suggesting delirium were not appreciated by the Young Turks. Wyndham Lewis recalled meeting William Orpen in France:

He came to our table and produced from his pocket a flask of whisky. 'Will y'have some?' he croaked in his quavering Dublin patter, which he had taken good care never to get rid of. 'It's good stuff – I know ut's good. It's from Haig's Mess. I gottut there this morning!'

I drank to the health of the High Command ... Upon hearing that I was with a battery in the Salient, he gazed in a half-mocking stare, twisting his eyebrows and smiling his wry Irish mockery at me.

'It's hell isn't it? It must be hell!' quickly he chattered under his breath.

I said it was Goya, it was Delacroix – all scooped out and very El Greco. But hell, no ...

'Ah yes, it must be hell!' he said. He pronounced hell, 'hail'.

'Hell sometimes for the infantry. But it's merely a stupid nighmare – it's not real.'

'Same thing!' said he.

Orpen however may be regarded as a pioneer of a style somewhere between what the Germans called *Neue Sachlichkeit* and the Italians *Realismo magico* (a term coined in 1919 by Giorgio de Chirico, who had spent the war in the Italian infantry, not at the front but reflecting on art in a barracks in Ferrara). The British, who have an excessive tendency to take their artistic labels from the French, have no term for this intermediate style, though one of its classic exemplars is *The Kensingtons at Laventie* painted in 1915 by Eric Kennington, who later specialized in portraits of individual frontline soldiers. Orpen's most striking war paintings stand somewhat on their own because of his odd sense of humour, but another artist who produced a *Neue Sachlichkeit/Realismo magico* type of picture, before the Germans and Italians found a label for the style, was Henry Lamb, whose *Advanced Dressing Station on the Struma* was painted for the Manchester City Gallery in 1920. From the German or Italian point of view the new style was a reaction to Expressionism or Post-Impressionism: from Kennington's or Orpen's or Lamb's point of view it was more directly a reaction to the war, and the problems of finding an iconological language in which to convey its realities.[8]

The man who succeeded most dramatically in finding the right painterly means of showing what was going on was Christopher Nevinson. A devoted disciple of Marinetti, the Italian Futurist, he had also known Picasso and was familiar with Cubism. In February 1915 he told the *Daily Express*, 'This war will be a violent incentive to Futurism, for we believe that there is no beauty except in strife, and no masterpiece without aggressiveness.' In 1913 Boccioni, the most considerable artist amongst the Futurists, had stated that they were working 'to destroy the old pictorial, idiotic, traditional, realistic, decorative, smoke-blackened museum stuff' and his programme went beyond what he regarded as the essentially traditionalist 'analytic enumeration' and emphasis on outward objective form of the Cubists: Impressionism, Boccioni wrote, was

> the first step towards the creation of a plastic organism constructed out of the pure lyrical interplay (of masses, lines, and lights) between object and setting... It points towards the *plastic fact*, towards creating what only we Italian Futurists have proclaimed and produced: the *style of sensation*, the *impression eternalized*, and *dynamism*.

Nevinson believed all that: the problem was how to reconcile this aggressive, cocksure celebration of modern forms and the modern spirit with what he had seen and felt as a hospital orderly in France. What for the Futurists was a celebration, with Nevinson became an indictment: his paintings show human individuals slotted together into a mass, like the components of a machine, or forced to become robot-like extensions of machines, or reduced at last to shadowy beings whose bandages have more individuality than their faces. As John Rothenstein later wrote, Cubism gave Nevinson 'an instrument in tune with the machines, which could represent a modern war with shattering effect ... it was a kind of magnificent shorthand, perfectly adapted to convey the simplified essence of a mechanized apocalypse'; but it was the apocalypticalness, not the cubishness, that Nevinson was concerned with. The critics responded enthusiastically to the way that Nevinson's formal technique fitted in with the physical appurtenances of machine-era warfare:

> Were there ever objects more appropriate for geometrical composition, for statement in terms of angles, curves and cubes, than guns and gun-carriages, lorries, planks and sleepers, aeroplanes, searchlights, the parallel rifles of troops on the march? The very steel helmets of the men in the trenches are so many ready-made arcs.

The Westminster Gazette saw Nevinson's way of depicting soldiers in positive terms: 'The soldiers themselves look as though they were the component parts of a formidable engine, drawn together by some irresistible attraction.' *The Times Literary Supplement* however recognized and endorsed Nevinson's evocation of the horrendously negative aspect of his subject:

> Nearly all war pictures in the past have been merely pictures that happened to represent war. Paolo Uccello's battle scenes are but pretexts for his peculiar version of the visible world. They might just as well be still life for all the effect the subject has had upon his treatment of it. Tintoret's battle scenes are parade pictures. Those of Rubens are like his hunting scenes or his Bacchanals, expressions of his own over-weening energy. In none of these, except perhaps in Lionardo's, was there implied any criticism of war, or any sense that it is an abnormal activity of man. The men who take part in it are just men fighting; they are not men seen differently because they are fighting, or in any way robbed of their humanity because of their inhuman business ...
>
> In Mr Nevinson's war pictures, now to be seen at the Leicester Gallery, there is expressed a modern sense of war as an abnormal occupation; and this sense shows itself in the very method of the artist. He was something of a Cubist before the war; but in these pictures he has found a new reason for being one; for his Cubist method does express, in the most direct way, his sense that in war man behaves like a machine or part of a machine, that war is a process in which man is not treated as a human being but as an item in a great instrument of destruction, in which he ceases to be a person and becomes lost in a process. The Cubist method, with its repetition and sharp distinction of planes, expresses this sense of mechanical process better than any other way of representation ... Samuel Butler imagined a future in which machines would come to life and make us their slaves; but

it is not so much that machines have come to life as that we ourselves have lost the pride and sweetness of our humanity; not that the machines seem more and more like us, but that we seem more and more like the machines.[9]

Not that *The Times Literary Supplement*'s reviewer was enamoured of Cubism:

There is the same incongruity between the cubist effort to see the visible world as a mechanical process and art itself. The cubist seems to force himself with a savage irony into this caricature of nature; we have emptied reality of its content in our thought and he will empty it of its content to our eyes… This irony we find in Mr Nevinson's pictures of the war, whether it be a despairing irony or the rebellion of an unshaken faith. He has emptied man of his content, just as the Prussian drill sergeant would empty him of his content for the purposes of war; and only a Prussian drill sergeant could consent to this version of man with any joy.

This seems to have chimed with what was increasingly Nevinson's own way of thinking. His experiences of machine-era warfare seem to have weaned him away, not merely from a Futurist admiration of machines, but from any interest in machines, or even in Cubism, with its simplified masses and straight lines and suggestion of mathematical relationships. In 1917 he was forbidden to exhibit a painting entitled *Paths of Glory* which showed two dead British soldiers face down beside a barbed wire entanglement, and was summoned to the War Office for an official reprimand when the picture was exhibited with a diagonal strip of brown paper bearing the word 'Censored' pasted across the two bodies. Apart from the steel helmets of the dead men there was nothing in the picture to suggest that it depicted the present: its painterly technique was as old as Manet. One almost suspects that for Nevinson the picture worked as well with the diagonal strip of brown paper as without: the message was 'Young men are being slaughtered uselessly', and it did not depend on the medium. A slightly later picture showing an overweight gentleman of somewhat Germanic appearance, with a distant look in his eyes, sitting on a chair with an anti-macassar next to a marble fire-place, bell-push and ornately framed oil painting, has its entire point in its title: *He Gained a Fortune but He Gave a Son.* The same message is contained in a poem written at about this time by Osbert Sitwell and dedicated to Siegfried Sassoon:

> His purple fingers clutch a large cigar –
> Plump, mottled fingers, with a ring or two.
> He rests back in his fat armchair. The war
> Has made this change in him. As he looks through
> His cheque-book with a tragic look he sighs:
> 'Disabled Soldiers' Fund' he reads afresh.
> And through his meat-red face peer angry eyes –
> The spirit piercing through its mound of flesh.
>
> They should not ask me to subscribe again!
> Consider me and all that I have done –
> I've fought for Britain with my might and main:
> I make explosives – and I gave a son ...

In both painting and poem, there is not much to take account of other than the message and the local colour, though the poem does suggest some ambiguities that may also be traceable in the painting. Sitwell's war profiteer is named Mr Abraham – presumably Jewish (surely Sitwell realised that Sassoon was Jewish too?). Is Nevinson's war profiteer Jewish too? He certainly doesn't look typically English. The Sitwell coal mines did rather well out of the war, and since neither Osbert nor his brother Sacheverell managed to get themselves killed, they stood to benefit eventually. Nevinson was himself a kind of war profiteer, making a better income painting the war than he would have done as a corporal fighting it. Perhaps his recognition of this contributed to his sense of defeat and depression. By 1917 he had lost his way as an artist, and seems never to have found it again.[10]

What Nevinson, in his best pictures, did for the frontline soldiers, Paul Nash did for the landscape of the war zone. His letters show him to have been a meticulous and highly intelligent observer of nature, but his pre-war artistic work seems feathery in concept as well as in composition. The war changed that. In 1917 he sketched the battlefield of Passchendaele, finding it 'the most frightful nightmare of a country more conceived by Dante or Poe than by nature ... one huge grave, and cast up on it the poor dead. It is unspeakable, godless, hopeless'. Some of the paintings he executed from these sketches in 1918 and 1919 have merely topographical captions – *The Mule Track*, *The Menin Road* – others had more polemical tides, *Void*, or *We Are Making a New World*. They all show a landscape denatured by human destructiveness, reduced to repetitive forms littered with shattered human artefacts, with humans visible, if at all, as vermin scuttling surreptitiously between cover: and, in the foreground of *The Menin Road*, a couple of beautifully-observed stems of sorrel growing in the mud, eloquently expressing the continuity of natural cycles amidst mechanised destruction. And it is remarkable how many details in his paintings are adumbrated in his letters: the shell holes filled with stagnant water which he wrote about to his wife, the 'black, brown and orange mould' thrown up by exploding shells, the smoke hanging in 'narrow bars of violet and dark' – these are all in *The Menin Road*. The 'headless trees' in his paintings can of course be seen in contemporary photographs too, though the 'landscape ... so distorted from its own gentle forms' is nowhere as painfully depicted as in *We Are Making A New World*. Nash was not the only artist to see that during the war man had reduced nature to a set of ugly abstract shapes. It was Wyndham Lewis who wrote:

War, and especially those miles of hideous desert known as 'the line' in Flanders and France, presented me with a subject-matter so consonant with the austerity of that 'abstract' vision I had developed, that it was an easy transition. Had you at that time asked me to paint a milkmaid in a landscape of buttercups and daisies I should probably have knocked you down. But when Mars with his mailed finger showed me a shell-crater and a skeleton, with a couple of shivered tree-stumps behind it, I was still in my 'abstract' element.

But none of Wyndham Lewis's creative efforts, whether literary or artistic, were ever as interesting as his programmes and commentaries. It was only really Nash and Nevinson who found in *avant-garde* art the means with which to paint Armageddon.[11]

4

TRUTH

In painting there may be no real distinction between what one wants to say and how one says it: after all, one does not actually *say* anything, one puts paint on a canvas. Some critics would claim the distinction does not exist in literature either; nevertheless this chapter deals primarily with *what* writers said about the First World War, and the next chapter primarily with *how* they said it.

From the very beginning governments recognized the propaganda value of supposedly authentic accounts of the fighting. At home the relatives of those at the front line, and all those others whose lives had been disrupted and energized by the mobilization of national resources, wanted – or thought they wanted – to know what was happening: abroad there were neutral states whose opinion-formers needed to be won over or at least placated. When the Swedish explorer Sven Hedin made his way to Germany to investigate the war, he was given every facility by the German Foreign Ministry and General Staff: the resulting book was regarded as a major coup for German propaganda. In Vienna authors like Rainer Maria Rilke, Hugo von Hofmannsthal, Stefan Zweig and Franz Werfel were employed (though not all at the same time) in the archives of the Ministry of War to write or touch up stories of frontline heroism suitable for use by the newspapers, while

Rudolf Konopa, Géza Mároti and other artists were sent to sketch at the front. In 1915 the British War Office permitted five correspondents from the London press to go out to the Western Front on a permanent basis, though despite the knighting of four of them after the war their work remains no more than higher journalism, written from the point of view of the onlooker. John Masefield's book on Gallipoli has already been mentioned. Successful aviators like Richthofen, Bishop and McCudden were officially encouraged to write up their exploits and managed to present themselves on paper as professional killers of no literary sensibility. Robert Nichols, the poet who had survived ten days within earshot of the front before having his nervous breakdown, was commissioned to write an account of the frontline work of the Royal Engineers but only managed two chapters. Nichols's later activities however suggest that officialdom, in Britain at least, may have attached less importance to literature than to painting; when he was sent on a propaganda mission to the United States in 1918 literature was only part of his remit. 'My first public act on landing was to place a wreath on the catafalque of Joyce Kilmer, one of their soldier poets. This created, I think, a favourable impression,' he reported, and he also gave interviews on 'the most modern developments of British Art, Literature and Music': but his chief responsibility was to help with the publicity for an exhibition of paintings by Christopher Nevinson, John Lavery and Wyndham Lewis. Perhaps it was recognized that art depended to a large extent on an institutional framework, but literature would go its own way whatever attempts were made to manipulate it.[1]

Literature in fact went in several directions. Ezra Pound – not in the armed forces – had a vivid impression of

> frankness as never before
> disillusions as never told in the old days
> hysterias, trench confessions
> laughter out of dead bellies

but for obvious reasons the bulk of what was written at the front, whether addressed to fellow soldiers or to loved ones at home, aimed at keeping up the spirits of both writer and reader. The French trench journal *On progresse* claimed, 'The rank stupidity of the Army and the vastness of the sea are the only two things which can give an idea of infinity', but it was *The Cambridge Magazine* back in England which printed Siegfried Sassoon's bitter denunciations of the war. The first page of the first issue of *The Dud* (the trench journal of 11th Battalion King's Shropshire Light Infantry) announced:

> The Editors are not setting out to reform the world, nor do they expect to create any undue sensation amongst literary circles. The origin of this paper – briefly stated – is as follows: the Editor and the Art Editor have long been sending contributions to the best known Journals, all of which have invariably been rejected! Therefore, they determined to publish their respective efforts and spite the publishers.
>
> If in so doing they amuse you for a few moments, then they will account their venture a success.

A fair specimen of the usual tone of whimsy in trench journals may be found in another *Dud*, this time produced by the 14th Battalion Argyll and Sutherland Highlanders:

> 'It's queer', said Black, 'how near we are to home. The gramophone is playing the latest revue rubbish, this cake was made by my sister only four days ago, and I am reading this week's *Punch.*'
>
> 'And I', I said, 'am trying to sleep', but the words were hardly out of my mouth before all thought of sleep vanished, for mother suddenly appeared in the dug-out, and the voice I loved best in the world said: 'The old story I see, James – breakfast in bed', and she smiled indulgently. 'By the way,

too, you don't look after your servants very well, those stairs haven't been dusted for *weeks.*' Poor mother! She also must have reversed engines in descending those stairs. Thank heaven she didn't come when it was wet.

'Will you have some tea?' I asked, 'we're just at breakfast – Bones!'

Bones appeared, lifted a dirty cup with a grimy paw, vanished into the darkness, and speedily reappeared with his vessel full of a brown tepid liquid. Mother did her best with it.

'He has a nice pleasant face,' she said, 'but he can't make tea, and, my dear boy, you must speak to him about the state of his hands.'

'Oh, they aren't so bad', said I uneasily, 'It's the shadows. It's pretty dark down here.'

'Disgracefully dark', assented mother. 'I could hardly find my way in, but', she added plaintively, 'I didn't dare to complain, I thought it was one of the hardships out here, perhaps.'

'We'll soon cure that', I replied stoutly, and lit a couple of extra candles. 'There, that's better.' It wasn't. Candles are hard to get, and in any case the cuttings from the *Vie Parisienne* became much too obvious. There was a gloomy silence whilst she regarded the walls of the dug-out...[2]

Some books were published which attempted to present honest, unbiased accounts of what was going on, but as the war prolonged itself attitudes with regard to what it was that was really going on necessarily changed. For the first eighteen months or so of the war the best writing about it by men in the firing line consisted of cool, detailed, rather detached prose accounts of what they had seen and of reflections, in both prose and poetry, on what they had experienced, though none of these were quite as disturbingly explicit as some of the statements handed in after the war by officers who had been taken prisoner, which remained buried in the War Office records for nearly eighty years. The detailed, rather detached prose accounts would come back after the war. From 1916 onwards however the intensification of the fighting and of its horrors shifted frontline writing in a new direction. It was no longer necessary to describe war to contemporaries who had seen it for themselves, or to the folks back home who had been saturated with first-hand accounts and obviously preferred something a little less unnerving, such as *The Love Letters of an Unknown Soldier: Found in a Dug-Out* (a best-seller in 1918), which purported to be the love letters of an unknown and probably dead artillery subaltern to an American girl he had met in Paris. The best frontline writing of the second half of the war was addressed to the discontents of one's fellow frontline soldiers. Michele Campana for example, finishing his book *Perchè ho ucciso?* ('Why did I kill?') in October 1918, wrote, 'Only my comrades can understand and like this book, because it is they who have created it with their blood and I who have faithfully transcribed it.'[3]

The best of this sort of writing came from the British army, and the best of all from Wilfred Owen, who thought, 'All a poet can do today is warn. That is why the true poets must be truthful':

Bent double, like old beggars under sacks,
Knock-kneed, coughing like hags, we cursed through sludge,
Till on the haunting flares we turned our backs
And towards our distant rest began to trudge.
Men marched asleep. Many had lost their boots
But limped on, blood-shod. All went lame; all blind;
Drunk with fatigue; deaf even to the hoots
Of tired, outstripped Five-Nines that dropped behind.

Gas! GAS! Quick, boys! –An ecstasy of fumbling,
Fitting the clumsy helmets just in time;
But someone still was yelling out and stumbling,
And flound'ring like a man in fire or lime...
Dim, through the misty panes and thick green light,
As under a green sea, I saw him drowning.

In all my dreams, before my helpless sight,
He plunges at me, guttering, choking, drowning.

If in some smothering dreams you too could pace
Behind the wagon that we flung him in,
And watch the white eyes writhing in his face,
His hanging face, like a devil's sick of sin;
If you could hear, at every jolt, the blood
Come gargling from the froth-corrupted lungs,
Obscene as cancer, bitter as the cud
Of vile, incurable sores on innocent tongues, –
My friend, you would not tell with such high zest
To children ardent for some desperate glory,
The old Lie: Dulce et decorum est
Pro patria mori.[4]

Poetry was the obvious medium for such statements, if only because its compression made it the most convenient format – Patrick MacGill was almost unique in claiming to be able to write at length in the trenches. Poetry also, despite Wordsworth's famous claim that it took its origin 'from emotion recollected in tranquillity', offered a kind of immediacy, which may be the reason why very little poetry written from a frontline perspective was produced once the war was over. The war poems of Anton Schnack and David Jones's *In Parenthesis are* perhaps the only notable exceptions. Wilfred Owen and Isaac Rosenberg had been killed in the last days of the war of course, but if they had survived it is unlikely they would have stuck with the war as a favoured subject: Owen amused himself with the idea that he intended 'To write blank-verse plays on old Welsh themes. Models: Tennyson, Yeats.' Sassoon, Graves, and Blunden survived to write more poetry but decided that prose offered the best medium for what they had left to say about their time in the army: in July 1919 Graves told Blunden, 'War poetry is played out I'm afraid, commercially, for another five or ten years. Rotten thing for us, but it's no good blinking at it.'[5]

It is sometimes claimed that, once the fighting was over, there was no real interest in war literature till the late 1920s, with 1929, the year of the book version of Erich Maria Remarque's *All Quiet on the Western Front*, R.C. Sherriff's *Journey's End*, Richard Aldington's *Death of a Hero* and Robert Graves's *Goodbye to All That* perhaps marking the breakthrough. At the end of the Second World War, when Godfrey Winn wanted to write up his experiences, Lord Beaverbrook told him:

> in ten years' time, the war will be 'news' again. It was last time. Remember *All Quiet?* In ten years' time, that's when you will get the sales. *Now's* the time for you to be out and about, with your nose to the scent. The war's over. The public are sick of war books, anything to do with the war. Ask your publisher, ask any bookseller. Now it's the future, the problems of reconstruction you should think about, write about, interest your readers in.

But Beaverbrook had his facts the wrong way round. Wilfrid Ewart's *Way of Revelation* enjoyed a brief vogue in 1921. (Fourteen months after his novel was published Ewart was dead, accidently shot by a New Year reveller in Mexico City.) Ernest Raymond's *Tell England*, one of the most celebrated of English war novels, came out in 1922. In the United States John Dos Passos's *Three Soldiers* was published in 1921. In Italy all the best work to appear about the war was in print by that year, with the exception of Carlo Salsa's *Trincee* ('Trenches'), which came out in 1924 and F.T. Marinetti's wartime notebooks, which remained unpublished till 1987: Gino Cornali's unimpressive *Un fante lassù* ('An Infantryman Up There') of 1934, later regarded as an important text by Nazi literary commentators, may be discounted. The year 1921 is also more or less the cut-off point for the Portuguese, who declared war on Germany in 1916 and thereafter made something of a speciality of insipid books with striking titles like *The Avalanche (1918)* and *The Macabre Symphony* (1920). The most influential of German war memoirs,

Ernst Jünger's *In Stahlgewittern*, was published in 1920, though six years later Jünger still thought 'it required a longer and harder labour for us to become clear about the meaning of events.'[6]

Like Jünger, Hugh MacDiarmid considered in 1923 that it was still too soon to come to terms with what their generation had lived through, claiming, 'the real literature of the war could not possibly be written for a few years – possibly for a good few years – if ever', and it may be a mistake to assume that the literature we have is the best we might or should have had. *In Stahlgewittern* might never have been published if Jünger's father had not put up the money to pay the printer. Georg von der Vring's *Soldat Suhren*, completed in 1923, was rejected by eighteen publishing houses before finally being accepted by a Swiss firm in 1927. Edmund Blunden hastened to set down his reminiscences in 1918 but did not publish them for ten years, finding it necessary to rewrite his text completely because, 'although in its details not much affected by the perplexities of distancing memory, [it] was noisy with a depressing gaiety then very much the rage.' Charles Carrington wrote down his memories of the Battle of the Somme and the Battle of Passchendaele in 1919 and 1920 but later confessed 'for several years modesty prevented me from showing them even to my friends'; eventually he published them under a pseudonym in 1929. Other manuscripts may have been not merely delayed but fumbled over for years before being finally binned. J.B. Priestley, who had enlisted in September 1914 and had been wounded twice in the trenches, did not publish anything about his experiences till the early 1960s, when what he mainly recalled was how disageeable it all was:

> Except at certain rare moments, and these were far outnumbered by their peacetime counterparts, I did not discover any deeper reality in war ... Its obvious one-sidedness soon made it seem to me a vast piece of imbecility.

At the time he had written to his father from the trenches of 'a vast exultation of the soul at the expense of the body', and one cannot help wondering if the negative picture he eventually gave in his memoirs was not coloured by creative blockages encountered over forty years earlier.[7]

War books, it should be remembered, were not simply caused by the war: soldier-writers were not simply virgin wombs who in 1914 were waiting to be impregnated by a dose of trench-fighting. When Siegfried Sassoon acknowledged, 'a war was needed to wake me up and give me my incentive to write', he did not mean that he had not written poems before 1914, merely that they had been rather dilettantish. And afterwards, though there were very large numbers of war books by authors who published nothing else, the majority of the best-known works were by professed men of letters, some of whom had already made a name for themselves before 1914: the war, however inescapable it seemed while everyone was in uniform, became just one out of a list of possible topics once peacetime necessities reasserted themselves. Both the books that were written and the moment at which their authors chose to write them related to the motivations and career strategies of a very disparate set of individuals.[8]

The choice of whether to write a war novel, a slightly fictionalized and tidied up memoir of what the author has really seen and felt, or a scrupulously faithful record in which a few of the more stomach-churning details have been supressed and a few names have been changed, has also to be seen in relation to certain characteristics which distinguish the majority of war memoirs from most other examples of autobiographical writing. War memoirs tend to say less about what the author did and who he met than about what he suffered and experienced passively. With a few arguable exceptions like Siegfried Sassoon's George Sherston sequence, they also give unusually little sense of their protagonists changing and developing as human beings, though in the four year period described the writers had often been promoted from junior dogsbody to positions of considerable responsibility. These books are unusual too in being written mostly by *young* men – sometimes still under thirty – and at a time when the events described were still recent and raw enough to give nightmares: that is to say, they were written in psychological conditions not dissimilar to those in which the romantic, subjective, whingeing type of first novel is generally produced.

Not surprisingly some war reminiscences seem to be more an exercise in forgetting than remembering. When Elliott White Springs left Culver Military Academy, Indiana, his class yearbook recorded. 'His ambition is to be a writer of dime novels.' Five years later he was a flight commander in the 148th Squadron of the US Army Air Corps and on the way to becoming America's sixth-ranking fighter ace: and not enjoying it. In July 1918 he wrote home:

> I'm all shot to pieces ... Few men live to know what real fear is. It's something that grows on you day by day, that eats into your constitution and undermines your sanity... While I am waiting around all day for the afternoon patrol, I think I am going crazy. I keep watching the clock and figuring how long I have to live ... When I go out to get in my plane my feet are like lead – I am just barely able to drag them after me.

Nothing of this appears in the sketches based on his experiences which he later published under the title *Nocturne Militaire*: in these the would-be dime novelist asserted himself with a vengeance.

> I got caught diving on a two-seater over by Armentières. I got underneath him according to the instructions and blue prints from GHQ – see page 14, paragraph 6, 'How to attack a two-seater'. I was all set to hit him with my first burst, but when I pressed my triggers nothing happened. Both guns had jammed and so did my heart! While I was trying to clear my guns, the two-seater began to manoeuvre, and before I woke up to what was happening, the observer had taken a good long crack at me and the hot oil was streaming back in my face to call attention to the fact that my oil lead was hit.

I started back at a thousand feet with the whole Hun army shooting at me and those that weren't shooting were throwing rocks and old shoes.

But perhaps Elliott White Springs really had forgotten his pre-mission nerves by the time he came to write *Nocturne Militaire*; perhaps in any case he had exaggerated his nervous prostration in his letter home out of a desire to obtain sympathy from his parents, or to inflict some obscure revenge on them. There is an element of posing in the wartime letter as much as in the post-war reminiscence, which is hardly surprising since the same man wrote both; but we cannot be sure that the authentic Elliott White Springs is to be found equidistant between the two poses, because we cannot know how many other poses there were in his repertoire.[9]

Any autobiographical writer has to choose what he feels to be an appropriate voice. Some may do so without quite realizing the range of possibilities on offer – though it took Edmund Blunden several years to get the undertone right in *Undertones of War*. Yet finding an appropriate voice is only a means to an end. The prime motive of most ex-servicemen who wrote about the war was nothing more or less than an urge to tell the truth about what they had experienced. As early as 1917 Vernon Bartlett stated in an 'Apologia' at the beginning of his *Mud and Khaki: Sketches from Flanders*:

There has been so much written about the trenches, there are so many war photographs, so many cinema films, that one might well hesitate before even mentioning the war – to try to write a book about it is, I fear, to incur the censure of the many who are tired of hearing about bombs and bullets, and who prefer to read of peace, and games, and flirtations.

But, for that very reason, I venture to think that even so indifferent a war book as mine will not come entirely amiss … If, to a minute extent, anything in these pages should help to bring home to people what war really is, and to remind them of their debt of gratitude, then these little sketches will have justified their existence.

Ernst Jünger wrote in 1920, 'I am not a reporter, I am not putting forward a collection of heroes, I don't wish to describe how it could have been, but how it was.' In 1925 Cyril McNeile remarked in the Preface to his novel *Shorty Bill:*

> Books on the war are no longer popular, but I cannot help thinking, from remarks that have been made to me, that there are still people who would like to be reminded, and others, of a younger generation, who would like to learn.

For T.W. White, author of an account of his escape from Turkish captivity, publication of his book in 1928 was an act of piety:

> My excuse for putting a war story before the public at so late a date is that I feel that this gist of a diary recording the doings and sufferings of prisoners of war in Turkey should be published, if for no other reason than as a tribute to those who died.[10]

Yet simply writing down the truth as one remembered it was not as easy as it sounded: as the Hungarian novelist József Lengyel later wrote 'If the author wished to write down everything, even the biography of an ant would fill more than a hundred volumes.' And though three or four years of military service might provide almost too many incidents to select from, while one was trying to make one's selection the memory itself was making a selection of its own. In the mid-1930s Victor Yeates did not find this a problem:

> I was writing a novel that was to be an exact reproduction of a period and an exact analysis and synthesis of a state of mind: for these purposes an overwhelming and untidy accumulation of detail seemed necessary.

But at exactly the same period John Gibbons was finding both details and states of mind increasingly hard to recall:

> *All Quiet on the Western Front* [the best-selling novel by Erich Maria Remarque] probably made a fortune for its publishers and for some gentlemen in Hollywood, but it could hardly have had any public at all from the men who had actually done the fighting ...
>
> I see that I shall have to write my own War Book. And I shall have to write it soon, if I am to get it into print in time for the next part of the War and before the thing is on us again. Also I shall have to get the story down before I have forgotten half of it. Which again is curious. For perhaps two years after 1918 I would wake night after night trembling with the nightmare of the filth and terror of the trenches; and now all that has long left me, and I catch myself remembering only the jolly bits and the funny stories of cheating the sergeant.

Less than five years after the war K.L. Harris, sitting down to compose an essay on his 'Service Experiences' for the RAF Staff course at Andover, noted that 'the distance of time that has elapsed has caused the incidents and impressions to become merged into one conglomerate mass, from which it is hard to extract the true metal and discard the dross.' Charles Carrington, who had written down his recollections of the Somme and Passchendaele in 1919 and 1920, thought in 1929 that 'no war book written now, ten or fifteen years after the event, can secure the authenticity attaching to these two stories.'[11]

Only a few months earlier Paolo Monelli had come to a similar conclusion, explaining:

> The man who undertook today, in good faith, to narrate his memories as a fighting man would write a false book. Not by his own fault, but because of the qualities of human nature. The most faithful and humble memory distorts long-past events.

The shells fall closer, the actions are enormously exaggerated, the periods of waiting lose their length, the intermediate moments disappear: the falsehoods and the rhetoric of others act unconsciously upon us. With what that should neither be conventional nor hypothetical could I now fill in the frightful silence that, in my memories, enwraps the battle of December 4th, 1917, on the saddle between Monte Tondarecar and Castelgomberto? Certainly that afternoon of fighting at close quarters, that struggle at a few dozen metres' distance, that wearisome disengaging from enemy encirclement, and those *mélées* round the machine-guns, must have been enveloped in a tremendous din; but, while I have still very clear recollections of the lie of the ground, the rocks, the mountain pines, the men, the wounded, the dead, the advancing German masses, the blood flowing from the forehead of corporal-major De Boni, and the wide, staring eyes of Altin, nothing remains to me of the voices, the shouts, the noises, or the explosions, as though I had lived through that scene – a vain image among other vain images – on the screen of a cinema.

Those critics were wrong who, rather disdaining these humble jottings of mine published immediately after the great tempest, said: 'Only the years to come will give us the books that really describe the war.' Completely wrong. The books that really describe war are those written shortly after the fight, immediately outside it. Even among these there are false ones, mark you, at least for us ex-soldiers, if our judgment – and some people doubt it – is to be of any value; false, because written by men in the back areas, or by boasters whom no war ever cured, or by people who took into the front line too many literary or humanitarian preconceptions.[12]

Other writers might have reasons for caution in misrepresenting what they had done or experienced. For example there are significant discrepancies between the account of being taken prisoner by the Germans that the poet F. W. Harvey handed in to the War Office at the end of the war and the account he subsequently published: he told the War Office 'I was captured on patrol', but in the book he wrote later he explained he was scheduled to lead a patrol and foolishly attempted to reconnoitre the patrol route in advance, on his own, telling only a corporal – a piece of unprofessional rashness senior officers would not have condoned. In this instance the misrepresentation was only in official paperwork, but other veterans may have found reason to be economical with the truth in their published writing in ways that might be now difficult to detect or verify.[13]

One thing was evident: it was not enough simply to have been there and seen it. Jean Norton Cru, in his analytical treatise *Témoins*, was not afraid to say when he thought frontline soldiers got it wrong: for example Roland Dorgelès, author of one of the classics of French war literature *Les croix de bois*, served fourteen months at the front but represented for Cru 'one of the most ignorant writers there is on the subject of combat experience and the sufferings of the common soldier'. André Bridoux complained:

> One could cite books that are false from softness, one might even say, feebleness, and from being intended to give an idea of war that would fit in with children's picture books, but one would find more that are false from excess and from wanting to shake the reader's nerves with a display of suffering and butchery. Apart from the fact that they are repugnant and useless, such descriptions are psychologically false, for the horror depended less on the spectacle itself than on one's state of mind at the time, and when one went into the line in a bad sector, seeing a wounded man, or even an empty stretcher, affected the imagination more than all the rubble over which one had marched up to the line.

Edmund Blunden was another who thought that it was difficult to strike the right note:

> a peculiar difficulty would exist for the artist to select the sights, faces, words, incidents, which characterized the time.

The art is rather to collect them, in their original form of incoherence. I have not noticed any compelling similarity between a bomb used as an inkpot and a bomb in the hand of a corpse, or even between the look of a footballer after a goal all the way and that of a sergeant inspecting whale-oiled feet. There was a difference prevailing in all things.[14]

In André Bridoux's view Blunden, an officer who spent much of his time at the front attached to battalion headquarters, needn't have bothered:

weeks, months, weren't enough to learn in: it needed years for the life of the soldier to get into one's skin, for one to take on its habits and its spirit; above all, it was necessary to have been a soldier, and I mean soldier, rank and file, for those who were only officers will always lack direct knowledge of the real rank and file, the essential component of the army.

Not everyone would have agreed with Bridoux. Cyril McNeile, later well-known as the author of the Bull-Dog Drummond series of thrillers, was a captain in the Royal Engineers when the war broke out: hence his pseudonym 'Sapper'. Apart from the fact that he won the Military Cross, was twice mentioned in despatches, and ended the war as a lieutenant-colonel commanding the 18th Battalion of the Middlesex Regiment, the nature of his frontline service is unclear: he was appointed brigade major (i.e. chief staff officer of an infantry brigade) in April 1917 but till he was appointed to command his battalion he would never, as an engineer officer, have had infantrymen under his direct orders. In 1917 he published a collection of short stories entitled *No Man's Land* dedicated 'To the Infantrymen', and in the Preface he wrote 'I offer these pages as a small tribute ... to the men who have saved the world – to the Infantrymen.' Apart from a couple of stories involving officers of the Royal Engineers, *No Man's Land* dealt with the life of the infantry from both the common soldier's and the subaltern's point of view: in a later work, *Shorty Bill* (1926) he took one of his Other Rank characters from *No Man's Land* and made him the central character. Though the sub-Kipling dialogue now jars somewhat, both books are convincing and, if read at a sufficiently early age, even moving. A better-known work is *Krieg* ('War', 1928) by Ludwig Renn, one of the classic accounts of the war from the ordinary soldier's point of view. The real identity of its author was Arnold Vieth von Golssenau, who had been a lieutenant in the Guards in Saxony when war broke out and commanded a company and later a battalion on the Western Front. He later explained:

> in the First World War ordinary soldiers often took the initiative if their officers were dead or absent. I wanted to give an account of these obscure individuals whom I had learnt to respect and love as the real heroes of the war. None of the war reporters or scribblers in the service of the ruling classes had written about them, because they did not know these soldiers and were forever on the look out for conspicuous deeds of personal heroism: and what came of that was empty phrases which we 'frontline swine' merely despised because they were all false or biassed.

Vieth von Golssenau (as one might have guessed) was a communist, having joined the party after his family lost its money in the inflation of the early 1920s: it is ironical that he should have adopted an authorial strategy similar to that of the creator of 'Bull-Dog Drummond'.[15]

Perhaps something similar but in reverse is evident in the volumes of Henry Williamson's *A Chronicle of Ancient Sunlight* that dealt with the war: in *A Test to Destruction* Williamson's protagonist/alter ego Phillip Maddison ends the war as a twenty-three-year-old acting lieutenant-colonel with a DSO whereas the twenty-three-year-old Williamson ended the war as a mere lieutenant with a couple of campaign medals.[16]

Humphrey Cobb went even further than Cyril McNeile or Ludwig Renn. An American citizen, he served in the Canadian Expeditionary Force as a teenager, and was wounded and twice gassed. His death from thrombosis in his mid-forties may have had its ultimate cause in his wartime injuries: he certainly had a close enough look at the war from the Canadian soldier's point of view to write a book about it. Instead he wrote *Paths of Glory* (1935), about soldiers in the French army who refused to advance in a doomed offensive, were court-martialled and executed by firing squad. He had read about such things happening in the French army, whereas in the Canadian Expeditionary Force the same scenario would not have been quite convincing.[17]

In rejecting personal experience in favour of a viable plot, Cobb was following in the footsteps of the author of the most famous of the American novels about the First World War: Ernest Hemingway's *A Farewell To Arms* (1929) in which the protagonist is with the Italian army from 1915 onwards: the defeat of the Italian army at Caporetto and the retreat to the Tagliamento, which provides the novel's climax, occurred while Hemingway was a cub reporter in Kansas City. Hemingway only arrived at the Italian front, as a Red Cross ambulance driver, the following June, and was wounded by an Austrian trench mortar three weeks later. The only battle he saw was the Italian army's defensive victory on the Piave, by which, at the time, he was most impressed:

> I was all through the big battle and have Austrian carbines and ammunition, German and Austrian medals, officer's automatic pistols, Boche helmets, about a dozen Bayonets, star shell pistols and knives and almost everything you can think of. The only limit to the amount of souvenirs I could have is what I could carry for there were so many dead Austrians and prisoners the ground was almost black with them. It was a great victory and showed the world what wonderful fighters the Italians are.

In retrospect however he decided the Piave was neither dramatic enough nor disastrous enough for his story-line, and posed problems of chronology. He may also have thought readers would be unable to sympathize with a red-blooded American hero who deserted his army when it was winning.[18]

The benefit of hindsight inevitably coloured even writing that purported to be honest reportage. 'The most successful war books of today', complained the Czech journalist Egon Erwin Kisch in 1930, 'present the facts of that time on the basis of the experiences, circumstances and views of today.' After he had had a considerable popular and critical success with his memoir *Good-Bye to All That* Robert Graves wrote to *The Times Literary Supplement* asking:

> But what is meant by the *truthfulness* of war-books? ... It was practically impossible (as well as forbidden) to keep a diary in any active trench-sector, or to send letters home which would be of any great post-War documentary value; and the more efficient the soldier the less time, of course, he took from his job to write about it. Great latitude should therefore be allowed to a soldier who has since got his facts or dates mixed. I would even paradoxically say that the memoirs of a man who went through some of the worst experiences of trench warfare are not truthful if they do not contain a high proportion of falsities. High-explosive barrages will make a temporary liar or visionary of anyone; the old trench-mind is at work in all over-estimation of casualties, 'unnecessary' dwelling on horrors, mixing of dates and confusion between trench rumours and scenes actually witnessed. General Crozier [of whom more later] honestly admits that his memory was in the later stages of his long service badly affected by the strain; but, as writers of books of this sort should, gives units, dates, places wherever possible as a pledge of intended truthfulness.

Graves's own deviations from strict accuracy include his endorsement of the picture in R.C. Sherriff's play *Journey's End* of company commanders awash with whisky, and some fashionable sneers at the Church of England:

> For Anglican regimental chaplains we had little respect. If they had shown one-tenth the courage, endurance, and other human qualities that the regimental doctors showed, we agreed, the British Expeditionary Force might well have started a religious revival. But they had not, being under orders to avoid getting mixed up in the fighting and to stay behind with the transport. Soldiers could hardly respect a chaplain who obeyed these orders, and yet not one in fifty seemed sorry to obey them ... the Roman Catholic chaplains were not only permitted to visit posts of danger, but definitely enjoyed to be wherever fighting was, so that they could give extreme unction to the dying. And we never heard of one who failed to do all that was expected of him and more. Jovial Father Gleeson of the Munsters, when all the officers were killed or wounded at the first battle of Ypres, had stripped off his black badges and, taking command of the survivors, held the line.

It is certainly true that three or four Catholic chaplains won the Distinguished Service Order for bravery under fire, as did the Rev. Michael Adler, 'Senior Jewish Chaplain to the Forces', and some clergymen of the Anglican Church preferred to go to the front not as chaplains but as combatant officers, including two men who were promoted to command battalions before being killed in action, the Rev. Bernard Vann, VC, MC and bar and the Rev. Percy William Beresford, DSO. The Rev. Robert Furley Callaway, a pre-war missionary in Africa who suffered eleven months of frustration as a military chaplain at a time when chaplains were confined to rear areas, obtained a combatant commission, took a communion plate and chalice with him to the front, and was killed during the Battle of the Somme in September 1916; and he was not the only Anglican clergyman who went to France first as a chaplain but later returned as a combatant. Other Anglican clergy served in the ranks. But the Rev. Theodore Bayley Hardy, VC, DSO, MC, a former headmaster who died of wounds complicated by pneumonia in October 1918 at the age of fifty-two and who was described by one battalion adjutant as 'the most wonderful man I have ever met', the Rev. Edward Mellish, VC, MC, the Rev. William Addison, VC and the Rev. Harry Blackburne, DSO, MC, seven times mentioned in despatches, afterwards Dean of Bristol, all distinguished themselves under fire as Anglican pastors. (No Catholic chaplain won the Victoria Cross.) One should also mention the Rev. P.T.B. 'Tubby' Clayton, founder of ToC H, and the Rev. G.A. Studdert Kennedy *aka* 'Woodbine Willie', both of whom won the Military Cross and who certainly did as much as any two men could to reverse the long-term decline of the Church of England's hold on the popular imagination. (Graves's suggestion that more effective chaplains could have started a religious revival, incidentally, is a direct crib from C.E. Montague's *Disenchantment*, published in 1922.) As for the jovial Father Gleeson, he is mentioned six times in Captain Stouppe McCance's *History of the Royal Munster Fusiliers* but only in his ecclesiastical character, and the War Diary of his battalion, which does not mention him, gives little indication that the Munsters ran out of officers during the First Battle of Ypres: *11 November 1914* (the worst day of the battle): '1.30 a.m. Line taken over. 8 a.m. Capt. Reymes-Cole killed by a sniper in B Coy Trenches. Attacks were made by enemy during the day. Lt Philby was killed. Night very wet; all quiet...', *19th November 1914* '7 officers granted 96 hrs leave out of country...' They would certainly not have sent seven officers home on leave if there had not been enough officers to command the surviving troops.[19]

Graves was later quite frank in admitting the degree of calculation that had gone into writing *Good-Bye to All That*: 'I have more or less deliberately mixed in all the ingredients that I know are mixed into other popular books, specifically food and drink, murders, ghosts, kings, one's mother, T.E. Lawrence and the Prince of Wales.' A similar calculatedness may have been behind the stream of grittily realistic war novels that followed in the wake of Erich Maria Remarque's best-selling *Im Westen Nichts Neues*, which was serialized in the influential Berlin newspaper *Vossische Zeitung* in November and December 1928. It appeared in book form during the following January and immediately became an international publishing sensation, its frankness on such topics as defecation, delousing and the patriotism of elderly non-combatants earning it hyperbolical reviews and vast sales wherever it appeared. The English translation, under the title *All Quiet on the Western Front* was reprinted eight times in April 1929 alone. (By the 1990s it had been translated into at least forty-nine languages, with world sales in excess of four million.) The military historian Cyril Falls noted sourly, 'it is common gossip that several writers sat down to produce one in the same vein after watching Herr Remarque's sales go soaring into the hundred thousands.' These writers may be taken as including J.F. Snook, author of *Gun Fodder*, a novel full of denunciations of officers and featuring a visit to a brothel in Calais; F. Haydn Hornsey, whose novel *Hell on Earth* describes a visit to what seems to have been the same brothel (apparently not a very appealing concern as neither author seems to have partaken of what was on offer); Charles Yale Harrison of the Canadian Expeditionary Force, author of *Generals Die in Bed*, in which the protagonist participates in a looting spree in Arras, sees his officer shot in the back, and surrendered German soldiers massacred by his comrades, and spends an entire ten days leave with a girl who picked him up in a Shaftesbury Avenue restaurant; and Helen Zenna Smith whose *Not So Quiet ... Stepdaughters of War* – note the title – was supposedly based on her experiences as an ambulance driver in France and Belgium and features bodily functions:

Pools of stale vomit from the poor wretches we have carried the night before, corners the sitters have turned into temporary lavatories for all purposes, blood and mud and vermin and the stale stench of stinking trench feet and gangrenous wounds...

– extramarital sex –

'And the men, making love to you one day and dead the next. I've been on leave twice with different subs and they're both dead.'

– and incomprehending mothers, rendered insensible by jingoism –

'I am proud of his blindness and his disability... If the sight of his blindness shames one of the cowards then he has not suffered vainly. As Shakespeare puts it...'

These four novels all appeared in 1930, but perhaps the most blatant attempt to cash in on the post-*All Quiet on the Western Front* mood came out in the early Summer of 1931: Wilfred Saint-Mandé's *War, Wine and Women*.[20]

Though now virtually forgotten, during the early 1930s *War, Wine and Women*, published by Cassell, one of the most respectable firms of the day, sold at least as well as Edmund Blunden's *Undertones of War* or Siegfried Sassoon's *Memoirs of a Fox-Hunting Man*. On 18 June 1931, *The Times Literary Supplement* carried an advert announcing '1st Edition Exhausted 2nd Impression Ready': the advert was framed in a decorative border of barbed wire, and showed a steel helmet, insouciantly tilted, strap hanging loose, a large butterfly perched on the crown and this art-work by no means misrepresents the contents of the book. (The barbed wire and the helmet were of course already stock symbols of the World War; the butterfly may have been the one seen by Paul Bäumer just before the bullet got him at the end of Lewis Milestone's 1930 film version of *All Quiet on the Western Front*.) The British Library's copy of *War, Wine and Women* is of the tenth edition of 1936: it was also published in a New York edition under the title *Sons of Cain*. (None of Wilfred Saint-Mandé's other books achieved a second printing.) *The Times*

Literary Supplement's anonymous reviewer confessed to having difficulty in deciding what to make of the book:

> If it were not extremely readable and exciting, it would not be worth puzzling over, so blatant are its faults and so bad its taste ... A man writing an autobiographical fragment is entitled to say what he likes about himself, but it is hard to believe that he would say of his wife – if a real wife – what is said here.

The book seems however to have been universally accepted as a genuine autobiographical memoir. In the American National Union Catalog for example it is cross-referenced under 'European War, 1914–1918 – Personal Narratives, English'.[21]

Although Wilfred Saint-Mandé claimed in the book to be a member of a family of wine-merchants, the offhand manner in which he refers to alcoholic merry-making does not seem to justify the inclusion of 'wine' in his title. The 'war' is obviously far more important. He tells how he enlisted in August 1914, served in the Ypres Salient, at the Battle of the Somme and during the German offensive of March 1918. He was wounded several times and in 1918 transferred to the Royal Air Force, becoming a pilot in a squadron of Bristol Fighters and shooting down six German aircraft before being himself shot down and wounded, his left arm being subsequently amputated. The fighter pilot bit is handled with the most cursory detail, but though the descriptions of trench warfare are much more leisurely and detailed, they are not especially individual or well-articulated:

> At 7.30 our barrage lifted, the whistles sounded and once more we clambered over the top. Once more Jerry swiftly got his machine-guns into position and mowed us down in heaps. The captain was one of the first to fall, blown to pieces by a shell. I felt sorry for him, for it is shocking to see a man rent asunder, even if he is a rotter. The religious man's prediction came true: his head was blown off by a trench-mortar bomb.

Smoke grew thicker over the battlefield, intense artillery fire
rolled, rumbled and thundered overhead and all round. Many
of my comrades fell, many to rise no more. (p. 286)

The only thing distinctive about this is the reference to the captain
and to the religious man's prediction coming true. There are scores
of better-written, more vividly realized, eye-witness accounts of the
battles of the First World War. Saint-Mandé was perhaps unusual
in the emphasis he gave to the smelly side of war:

The swollen corpses lying out in front were punctured by bullets
or burst spontaneously and sent over the vilest of stinks. (p. 222)

or:

The usual chemical-soaked blanket hung in the doorway and
the ventilation was nil. The steam from our wet clothes, and the
sweat from our filthy bodies, concocted the vilest fog I've ever
known. I fell asleep from utter exhaustion, and in spite of the
lice, did not wake until next morning. (p. 262)

Saint-Mandé also devoted particular attention to the loathsome
and horrendous injuries suffered by the combatants, for example:

A bomb had burst in his face, destroying both eyes and
mutilating him so frightfully that he would have been better
dead. There was a bloody hole where the nose had been and
the lower jaw was shattered so that the mouth hung askew in
a horrible grimace. I wish a photograph of that charnel-house
could be hung in every school in the world. (p. 155)

The last sentence quoted is perhaps a give-away: photographs of
war-mutilated faces and limbs were often employed by anti-war
propagandists in the 1920s and 1930s and Saint-Mandé's lingering
on such details seems to suggest a similar propaganda intention:
and, clearly, it was welcomed as such by his readers.[22]

The horrific descriptions are set off by literary disquisitions, philosophizing and accounts of sexual adventures. This combination of elements reminds one a little of Frank Harris's *My Life and Loves*, the first volume of which had been printed in Paris in 1922. *War, Wine and Women* is a would-be classic evocation of a young man at the outset of adulthood, bursting with intellectual and sexual energy, caught up in the death-machine of the world war. The intellectual energy aspect is not entirely convincing. Saint-Mandé claimed in his book that he had won 'a modern languages scholarship at Oxford' just before the outbreak of war (as well as playing cricket and rugby for his school). He presents himself as knowing some Italian, and is able to quote the relatively obscure late seventeenth-century Italian poet Vincenzo da Filicaja (p. 23). His French of course is excellent, and he not only recounts word for word a number of stilted conversations in that language, and refers to his reciting verses by Béranger, Hugo and Deroulède, but also quotes verbatim from Lamartine, Buffon and Ronsard. His German was also evidently fluent as he was able to act as interpreter when a German prisoner is interrogated, and to understand him when he announced 'It is time the *dulce et decorum est pro patria mori* stunt be shown up' – a rather tricky sentence in the original German, surely, especially in view of the different pronunciation of Latin Saint-Mandé would have learnt at school in Britain (p. 383). Earlier he lingers over a 'copy of Lessing's "*Laocoon*" that I had taken from a dead German'. He is fascinated by and repeats to himself the lines:

As the depths of the sea always remain calm, however violently the surface may rage, so the expression in the figures of the Greeks, under every form of passion, shows a great and self collected soul... (p. 301)

As it happens, these words, in the first paragraph of the first chapter of *Laokoon*, are not by Lessing himself but are a quotation from Winckelmann; considering that they are difficult to translate from the original German the fact that Saint-Mandé's version scarcely differs from that given in E.C. Beasley's translation, published in 1888 by Bohn's Shilling Library, reminds one that while great minds think alike hacks prefer to copy from one another.[23]

Needless to say, English Literature is not neglected. Saint-Mandé only got round to Oscar Wilde's *Picture of Dorian Gray* and Thomas Browne's *Religio Medici* after the war and never seems to have got round to Milton or Wordsworth at all, but R.L. Stevenson's *Travels with a Donkey*, J.A. Froude's *Short Studies in Great Subjects* and Henry Fielding's *Journal of a Voyage to Lisbon* provide timely quotations. In a characteristic passage Saint-Mandé describes his liaison with 'a most voluptuous woman' who has abandoned her husband, 'a typical American with big spectacles and a clean-shaven face' (p. 430). He gives her a lesson on early eighteenth-century English Literature and she admits that she 'had at one time tried to read Hegel and had given it up as hopeless.' Fortunately there is a copy of Thoreau's *Walden* in the bookcase and the narrator is able to turn up a favourite passage. After that the woman changes into silk pyjamas and they have sexual intercourse. (pp. 436–9)

Unfortunately it was not always possible to maintain this intellectual level, for as Saint-Mandé confesses:

One often reads highfalutin accounts of philosophic meditations on the battle-field. For my part I lived like a brute. My mind was numbed and incapable of any thought, beyond brooding over the fiendish discomforts that we had to endure. (p. 407)

Nevertheless, shortly before the great German offensive of March 1918, he asks his parents to send 'a few books, including if possible:

Aucassin et Nicolette
The Decameron
The Memoirs of Benvenuto Cellini

The Plays of Aristophanes
Representative Men, Emerson
Principles of Human Knowledge, Berkeley (p. 519)

This list probably gives a fair representation of the author's intellectual interests at this juncture. But there was one other preoccupation which evidently predominated, for it receives the main emphasis in the text as well as in the title of *War, Wine and Women.*

Wilfred Saint-Mandé is not one of your unscrupulous sexual opportunists. A young peasant woman with two small children offers herself, 'pressing against me and exacerbating my desire', but he remembers 'the words of Christ that if a man offended a little child it were better for him to hang a millstone round his neck and drown himself in the depths of the sea', and muttering *'parce que vous avez des enfants'* he 'strode rapidly down the hill, afraid my resolution would weaken unless I hurried.' (p. 279) A little earlier, recovering from wounds behind the lines, he had showed less firmness. Marie, a young barmaid whose parents had been executed by the Germans as *franc-tireurs*, is eager to give herself to him:

> I could not be sure whether it was to prove her love or merely to satisfy her sex-impulse. In the trenches I yearned for such an opportunity with all the fervour of a strong and healthy frame. But when it was offered I had scruples. It seemed dishonourable to have sexual intercourse with a girl whom one would never see again, and my early education implanted in me a wholesome respect for virginity.

On Marie's birthday however they 'drank old wine out of bottles covered with cobwebs' and he allowed himself to be over-persuaded. 'That night was the prelude to many others.' (pp. 249–50)

But Saint-Mandé's best adventures are with Anglo-Saxon girls. When he first meets Jean, his future wife, they merely discuss

Platonic Love and cuddle on a greatcoat spread out on a mossy bank at the foot of an old oak (pp. 100–102). While he is away at the Western Front Jean marries a wealthy, well-connected man three times her age who, instead of consummating the marriage, runs off to Paris to be with his mistress and to have a VD cure. When Saint-Mandé is wounded he is taken to her stately home which, as part of the war effort, she is running as a hospital, and it is not long before she summons him to her private quarters. She tells him that she still loves him and, despite having recently been wounded in the left arm and right shoulder, he carries her to a couch:

> The fragrant perfume of her hair, the freshness and flexibility of her body, the delightful caresses and prolonged kisses, the exquisite softness of her skin and the beauty of her face, all enraptured me to such a pitch that the world and the war were forgotten in those divine moments. (p.171)

But, perhaps because Jean was his future wife, Saint-Mandé gives less by way of explicit detail than in the case of some of his other adventures. There is Daphne, for example, who has read 'for Honours in Philosophy of all things' at Newnham College, Cambridge, and has been briefly married to a captain in the Scots Guards who 'lost both legs at Le Cateau, and shot himself rather than live the life of a *cul-de-jatte.*' (p. 110) They meet in a night club before Saint-Mandé embarks for France and after two minutes' conversation they ensconce themselves in an alcove:

> Daphne placed her feet on a balcony rail in front and pulled back her skirt to avoid creasing it at the knee. The fine silk stockings emphasized the slender ankles and shapely calves. I kissed her while caressing the firm little breasts which stood out challengingly, instead of drooping like the flaccid apologies one sees on so many anaemic maidens, who starve their bodies to keep them slim, and sacrifice their health in the process. (p. 109)

But Saint-Mandé has more than sex and anorexia on his mind:

> 'Were you brought up in a Christian home?' I wondered.
> 'Why do you ask?'
> 'Merely to know if your emancipation from the servile thraldom that masquerades as Christianity was similar to my own.' (p. 114)[24]

Though not above going with French prostitutes providing they seemed to be amateurs (pp. 312–4) and enjoying a tender friendship with an American nurse (pp. 365–7) Saint-Mandé also has a significant relationship with the American lady who had given up on Hegel:

> Her figure was slim but not thin. The waist was very slim but the buttocks were well developed and moved up and down with a peculiar snaky motion as she walked. The legs were shapely even when naked. (p. 430)

She is at least ten years his senior – not yet in need of surgical stockings it seems, though it may have been a mistake to leave off her stays. Another promising encounter with an older woman – the wife of the vicar back home, no less – soon approaches its consummation:

> 'Wilfred, what would the world be without love – I mean passionate, rapturous embraces?' she asked suddenly.
> 'Not worth living in,' I replied fervently, rushing at her and crushing her in my arms. (p. 450)

They are interrupted by the return home of the vicar; but one can see why Jean often seems to wish to break off their engagement.

Needless to say, so enthusiastic an indulger of healthy natural urges had no time for perversion. At one of the many base hospitals he passed through, he 'picked up a book called *"A Rebours"* by Huysmans and sat up half the night reading it.' His verdict on the book may well give an idea of what his literature classes were like in later years when he was a university lecturer:

> The curious hero of the work is one Des Esseintes, who is morbid and decadent in every possible way. The book is a series of filthy scenes wrapped up in an odour of mysticism. Years later I read Oscar Wilde's *'Picture of Dorian Gray'*, and was struck by the resemblance between the two books ... The book, neurotic and morbid as it is, is written with much talent; it is an able study of a diseased soul. (p. 381)

The sheer philistinism of all this seems almost a guarantee of authenticity but in the preface to one of his later books Saint-Mandé confessed that *War, Wine and Women* 'was meant to be nothing more than a novel with war as a background'. At first glance this seems no more than a change of marketing strategy, since the book had obviously been received as a true account and, however much exaggerated and padded out, would probably strike the most sceptical reader as *mainly* autobiographical. The suspicion that Wilfred Saint-Mandé is a pseudonym – taken from the name of a Paris suburb – is not in itself cause to doubt the book's authenticity: many memoirs of the First World War were published pseudonymously. The account given of Saint-Mandé's descent from a French emigré family which 'never deserted the wine business in London, which is still today one of the most important in the country' is demonstrably fictitious but this is not in itself of major importance. What is crucial to the status as an authentic memoir of *War, Wine and Women* is that, while it purports to be an account of the experiences of an infantryman in and out of the trenches, the British Army has no record of the author ever having served in an infantry regiment.[25]

There seems to be no question that Saint-Mandé was of military age during the First World War, and that he was physically fit for combatant service: during the last months of the war he was in the Royal Air Force as a trainee. He seems to have claimed after the war to have been in the Royal Field Artillery, in which case he may have been issued with a rifle, but of course personnel in the artillery never advanced against German entrenchments on foot. And though many artillerists were decorated for gallantry during the First World War, the author of *War, Wine and Women* was not amongst them. His protagonist found that one new officer 'was very impressed by my [medal] ribbons' (p. 477) and the American older woman had read in the newspapers how he 'had already become distinguished' (p. 431): the real-life author is not on record as having obtained even the usual campaign medals. Given the amount of equipment involved in artillery work, it is even possible that the author never served near the front, but only somewhere far in the rear or in Britain.

Wilfred Saint-Mandé's real name was John Henry Parkyn Lamont and at the time of writing *War, Wine and Women* he was senior lecturer in French at Transvaal University College, Pretoria, which became the University of Pretoria during the period he worked there. Actually he was the only member of the French department and got away with giving his qualifications in the university calendar as M.A. (Wales) and B. ès L. (Besançon), the latter title being the professionally worthless baccalauréat, equivalent to GCE A-level or graduation from High School.[26]

War, Wine and Women belongs to the period during which Frank Harris's *My Life and Loves*, James Joyce's *Ulysses* and D.H. Lawrence's *Lady Chatterley's Lover*, though (or because) banned in Britain, were establishing their reputation as classics of sexual frankness, and it was not long since Robert Keable, an ex-missionary, had enjoyed a runaway success with *Simon Called Peter*, a novel about an army chaplain who, as his faith wobbles in the rear lines in France, betrays his chaste almost-fiancée Hilda in the liberated embrace of a fast-living nurse named Julie. Sex had also been one of the things *The Times Literary Supplement*'s reviewer had objected to in *All Quiet on the Western Front* when complaining of Remarque's 'preoccupation with bodily functions', though in fact *All Quiet on the Western Front* was positively virginal by comparison with another book published in Germany in 1929, Hans Otto Henel's *Eros im Stacheldraht* ('Eros in the Barbed Wire') which deals with frontline brothels, venereal disease, marriages failing because the husband is at the front, etc. The reaction against nineteenth-century pieties, already evident before 1914, received enormous impetus from the First World War, especially since many younger men came to believe that those who were the most mealy-mouthed about sex and religion were also the most prone to romanticizing the slaughter in the trenches. This equation is very evident in, for example, Aldington's *Death of a Hero* and Henel's *Eros im Stacheldraht*, and is one of the sub-texts of *Lady Chatterley's Lover*.

Amongst those who saw themselves in the vanguard of the assault on prudery and hypocrisy was Henry Parkyn Lamont, M.A., B. ès L. In one of his later works, *Halcyon Days in Africa*, describing the experiences of the young 'Professor of French at Krugersburg University College', his protagonist encounters a Miss Elizabeth Werger at a conference of the Senate of the University of South Africa, held at Murraytown; running into her later on the same day he goes back to her hotel room where she declares, 'I want you to give me a baby.' He obliges but some months later receives a tear-stained letter from her informing him that she has killed herself: amusing herself in Berlin while awaiting the birth of their child, she has contracted syphilis. ('Drink and drugs destroyed my will. I sold my soul for cocaine. Night after night I lowered myself to hell.') The thought of her disease rotting not only her lovely body but also her unborn child has driven her to suicide. This book was published by Eric Partridge's Scholartis Press but, despite Partridge's well-known scatological sympathies, the narrative is on occasion interrupted by rows of asterisks, though given the unevenness of Lamont's prose style it is difficult to tell which parts of the *mise en scène* have been bowdlerized. That was in 1934. Next year Lamont brought out two novels with the obscure firm of Lincoln Williams. The Foreword of *The Devouring Flame* announced 'Like certain other efforts of mine, it has been mutilated in order to ensure reasonably safe publication.' He also complained that 'there are, unfortunately, many evilly-disposed persons who persistently misrepresent the high moral purpose of my work.' The Foreword of *No Repentance* discusses the public reaction to *War, Wine and Women*:

'Nasty', 'Disgusting', 'Pornographic' and 'Revolting' were hurled at me for not remembering that England is the last refuge of sexual cant, prudery and hypocrisy. I used to think America would beat us in this respect, but even there, *Ulysses* has been admitted, whereas it is still banned here.[27]

Lamont was also abreast of fashion in having a chip on his shoulder about social class. The imaginary family background of affluent wine-merchants and the improbable open scholarship to Oxford have already been noted. The women bedded by the protagonist of *War, Wine and Women* all seem to have been picked for their connections as well as their looks. The young French woman with children whom he rejects is merely a peasant 'whose husband was in a road gang' and who is worried about the cost of living (p. 279) but Jean, his future wife, has a notably rich and snobbish family, Daphne with her Newnham degree and Guards Brigade husband clearly has a superior background, Juliet the American nurse has puritanical but rich and materialistic parents (p. 365) and the American Lady who had discovered the hopelessness of Hegel is married to a wealthy banker (p. 430). Even Marie Masson, whose parents have been shot as *franc-tireurs*, 'had been able to secure part of her father's fortune, with which she acquired the modest inn' (p. 248).

Though more than once urged to apply for a commission (pp. 309, 410), the narrator of *War, Wine and Women* has little time for most of the officers set over him through the workings of the British class system: 'a tall dark fellow with an evil scowl [who] delighted in punishing men for the slightest offence' (p. 80), 'he looked a raving maniac and had probably been drinking. He flourished his revolver, and seemed ready to use it' (p. 197). Not all the officers are like this of course but those who are not, like Captain Ray (p. 310) and Captain Ewen (pp. 466–7), are presented as exceptions. One of the rare 'good' officers acknowledges:

> 'I admit there are both officers and non-coms who make one sick. ... They lack the most elementary qualities of leadership and make up for it by bullying and cursing the men.' (p. 200)

This kind of thing found a ready audience in the 1930s. Both the disastrous casualties of the First World War and the post-war failures on the economic and social front were widely thought to be the fault of traditional governing classes which nevertheless remained the model for social emulation. Charles Carrington had complained in 1929 that, 'After the war was over a fashion set in for decrying the efforts and defaming the characters of all those in authority in the war.' Lamont's combination of snobbishness and anti-authoritarianism, while typical of the period, was also perhaps a reflection of the fact that his own rise in the social scale had not been entirely unproblematic.[28]

War, Wine and Women must be regarded as a successfully calculated piece of book-making – one that brought its own poetic retribution in the failure of Lamont's later books to meet his expectations – and as such presumably related more to the author's assessment of what readers expected than to personal agonies that needed to be exorcized. And yet the author *was* in the war, and though not killed or, like his protagonist, mutilated, the war presumably made as big a hole in his life as it did in the lives of other participants. *War, Wine and Women* may be tosh but it is still an ex-serviceman's best attempt to salvage some sort of literary statement from what he had lived through. It is worth noting too that the authors who, a century after the war, are now regarded as having offered *the* classic statements of what it was like to serve in the front line – Sassoon, Graves, Blunden – provide essentially nostalgic evocations of a *pre-war* sensibility confronted with the horrors of twentieth-century warfare: Lamont presents a sensibility that to a great extent was created (and coarsened) by the war. The fact that university professors nowadays tend to prefer the Sassoon, Graves, Blunden version may say more about professors than it does about literature of the 1920s and 1930s.

War, Wine and Women may be taken as representing one extreme, but even those writers at the other end of the spectrum of veracity, who made it their mission to tell the unvarnished truth, however unpleasant or discreditable to themselves personally, might have problems with objective and ascertainable fact. During the 1930s Frank Percy Crozier (reputedly the best brigade commander in the British army during the First World War, though in retrospect horrified by how much he had enjoyed it) was making a second career for himself as a platform speaker in the cause of world peace, and one of the ideas he was anxious to put across was that it was quite normal for soldiers to be exhilarated by combat, and to be carried forward on a surge of homicidal glee. At the same time he never forgot how good he had been at his job and nurtured a considerable resentment with regard to the circumstances which led to the loss of half his brigade on 9 April 1918.[29]

The only thing most people know about the expeditionary corps which the Portuguese sent to the Western Front in 1917 is that in April 1918 the second of the German spring offensives was directed against the section of the line held by the Portuguese 2^a *Divisão*, resulting in a break-through on a nine mile front: it was two days later, with the gap in the British front still widening, that Haig issued his famous order of the day, 'With our backs to the wall and believing in the justice of our cause each one of us must fight on to the end.' The 119th Infantry Brigade, which Crozier commanded, had been immediately next to the Portuguese on their left flank. Of his three infantry battalions, the 18th Battalion Welch Regiment lost all but its Commanding Officer, signalling officer and twenty Other Ranks, and the 13th Battalion East Surrey Regiment lost eighty-nine killed and wounded and 455 'missing'.[30]

In his war memoirs, *A Brass Hat in No Man's Land*, published in 1930, Crozier recorded that the Portuguese simply bolted, adding:

> The uniforms of the Germans and Portuguese are not dissimilar. Hundreds of Portuguese were mown down by our machine guns, and rifle fire. After all, 'fire at all field grey advancing towards us', was a legitimate order!

The Portuguese authorities learnt of Crozier's remarks from a review in the *Daily Mail* and complained to the British Ambassador in Lisbon. The latter passed on the complaint to the Foreign Office in London:

3rd May, 1930

Sir,

    At an interview which I had with the Minister for Foreign Affairs yesterday His Excellency showed me a copy of the *Daily Mail* in which was published, under fairly sensational headlines, a review of a book upon the War recently written by a certain Brigadier-General Crozier. Commander Branco pointed with great indignation to references made by the Brigadier to the behaviour of the Portuguese Army in France – references which he stigmatised as completely unfounded and most malicious. He asked me whether something could not be done in the matter and requested that I should, at any rate, call the attention of my Government to the publication in question.

2. I told His Excellency that, as he knew, the press was completely free in England to publish what it liked on condition that it was ready to run the risk of actions for libel; and, although my knowledge of the law was limited, I did not think that the Portuguese Government could successfully prosecute the *Daily Mail* for the article which he had showed me. I must confess that I had hardly ever in my life read a number of the *Daily Mail*, nor was it one of the newspapers taken in by any member of my staff. The paper carried no weight with any sensible person in England, and made a speciality of sensational news and headlines. Nor had I read the Brigadier's book but, judging by the passages in the review which he had shown me, it appeared to me to be one of those numerous publications issued since the War by disgruntled people who considered that their military genius had not been adequately recognised by the British authorities and who, under a regime less humanitarian than our own, would probably never have had the opportunity of publishing anything at all. I promised, as he had asked me, to draw your attention to the article in question.

3. I regret to say that I did not take note of the issue of the *Daily Mail* of which Commander Branco complained, but I will endeavour to ascertain this and send the Department of the Foreign Office concerned a private note indicating the date.

I have the honour to be with the highest respect, Sir, Your most obedient, humble Servant,

F.O. Lindley

The Foreign Office does not seem to have been especially concerned, and the matter was dealt with at a junior level. Charles Duff, a press officer, minuted,

> What Brig. Gen. Crozier says about the Portuguese is substantially true: I was attached to them as interpreter for several months & I think Brig. Gen. Crozier lets them off very lightly.

R.A. Gallop, formerly second secretary at the Athens legation, and not yet thirty, noted,

> I do not think anything would be gained by asking the WO [War Office] whether they can substantiate Gen. Crozier's charges and have amended the draft [letter to the Lisbon embassy] accordingly. Unless the Portuguese MFA [Minister of Foreign Affairs] reverts to the question with Sir. F. Lindley I think no further action need be taken.[31]

Interestingly enough the Director of Personal Services at the War Office, Major General G.S. Clive – later Sir Sidney Clive – rather liked Crozier's book, minuting 'his experiences are … of more value to those who want to know what war means than any I have found in other books on the war.' The King disagreed, regarding Crozier as 'an undesirable person' whose book should be allowed to 'sink back in the mud from which it emerged'. This was not of course Brigadier General Crozier's view, and in a subsequent book, an anti-war tirade entitled *The Men I Killed*, he again referred to the Portuguese troops' disorderly retreat across his section of the line, stating 'I ordered the shooting, by machine-gun and rifle fire, of many Portuguese, in order to stem the tide.' This time it was a Portuguese newspaper *Diario de noticias* which drew the matter to the Portuguese government's attention, and again a complaint was forwarded to London. At the prompting of Sir George Mounsey, assistant under-secretary of state at the Foreign Office – i.e. no. 4 in the official hierarchy – the question was referred to Stephen Gaselee, the Foreign Office's librarian and adviser on literary matters. Gaselee minuted:

> The General is now dead *(vile damnum)* and it might almost be worth while quoting to the Portuguese the words in the *Times* obituary notice about his last publication:
>
> 'In kindness to him his last book, *The Men I Killed*, is best forgotten. Most of it was written in the worst of taste. The allegations he made against the conduct of soldiers at the front aroused great indignation among ex-Service men and the relatives of those who lost their lives in the War.'
>
> In fact, we are just as angry as the Portuguese.

Mounsey added a final note to the file:

> Good, then we can make our assurances whole-hearted.[32]

There is no doubt that Crozier was an excitable, over-emphatic individual, and a great believer in the idea that in the heat of battle it was natural for men to be carried away by blood-lust. Here is part of his account of the events of 9 April 1918:

> Strictly from the military point of view I have no regrets for having killed a subaltern of British infantry on that same morning I ordered our machine-guns and rifles to be turned on the fleeing Portuguese. It happened on the Strazeel Road. It was a desperate emergency. I had to shoot him myself, along with a German who was running after him. My action *did* stem the tide; and that is what we were there for.
>
> Vividly, I still remember that scene. It might have been only yesterday. Never can I forget the agonized expression on that

British youngster's face as he ran in terror, escaping from the ferocious Hun whose passions were a madness and who saw only red.

As I stood on the road, almost alone, after the incident, a car drove up. In it were a GSO2 and a CRE. One of them shouted out to me. Was all well? And he looked at the smoking revolver in my right hand.

Yes – all was well! And I *laughed*.

Perhaps you, reader, would not have laughed …

I do not believe, had you been in my shoes, that you would have known either what you might do next or what you might have done. It is even conceivable that you might have run away, too, and not known it. I nearly did.

But we only have his word for it. There may have been no one else nearby when he shot the British subaltern but it is odd that there is no confirmation from other sources of his ordering his men to fire on the Portuguese. The war diaries of the 119th Infantry Brigade, its three component infantry battalions and the 40th Battalion Machine Gun Corps, which manned the Vickers Guns in Crozier's brigade area, are all available in the The National Archives at Kew. The 119th Infantry Brigade diary, the 21st Middlesex diary and the 'Narrative of Events 9th April to 14th April 1918', written on 16 April to supplement the exiguous diary of the virtually defunct 18th Welch, mention the Germans on the Portuguese front, but make no reference to Portuguese troops as such. The 13th East Surrey diary states, 'the enemy broke through the Portuguese on our Right flank, and the Battalion was surrounded'. The 40th MGC's 'Report on Operations 9th–14th April' says the enemy 'having pressed back the *Portuguese* were gradually encircling our men'. There are no other references to the Portuguese, let alone to shooting them.[33]

Brigadier-General Crozier's soldier servant, David Starrett – later a close friend – left his own account of the events of 9 April 1918, in a typescript that may be examined in the Imperial War Museum. He wrote that, 'Some "Pork-and-Beans" as we called the

Portuguese appearing, they were chased away as huntsmen chase foxes.' He makes no mention of their being fired on with rifles and machine guns, and his huntsmen image scarcely suggests that this was what he had in mind: even a member of the servant class would have known huntsmen do not shoot foxes.[34]

Nor did Crozier refer to the machine-gunning of the Portuguese in the letter he wrote in September 1927 to Brigadier General James Edmonds with the object of establishing that he had been certain beforehand that the Germans would attack and that his superiors had ignored his suggestions for precautionary measures, though he did take the opportunity to reflect both on the Portuguese and on his own Corps Commander:

> But the most astounding thing of all to my mind was the mentality which permitted the Portuguese to hold the line *at all!!* and thus expose the whole front to danger.
>
> I have no wish whatever to make insinuations against Du Cane, my Corps Cdr of those days, with whom I have been on terms of Friendship for years but I do say that the Corps was 'thinking wrong' in early 1918.

Given the combative tone of this letter, it may even seem a little odd that Crozier makes no allusion to something to which he was later to attach some considerable significance.[35]

It is worth noting that Crozier nowhere states that the advancing German troops were mixed up with the retreating Portuguese, or were immediately behind them, or were using them as a screen. Despite his claim in *The Men I Killed* that he saw a British subaltern being chased down a road by a German soldier and shot them both with his revolver, there would generally have been some distance between fleeing British and Portuguese and attacking Germans – in fact an official report drawn up a month later specifically states that 'the enemy were not in close pursuit' of the retreating Portuguese. Consequently there would have been no reason why British troops would have wanted to fire on the Portuguese, at a time when it would have been desirable to conserve ammunition for the Germans. Crozier may well, in his anger and excitement, have ordered his troops to shoot at the Portuguese, but even if he did see a mob of Portuguese being mowed down by a traversing machine gun, in the midst of a large-scale battle he would have had no way of being sure which machine gun it was that fired the bullets, even if he had been standing right next to the machine-gunner responsible. And in 1930 he stated merely that the Portuguese had been shot and that this was consistent with orders: the claim that he had specifically instructed them to be shot only materialized in 1937.[36]

Other accounts of the Portuguese collapse fail to provide a clearer picture of what actually happened. A report signed by the Army Commander, General Sir Henry Horne stated, 'The Portuguese were not retiring. They were in flight, many without arms, some with their boots off, some half dressed,' but a senior British officer captured in the battle told the Official Historian thirteen years later, 'The number of Portuguese in the Prisoner of War cage behind LA BASEE, complete with kit, made us think they had either been bribed to walk over or had done so on their own.' The only other reference I have found to the Portuguese being machine-gunned by the British (apart from a confidential letter to the Official Historian which the latter seems to have discounted) is in F. Haydn Hornsey's *Hell on Earth*, published two months after *Brass Hat in No Man's Land*. Hornsey was apparently in the 11th Battalion Suffolk Regiment in the 34th Division, separated from the Portuguese by Crozier's brigade and the 121st Brigade, and he describes the incident as having occurred on the fifth or sixth day of the German offensive, by which time the Portuguese had been withdrawn from the line. He mentions that the Portuguese 'wore a uniform which at a distance resembled the field grey of the Germans'. Crozier had made the same point: one suspects Hornsey added the passage at the last minute after he had read Crozier's book.[37]

There is no doubt however that the Portuguese brigade next to Crozier's, the *4ª Brigada de Infantaria*, also known as the

Brigada do Minho, was more or less obliterated: but the two other Portuguese brigades in the line further away from Crozier's machine guns lost almost as heavily – in fact both contained a battalion that suffered heavier casualties than the hardest hit battalion in the 4^a *Brigada* – and considering that almost 90 per cent of the losses were Prisoners of War rather than fatalities the two hundred or so dead of the 4^a *Brigada* do not seem too numerous to attribute to the unassisted effort of the attacking Germans. A century later the details do not perhaps matter very much – is responsibility or guilt simply a question of who gave or obeyed orders? For our purposes the most interesting aspect is how unconvincing Crozier's efforts were when he tried so manfully to tell the truth.[38]

Perhaps the real point is that every attempt to tell the truth is as much a matter of motives and previous commitments as making up lies and inventing falsehoods.

5

TECHNIQUE

It is the message of First World War literature rather than its technique that one remembers, yet in 1914 many younger writers were as preoccupied by questions of technique as the painters of the day.

In the event the only movement related to literature to obtain significant additional energy from the First World War was Surrealism, which was robbed of its founding father during the war itself and did not emerge into the public gaze till the mid-1920s. Guillaume Apollinaire, the most influential of Surrealism's pioneers, volunteered for the French army – he was a Russian citizen – rose from private to *sous-lieutenant*, and seems to have had a marvellous time, a kind of second adolescence without hang-ups, till wounded in the head in March 1916. He died in Paris from influenza and emphysema two days before the Armistice, and as with other writers who die relatively young one can only speculate whether his extinction came before or after he had had a chance to produce his best work. What is most striking however about his wartime writings, and those of his *avant-garde* associates, was how much they had in common with the work of other combatants.

Apollinaire's enjoyment of the war seems to have had little philosophical rationale, and his poetry suggests that what appealed to him most were the spectacular stage effects, and perhaps the ever present sense of menace:

Que c'est beau ces fusées qui illuminent la nuit
Elles montent sur leur propre cime et se penchent pour regarder
Ce sont des dames qui dansent avec leurs regards pour yeux
    bras et coeurs

J'ai reconnu ton sourire et ta vivacité

C'est aussi l'apothéose quotidienne de toutes mes Bérénices
    dont les chevelures sont devenues des comètes
Ces danseuses surdorées appartiennent a tous les temps et à
    toutes les races
Elles accouchent brusquement d'enfants qui n'ont que le
    temps de mourir

(How lovely the rockets which light up the night
They rise to their limit and stoop to look
They are dancing women attentive to eyes arms and hearts

I recognized your smile and your liveliness

They're also an everyday apotheosis of all my Berenices
    whose hair has become comets
These gilded dancers belong to every age and every race
They off-handedly bring forth children who have only time
    to die)

(The poem of which this is part is entitled 'Merveille de la guerre',
'Wonder of War'.) One can see the same frigid detachment in Paul
Éluard's

Toujours, très lente
Camions, canons, mi-roues renouvelées dans les blés

('For ever and ever, very slowly, wagons, field-guns, half-wheels
renewing themselves in the corn fields'). Yet though the concept

of Surrealism had still to be officially promulgated, the Surrealist quality of the war was recognized by great numbers of those who fought in it. Éluard's phrase, 'the machine gun, like a person stammering', Apollinaire's comparison of the noise made by a salvo of shells exploding to the sound of four people shaking a carpet to make the dust come out, or Blaise Cendrars's description of an artillery barrage as resembling 'old puffers entering the station ... locomotives in the air, invisible trains, concertinaings, collisions ... Gratings. Slurrings. Hootings. Whinnyings ... Chimaeras of steel and mastodons in rut', had their counterpart in the writings of frontline veterans of much more limited literary ambition.[1]

For the civilians herded into the ranks the sounds of shell and bullet were strange and unexpected as well as frightening and called out for description. At close quarters an artillery barrage sounded 'as though the earth were cracking up like an egg of super-gigantic proportions tapped by a gargantuan spoon': it created, according to the same witness, 'A veritable crescendo of sounds, so continuous as to merge and blend into a single annihilating roar, the roar of a train in a tunnel magnified a millionfold: only the rattle of the machine-gun barrage, like clocks gone mad, ticking out the end of time in a final breathless reckoning, rises above it.' At a greater distance it was 'like someone kicking footballs – a soft bumping, miles away', or a noise, felt rather than heard 'like the beating of one's heart after running'. A German infantry officer recalled, 'If you put your hands over your ears and then drum your fingers vigorously on the back of your head, then you get some idea of what the drumfire sounded like to us.' The sound of an approaching shell, it was claimed, 'can be imitated by a suitable rendering of the sentences, "Who are you? I am (these words being drawn out to full length) – (a slight pause) – Krupp (very short and sharp!)"' Similarly, Ford Madox Ford wrote of how shells made a noise like 'We ...e ...e ...ry!' explaining, 'Shells always appeared tired of life. As if after a long journey they said: "Weary!" Very much prolonging the 'e' sound. Then "Whack!" when they burst.' Much the same idea appears in a little poem with the title 'De varendo Bom' ('The incoming shell') by Johan De Maegt of the Belgian Army:

Daar!
ik gier
ik ren
er heen! Hier! hier! hier!
Ik kom
Au! ik ben
de bom!
Bom!

('There! I howl. I race. away! Here! here! here! I'm coming. Ouch! I am the shell! Boom!')[2]

Some writers attempted to marshal all the onomatopoeic resources of their language, just as Robert Southey had done a hundred years earlier in a poem for children about a waterfall:

The Cataract strong
Then plunges along,
Striking and raging
As if a war waging
Its caverns and rocks among:
Rising and leaping,
Sinking and creeping,
Swelling and sweeping,
Showering and springing,
Flying and flinging
Writhing and ringing ...

The repetitive 'i' sounds and the concussive 'n's in Isaac Rosenberg's lines 'And shells go crying over them/From night till night and now' were no serendipitous accident, nor were the concussives of Johan De Maegt's

De vlammen loeien, dampen, gulpen,
de roode gensters huilen rond;
Ze slaan, ze slaam, de duizend smeden,
al drupt hun roode bloed op grond,

('Flames bray, smoke spouts, the red sparks whine around; they
strike, they strike, the thousand blacksmiths drip their red blood
on the ground'), or the sibillants of Nikolai Gumilev's

Kak sobaka na tsyepi tyazhyeloi
Tyavkayet za lyesom pulyemyet
I zhuzhzhat shrapneli, slovno pchyeli
Sobiraya yarko-krasni med.

('Like a dog on a heavy chain barks a machine-gun in the wood
and shrapnel buzzes like bees gathering bright red honey.') The
most successful ventures with this technique during the First World
War were by the German poet August Stramm, though admittedly
one of his efforts was taken up by several German newspapers and
printed as an example of what war poetry should *not* be like. This
is his poem 'Granaten' ('Shells'):

Das Wissen stockt
Nur Ahnen webt und trügt
Taube täubet schrecke Wunden
Klappen Tappen Wühlen Kreischen
Schrillen Pfeifen Fauchen Schwirren
Splittern Klatschen Knarren Knirschen
Stumpfen Stampfen
Der Himmel tapft
Die Sterne schlacken
Zeit entgraust
Sture weltet blöden Raum.

('Knowledge stops – only perception weaves and deceives – dove deafens terrible wounds – flap fumble burrow shriek – shrill pipe spit whirr – splinter chip creak crunch – stump stamp – the sky trudges – the stars become slag – time becomes more horrid – stubbornness populates stupid space.')[3]

It was easier though to make up one's own onomatopoeic words. This had been done by Aristophanes and, on a modest scale, by Tolstoy in *War and Peace* ('*Trakh-ta-ta-takh!* came the frequent crackle of musketry'). Early in 1914 the Futurist writer F.T. Marinetti made this practice a particular feature of a book intended to present the noises and atmosphere of the Balkan Wars in the Futurist idiom:

> **tza tzu tatatatatata** la gomena puzzare fumare crrr prac-prac troppo tardi inferno al diavolo il ponte angolo ottuso arco teso gonfiare il suo ventre **apriiiiirsi aaaaahi patapum-patatraack** maledizione canaglia canaglia gridare gridare uriare muggire **scoppio di cuori turchi** squarciagola sfrangiarsi scapigliamento di **hurrrrrrraaah tatatatatata hurrrrrraaah tatatatata** PUUM PAMPAM PLUFF **zang-tumb-tumb hurrrrraaah tatatatatata hurrrraaah**

(Even the ordinary vocabulary of this is syntactically so jumbled that it is scarcely translatable.) In English onomatopoeic words like 'twang' and 'boom' and 'crash' had been acceptable usages as far back as the sixteenth century: 'ping', for the noise made by a rifle bullet, seems to have entered the language in the nineteenth century; but onomatopoeic coinages seem to be especially characteristic of twentieth-century English, and can be seen as an aspect of the democratization, vulgarization, vernacularization of language in the era of the mass-market and mass-democracy, as in Henry Williamson's *The Patriot's Progress*:

> Drubber drubber drub continuous gunfire over and through all the living and the dead ... Brutal downward dronings of 5.9's. Ruddy flashes in front. Cra-ash. Cra-ash. Cra-ash.

John Bullock breathed faster. Cries from far in front. Drivers crouched over their mules. For Christ's sake get a move on in front! They waited. The woo-r, woo-r, woo-r plop, woo-r plop, of gas-shells, the corkscrewing downward sigh, the soft plop in the mud. Another and another. Gas-shells – them. From behind a voice crying, 'Pass the word up from the Second-in-Command to move on!' Other messages. Erz-z-z-z-z-ZAR, another salvo over them like runaway tramcars, red-smoky glares and spark-scatters and colossal rending crashes.[4]

Everyone could invent their own sound-imitating string of letters. For Robert Graves the noise a shell made was 'whoo-oo-ooo-oooOOO-bump- *Crash!*' followed by 'a curious singing noise in the air, and then flop! flop! little pieces of shell-casing came buzzing down all around'. J.D. Strange transcribed the sound of an incoming shell as 'Wheeeeee-ee-hurrunch!' but Cecil Lewis thought it was more a case of 'Wheeeeee … wheeee … whee–ow … whe–ow … whow .. whow . whow … Zonk!' According to Richard Aldington a complete salvo made a crescendo noise, *'zwiing, crash! craash! claaang'*. Bernard Adams described trench mortars as going 'whizz-sh-sh-sh-h-h' – silence – *'thud'* and the sound of a richocheting rifle bullet as 'Ping-g-g-g,' while for Ford Madox Ford the noise of a passing bullet was *'f-r-r-r-r-r!* A gentle purring sound!' and shellfire went 'Pam… Pamperi! … Pam! Pam! … Pa … Pamperi … Pam! Pam! … pampamperipampampam … Pam …' For Hugh Dalton machine-guns made a 'wooden-sounding *clack-clack-clack'*, whereas Richard Aldington wrote of the 'Zwiss, zwiss, zwiss, zwiss … of bullets, following the rapid rat-tat-tat-rat-tat-tat-rat of a machine-gun'. For Ford Madox Ford, or Ford Madox Hueffer as he was then called, it was more of a *wukka wukka* noise:

Then, far away to the right thro' the moonbeams
'Wukka Wukka' will go the machine-guns,

And, far away to the left
Wukka Wukka.
And sharply,
Wuk ... Wuk... and then silence
For a space in the clear of the moon.[5]

Of course it was not always possible to identify what it was actually making a noise:

We ducked, then got up again and witnessed the horrifying spectacle of Harvey blown into the air. I shuddered as a piece of something hit my helmet with a 'tink'. It might be a piece of Harvey's skull!

And often enough the sounds were in elaborate combinations even when one was some miles to the rear:

Shells falling on a church: these make a huge *'corump'* sound, followed by a noise like crockery falling off a tray – as the roof tiles fall off. If the roof is not tiled you can hear the stained glass, sifting mechanically until the next shell. (Heard in a church square, on each occasion, about ninety yards away.) Screams of women penetrate all these sounds – but I do not find that they agitate me as they have done at home.

Nearer the firing line the orchestration of different varieties of killing device was even more complex:

Close by, a quickfirer is pounding away its allowance of a dozen shells a day. It is like a cow coughing. Eastward there begins a sound (all sounds begin at sundown and continue intermittently till midnight, reaching their zenith at about 9 p.m. and then dying away as sleepiness claims their makers) – a sound like a motor-cycle race – thousands of motor-cycles tearing round and round a track, with cut-outs out: it is really a pair of machine guns firing. And now one sound awakens another. The old cow coughing has started the motor-bikes: and now at intervals of a few minutes come express trains in our direction: you can hear them rushing toward us; they pass going straight for the town behind us: and you hear them begin to slow down as they reach the town: they will soon stop: but no, every time, just before they reach it, is a tremendous railway accident. At least, it must be a railway accident, there is so much noise, and you can see the dust that the wreckage scatters. Sometimes the train behind comes very close, but it too smashes on the wreckage of its forerunners. A tremendous cloud of dust, and then the groans. So many trains and accidents start the cow coughing again: only another cow this time, somewhere behind us.

The closer one was, the less pleasant the sounds:

More terrible – not to be forgotten – were the salvoes of the German batteries close in front, which fired almost together every three minutes. Boom-boom-boom-boom – they threatened to burst the brain, they caused a racking headache, these terrible tornadoes of sound. The machine-gun and the rifle-fire were as nothing after these. The rat-tat-tat, the clack-clack, the ping-ping sent their messages well overhead to the trenches behind and the still-advancing troops. Much other noise came to puzzle the ears, to weary the brain: the faint shouting of men, the clink-clink of the entrenching-tools as soldiers dug themselves in, the great hollow explosions which resounded afar off amid the ruins of Aubers and Neuve Chapelle.

And the groans, the moans, the crying of those who lay around!

Richard Aldington described a battle as 'an immense rhythmic harmony, a super-jazz of tremendous drums, a ride of the Walkyrie played by three thousand cannon. The intense rattle of the machine-guns played a minor motif of terror.' Wilfred Owen played with the idea that these noises carried some sort of message:

> The Bullets chirped – In vain! vain! vain!
> Machine-guns chuckled – Tut-tut! Tut-tut!
> And the Big Gun guffawed

But in another of his poems it was simply a matter of 'the monstrous anger of the guns, / Only the stuttering rifles' rapid rattle'.[6]

It was not only the British who went in for the game of trying to find exact equivalents for the sounds of modern warfare. French artillerist Paul Lintier was reminded of the sea:

> From the unknown country beyond the hills came the terrific noise of the battle: the rattle of musketry and the roar of machine-guns, like great rollers being sucked back on a pebbly shore, and the thunder of artillery enveloping and uniting all these noises into a single voice like that of a storm in mid-ocean, with heaving, crashing waves, deep, thudding undertones and the shrill whistle of the wind through the surf.

Henri Barbusse wrote of 'les sifflements et les tapements des balles, le souffle des obus qui passent: des rugissements et des miaulements, trés exactement, et des halètements de locomotives lancées à toute vitesse', the whistling and pattering of bullets, the whisper of passing shells, roarings and miaowings, literally, and the panting of locomotives hurtling at full speed. Jean Galtier-Boissière noted down the sound of shrapnel as 'Dzin-baiing! ... Psiou ... Brainggn! ... Dzin ... brâon ... Dzion ... brâon ... Dchin ... bingh!' The combination of noises made by machine guns mounted on motor vehicles inspired one French armoured car unit to christen their unit magazine *TacaTacTeufTeuf*. In the Portuguese army Diego de Camo Reìs wrote of being mortared:

Os stilhaços gemendo fazem: pim!
Pelo grande zunido, pelo som
Parece-me que valsam junto a mim!
Os patifes dos boches dizem! Pum! …
Vejam que o sólido muda de tom
E não façam connosco Pim–pam–pum!

('The moaning splinters go: pim! Through the great noise, through sound, seems to me they are waltzing near me. The boches's bastards say: Pum! See how the solid changes tone. Don't do Pim-pam-pum! With us.) Ali Riza Eti, serving with the Ottoman Third Army is eastern Anatolia, described in his diary how Russian rifle bullets made a *civ*, *civ*, *civ* sound, whereas a shrapnel shell made a *ciiib*! noise when it burst. For the German writer Otto Riebicke, bullets went 'päng … päng', grenades 'rrrumsch … rrrumsch', machine guns 'rattarattatt'. In his novel *Krieg* Ludwig Renn, according to a British critic, 'imitates the noise made by the shells with a meticulous care that is almost comic': 'S – kramm! ram! ram! ram! ram! … Sch – p! [a dud] … Bramm! … Wramm … Ramm! App! Ramms! Karr! … Pramm! harp! Kötsch! Rur-rum-pa! ra! hrätsch! Parr! … Ra – Ramms! S-parr! Schr – kräpp!' Werner Beumelburg, who almost certainly disapproved of Renn's work, followed his example in this at least: 'sssss kreng … Sssss … kreng krach. Sssss … petsch [another dud] … Sssss … sssss … wwumm wwumm'. He even made a kind of joke of it:

How many men have you got left? … A nice simple calculation. … There were thirty-four of you at Azannes … wummm rrranggg …. Comma, line. Got it? Go on. Twenty-four in the Orne Gorge … krrranggg rrenggrrenggrrrenggg … write it down in a column, subtract … sss krrangg … four from four equals zero … wummm krrranggg … three from four leaves one … rrrang brummm … makes ten …[7]

Even neutrals got in on the game. Thomas Dinesen, the brother of

Karen Blixen, joined the Canadian army, won the Victoria Cross
and wrote his memoirs – in his native language, which was Danish:

> Hele natten igennem drøner kanonerne, med spredte skud, både
> nær ved og langt, langt borte mod nord og syd ... bum – – –
> bum – – bum bum – *BUM!* lige bag os, – og vi hører granaterne
> suse gennem luften. De små, langt borte, knirker som en cykel
> på en grussti; andre hvæser tæt over hovedet på én som en
> Rolls-Royce i fuld fart. De engelske maskingeværer skratter,
> med mellemrum, natten igennem, – da-da-da-da – – – – da-da-
> da-da-da-da – – – – – da-da-da –, men de bør jo ikke være farlige
> for os, selv om kuglerne pister lige over vore hoveder.
>   *SVUP!* der ryger en dart, en stor granat fra en
> skyttegravsmorter, op et sted ovre i mørket fra Frits' forreste
> linie, 2-300 meter borte.

This was translated into English, with the orthography of the
sound- effects revised to suit an English readership:

> boom ... boom ... boom ... boom-boom ... *BOOM!* Just
> behind us we hear the shrapnel whizzing through the air. The
> small shells, when far away, creak just like a cycle on a gravel
> path; others hiss immediately above one's head, like the sound
> of a big Rolls-Royce going at top speed. In between, comes
> the sound of the English machine-guns, suddenly stopping,
> then commencing again all through the night: *dah-dah-dah
> ... dah-dah-dah ... dah-dah-dah-dah!* Of course, they ought
> to be our best friends, but all the same some of the shots come
> very close, whizzing just above our heads! SWU-UPP! ...[8]

Yet no amount of ingenuity in transcribing sound effects could
provide a basis for a sustained literary treatment of the war, and
though the *idea* of war literature had emerged clearly enough in
the later nineteenth century, it seems that developments in literary
technique – more especially in poetry – gave less direct assistance

to writers than the developments in painting in the two decades before 1914 did to artists.

In poetry, in Britain, the Imagist movement seemed initially to offer some useful prescriptions on how to write a war poem, though a manifesto published in 1915 was anxious to deny their novelty:

> These principles are not new; they have fallen into desuetude. They are the essentials of all great poetry, indeed of all great literature, and they are simply these:
>
> 1. To use the language of common speech, but to employ always the *exact* word, not the nearly exact, nor the merely decorative word.
>
> 2. To create new rhythms – as the expression of new moods – and not to copy old rhythms, which merely echo old moods …. In poetry, a new cadence means a new idea.
>
> 3. To allow absolute freedom in the choice of subject. It is not good art to write badly about aeroplanes and automobiles; nor is it necessarily bad art to write well about the past. We believe passionately in the artistic value of modern life, but we wish to point out that there is nothing so uninspiring nor so old-fashioned as an aeroplane of the year 1911.
>
> 4. To present an image (hence the name: 'Imagist'). We are not a school of painters, but we believe that poetry should render particulars exactly and not deal in vague generalities, however magnificent and sonorous …
>
> 5. To produce poetry that is hard and clear, never blurred nor indefinite.
>
> 6. Finally, most of us believe that concentration is of the very essence of poetry.

These words were written by Richard Aldington, but his poetic practice was less impressive than either his preaching or, later on, his novel *Death of a Hero*:

These antique prostitutions –
Am I dead? Withered? Grown Old?
That not the least flush of desire
Tinges my unmoved flesh,
And that instead of women's living bodies
I see dead men – you understand? dead men
With sullen, dark red gashes
Luminous in a foul trench?[9]

In fact almost none of the best English poetry of the First World War is technically innovative: Wilfred Owen's panting half-rhymes are in no sense as mould-breaking as the experiments of Ungaretti in Italian and Stramm in German:

It seemed that out of battle I escaped
Down some profound long tunnel, long since scooped
Through granites which titanic wars had groined

Yet also there encumbered sleepers groaned,
Too fast in thought or death to be bestirred,
Then, as I probed them, one sprang up, and stared ...

One may even read something of a hidden agenda in T.S. Eliot's claim that David Jones belonged to the same innovative generation as himself, James Joyce and Ezra Pound, for Jones's *In Parenthesis*, unlike the rest of the best poetry of the war, was written years afterwards, long after Owen and Rosenberg had been carried to their graves on the battlefield.[10]

There is indeed no mention of Owen and Rosenberg in Eliot's correspondence: his verdict on a public reading of war poetry in October 1917 was 'the only one who has any merit is a youth named Siegfried Sassoon (Semitic) and his stuff is better politics than poetry.' The word 'youth', though not totally inappropriate when applied to Sassoon's habitual demeanour, was probably meant satirically: already in his thirties, Sassoon was two years older than Eliot. The degree to which the creator of 'Prufrock' was disengaged from what was going on is suggested by a bogus letter, purportedly by a lady named Helen B. Trundlett, which he wrote shortly afterwards as a space-filler for a literary journal he helped edit: this spoof described the 'dross' in Rupert Brooke's earlier poetry as having been 'purged away (if I may be permitted this word) in the fire of the Great Ordeal which is proving the well-spring of a Renaissance of English poetry.' This is meant to be ironic, for Eliot thought otherwise. He may already have been working out his ideas for his influential essay on 'The Metaphysical Poets', first printed in 1921, in which he put forward the idea of a 'dissociation of sensibility' which had prevented English poets since the seventeenth century from writing genuine poetry about their intellectual and moral concerns: a point of view that implies a complete dismissal of the attempts of Owen and other First World War poets to give poetic form to their experiences.[11]

Owen himself claimed of his own work 'The Poetry is in the pity', and some of the most successful poems of the war years depend on their subject, tragic context and the chance memorable phrase rather than any real poetic excellence. Both Rupert Brooke's

> If I should die think only this of me
> That there's some corner of a foreign field
> That is for ever England

or Alan Seeger's

> I have a rendezvous with Death
> At some disputed barricade

would have weathered less well if their authors had survived to edit the *Daily Telegraph* or become ambassador at Stockholm, though neither the hill-top olive grove on Skyros where Brooke was buried nor the meadow near Belloy-en-Santerre where Seeger was riddled by a traversing machine gun was quite what their poems evoked. One suspects in any case that luck has a great deal to do with the reputation of such pieces: Ewart Alan Mackintosh, a classical scholar at Christ Church, produced a couple of volumes of rather late-Victorian verse, of which one poem at least is as fine as anything Brooke or Seeger wrote, even if later readers might have preferred to have foregone 'the crash of Victory' in the last stanza quoted – though perhaps after all it conveys well enough the callous satisfaction of a man throwing hand grenades ('a bomber') when one of his grenades detonates exactly where he intended:

Though grasses grow on Vimy,
And poppies at Messines,
And in High Wood the children play,
The craters and the graves will stay
To show what things have been.

Though all be quiet in day-time
The night shall bring a change,
And peasants walking home shall see
Shell-torn meadow and riven tree,
And their own fields grown strange.

They shall hear live men crying,
They shall see dead men lie,
Shall hear the rattling Maxims fire,
And see by broken twists of wire
Gold flares light up the sky.

And in their new-built houses
The frightened folk will see
Pale bombers coming down the street,
And hear the flurry of charging feet,
And the crash of Victory.[12]

Mackintosh's verses seem to owe something to the tone and pace of a much better-known piece by John MacCrae:

> In Flanders fields the poppies grow
> Between the crosses, row on row
> That mark our place: and in the sky
> The larks still bravely singing, fly
> Scarce heard amid the guns below.

MacCrae himself, who had been born in 1872 and had served as a major in the Royal Artillery during the Boer War, had been one of those who had thrilled to A.E. Housman's *A Shropshire Lad* when it had first become famous in the late 1890s, and despite the differences in prosody one is probably justified in seeing Housman as the most influential of his literary forebears. (Poppies growing on the broken ground of a battlefield had however been noted as far back as the seventeenth century, the 'scarlet sheet' of poppies on the site of the Battle of Landen looking 'as if last year's blood has taken root, and appeared in this year's flowers'.)[13]

Rupert Brooke also had his imitators, though the echo of his famous sonnet in the first line of the following is presumably ironic:

> If I should die, be not concerned to know
> The manner of my ending, if I fell
> Leading a forlorn charge against the foe,
> Strangled by gas, or shattered by a shell.
> Nor seek to see me in this death-in-life
> Mid shirks and curses, oaths and blood and sweat,
> Cold in the darkness, on the edge of strife,
> Bored and afraid, irresolute, and wet.
>
> But if you think of me, remember one
> Who loved good dinners, curious parody,
> Swimming, and lying naked in the sun,
> Latin hexameters, and heraldry,

Athenian subtleties of δηζ and τοιζ,
Beethoven, Botticelli, beer, and boys.

(The author, Phillip Bainbrigge, had been a sixth-form master at
Shrewsbury before his call-up and though he had at least one close
friend who was gay the reference to 'boys' is unlikely to have any
homoerotic significance – even if the war did play havoc with
pre-war cautions.)[14]

Other poets chose less obvious models, for example Keats:

A little moment more – O, let me hear
(The thunder rolls above, and star-shells fall)
Those melodies unheard re-echo clear
Before the shuddering moment closes all.
They come – they come – they answer to my call,
That Grecian throng of graven ecstasies,
Hyperion aglow in blazing skies,
And Cortez with the wonder in his eyes.

Southey perhaps (but with a curious prefiguring of the poem by
Wilfred Owen quoted a couple of pages back):

I tracked a dead man down a trench,
I knew not he was dead.
They told me he had gone that way,
And there his foot-marks led.

The trench was long and close and curved,
It seemed without an end;
And as I threaded each new bay
I thought to see my friend.

I went there stooping to the ground.
For, should I raise my head,
Death watched to spring; and how should then

A dead man find the dead?

At last I saw his back. He crouched
As still as still could be,
And when I called his name aloud
He did not answer me.

The floor-way of the trench was wet
Where he was crouching dead:
The water of the pool was brown,
And round him it was red.

I stole up softly where he stayed
With head hung down all slack,
And on his shoulders laid my hands
And drew him gently back.

And then, as I had guessed, I saw
His head, and how the crown –
I saw then why he crouched so still,
And why his head hung down.

Or possibly Browning:

Who but the guns shall avenge him? *Battery – Action!*
Load us and lay to the centremost hair of the dial-sight's
  refraction;
Set your quick hands to our levers to compass the sped soul's
  assoiling
Brace your taut limbs to the shock when the thrust of the
  barrel recoiling
Deafens and stuns!
Vengeance is ours for our servants: trust ye the guns!

A.P. Herbert, in *The Bomber Gipsey*, obviously took his title from

Matthew Arnold, though one of the poems in this collection, 'Beaucourt Revisited', echoed William Johnson Cory's 'They Told Me, Heraclitus ...':

I wandered up to Beaucourt, I took the river track
And saw the lines we lived in before the Boche went back ...

Charles Sorley's best-known poem, found in his kit-bag after he was shot through the head, suggests a debt to Christina Rossetti:

When you see millions of the mouthless dead
Across your dreams in pale battalions go,
Say not soft things as other men have said,
That you'll remember. For you need not so.
Give them not praise. For, deaf, how should they know
It is not curses heaped on each gashed head?
Nor tears. Their blind eyes see not your tears flow.
Nor honour. It is easy to be dead.
Say only this, 'They are dead.' Then add thereto,
'Yet many a better one has died before.'
Then, scanning all the o'ercrowded mass, should you
Perceive one face that you loved heretofore,
It is a spook. None wears the face you knew,
Great death has made all his for evermore.

Isaac Rosenberg, despite his admiration for Walt Whitman ('I have written a few war poems but when I think of "Drum Taps" mine are absurd') and his qualified view of Blake ('The drawings are finer than his poems'), seems to have modelled himself more on the latter:

I snatched two poppies
From the parapet's ledge
Two bright red poppies
That winked on the ledge

Even in his 'Break of Day in the Trenches' there is an echo of Blake, with a rat instead of a tiger:

What do you see in our eyes
At the shrieking iron and flame
Hurled through still heavens?
What quaver – what heart aghast?[15]

Similar lines of descent will be traceable in the work of French and German war poets: and the oddest instance of a wartime poem, or rather song, that derives from an earlier model is an English adaptation of a German original. There are innumerable different versions of this song. 'The German generals crossed the Rhine ...', or perhaps they were merely officers, no rank specified, and there may have been three of them, and it may have been the *line* rather than the Rhine – front line? Armistice line? Different versions have different refrains: '*Skibboo, skibboo, ski-bumpity-bump skibboo!*' or '*Taboo, taboo, tabollocky eye taboo!*' but the most usual is '*Parley-voo*', which provided the name by which the song was known in the neighbourhood of Colchester barracks where this author first heard it in the late 1950s: the title *Mademoiselle from Armentières*, which is sometimes used, properly refers only to the tune:

The German generals crossed the line, *parley-voo*

The German generals crossed the line, *parley-voo*

The German generals crossed the line
To fuck the women and drink the wine
Inky-pinky parley-voo

They came to the door of a wayside inn, *parley-voo*

They came to the door of a wayside inn, *parley-voo*

They came to the door of a wayside inn
Pissed on the mat and walked right in
Inky-pinky parley-voo

'O landlord have you a daughter fair, *parley-voo*

O landlord have you a daughter fair, *parley-voo*

O landlord have you a daughter fair
With lily-white tits and golden hair?'
Inky-pinky parley-voo

This is undoubtedly derived from Ludwig Uhland's well-known ballad 'Der Wirtin Töchterlein', written in 1809 and published in his *Gedichte* of 1815:

Es zogen drei Bursche wohl über den Rhein
Bei einer Frau Wirthin, da kehrten sie ein
'Frau Wirthin! hat Sie gut Bier und Wein?
Wo hat Sie Ihr schönes Töchterlein?'

In Uhland's version the landlady (not landlord) takes the three *Bursche* (batmen or orderlies, or perhaps merely 'lads') to a bedroom and shows them her daughter's corpse, and each of the orderlies declares that he had been in love with her. In the British First World War version

At last they got her on the bed [repeated twice, with refrain]
And shagged her till her cheeks were red
And then they took her to a shed [repeated twice, with refrain]
And shagged her till she was nearly dead
They took her down a shady lane [repeated twice, with refrain]
And shagged her back to life again.

How and when the transformation of Uhland's verses occurred is a mystery: Eric Partridge, the folklorist of English filth, thought it might even have happened as far back as the time of Waterloo, though there is no real evidence to sustain this theory. At any rate 'Parley-voo' serves both as a warning against trying to 'explain' poems in terms of their sources and as a useful corrective for those who wish to think of the British trenches as populated solely by idealistic young poets who were half in love with each other.[16]

Prose writers also needed models. If there was less difficulty, *pace* Blunden, about tone and phrasing than with poetry (prose being closer to everyday discourse) there was more difficulty with regard to structure and organization, since a novel or a book-length memoir would have to contain far more words than a poem: as Somerset Maugham explained in the Preface to his collection of short stories based on his First World War career as a British secret service agent,

> Fact is a poor story-teller. It starts a story at haphazard, generally long before the beginning, rambles on inconsequently and tails off, leaving loose ends hanging about, without a conclusion. It works up to an interesting situation, and then leaves it in the air to follow an issue that has nothing to do with the point; it has no sense of climax and whittles away its dramatic effects in irrelevance. There is a school of novelists that looks upon this as the proper model for fiction. If life, they say, is arbitrary and disconnected, why, fiction should be so too; for fiction should imitate life. In life things happen at random, and that is how they should happen in a story; they do not lead to a climax, which is an outrage to probability, they just go on. Nothing offends these people more than the punch or the unexpected twist with which some writers seek to surprise their readers, and when the circumstances they relate seem to tend towards a dramatic effect they do their best to avoid it. They do not give you a story, they give you the material on which you can invent your own.[17]

One model was *War and Peace*. Wilfrid Ewart's debt to Tolstoy was acknowledged by his biographer:

> The next idea was to give to England a book which might be the equivalent of Tolstoy's *War and Peace*. He read the whole of *War and Peace* with that in mind. His greatest difficulty was naturally the technical one of novel-writing. He had the experience, he had the gift of writing, but he had no known equipment for telling a story.

The result was *Way of Revelation*, which enjoyed considerable success when it was published in 1921. The *Times Literary Supplement* wrote:

> The central figures of the drama – Adrian Knoyle and Eric Sinclair – stand on the threshold of adventure. Adrian has become engaged, unofficially, to Lady Rosemary Meynall, while his friend maintains a desultory courtship of Faith Daventry. Then comes the war, and the remainder of the book is devoted to a study of the reactions of this set of characters to the new conditions.
>
> It is of course, the obvious way in which to treat the war. The same thing has been done a great many times already, occasionally with success. *Way of Revelation* conforms to the pattern. There is no story. Pictures of warfare and trench routine alternate with pictures of London society. Most of the women fill a portion of their spare time with nursing and charity entertainments. Some of the men obtain soft jobs at the Admiralty. The majority of them go to France, where some are killed and whence others return maimed ... In the treatment of an obvious theme he has made use of the obvious characters, the obvious situations, the obvious emotions, and yet, because of his sincerity, because of his faith in his vision of life, he has reached, through the obvious, to the universal.[18]

British recruitment poster, 1915.

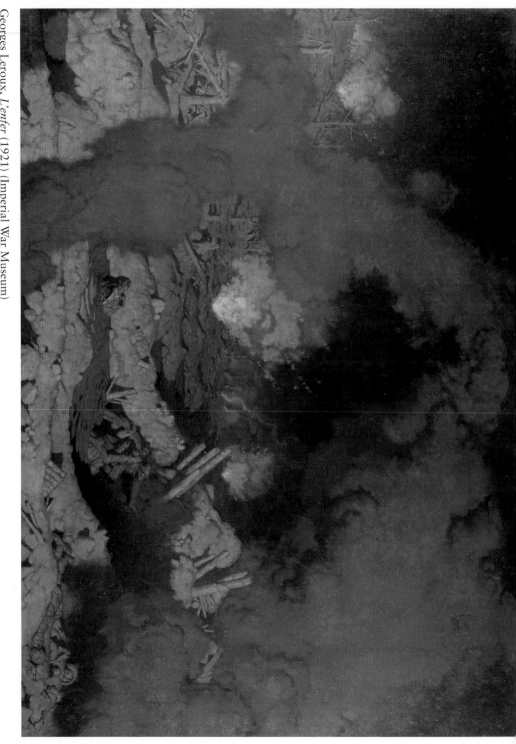

Otto Dix, *Flanders* (1934–6) (Nationalgalerie, Berlin)

Christopher Nevinson, *Marching Men* (1916) (Imperial War Museum)

Left: Henri Barbusse.

Below left: Wilfred Owen.

Below right: Siegfried Sassoon.

Bottom: Futurists Russolo, Carra, Marinetti, Boccioni and Severini in Paris, 1912.

'Help us to win! Subscribe to the War Loan' by Fritz Erler (1868–1940).

Above left: Giuseppe Ungaretti.

Above right: T. S. Eliot.

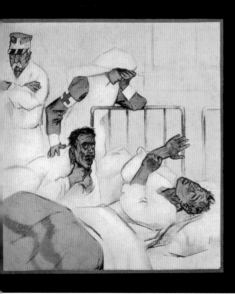

Gassed !
– another Victory
for KULTUR

Drawn by
Louis Raemaekers
for The Century Magazine

Barron Collier Series of Patriotic Cartoo

The Century Magazine, New York 1916.

Christopher Nevinson, *French Troops Resting* (1916) (Imperial War Museum)

THE SPHERE

AN ILLUSTRATED NEWSPAPER FOR THE HOME   With which is incorporated "BLACK & WHITE"

Volume LXVI. No. 858.   {REGISTERED AT THE GENERAL} {POST OFFICE AS A NEWSPAPER}   London, July 1, 1916   Price Sixpence.

DRAWN BY F. MATANIA. FROM MATERIAL SUPPLIED, 1916

The Sphere, 1 July 1916.

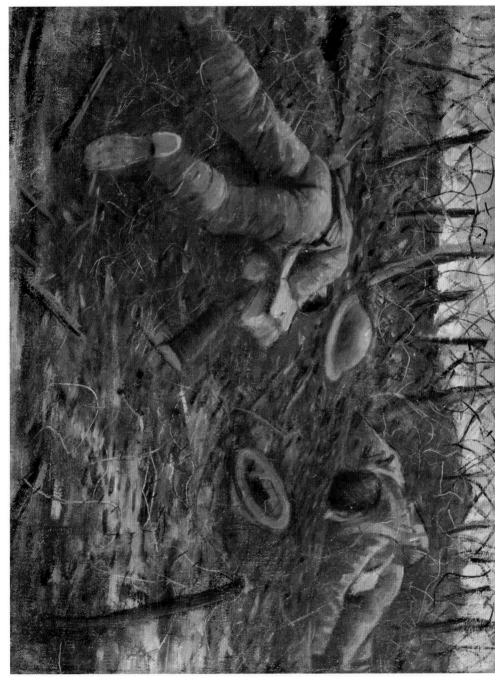

Christopher Nevinson, *Paths of Glory* (1917) (Imperial War Museum)

Paul Nash, *The Mule Track* (1918) (Imperial War Museum)

Paul Nash, *The Menin Road* (1918) (Imperial War Museum)

Above left: Robert Graves.

Above right: Guillaume Apollinaire.

Below: American artillery, 1918.

Norman G. Arnold, *The Last Flight of Captain Ball* (1919) (Imperial War Museum)

Above left: Wounded with the 4th Ambulance Corps, American 1st Div. in a church, 1918.

Above right: Ford Madox Ford.

The ruins of Bailleul, September 1918.

Another, perhaps more impressive, attempt to integrate the war into the working out of the protagonist's emotional life was Ford Madox Ford's *Parade's End* tetralogy (1924–28) in which Tolstoy's Pierre Bezukhov becomes anglicized (though with a Dutch surname) as a captain in the Glamorganshires whose Edwardian values place him at a disadvantage when confronted with the era of the world wars. Gilbert Frankau's *Peter Jackson: Cigar Merchant* and Richard Aldington's *Death of a Hero* may be seen as variations on the *War and Peace* model too (though the critic F.R. Leavis also noted in *Death of a Hero* 'tributes to Samuel Butler and Mr Aldous Huxley' and the occasional 'patch of H.G. Wells [and] of D.H. Lawrence'), but not inappropriately the war novel most reminiscent of Tolstoy was written by a Russian. Peter Nikolayevich Krasnov, a colonel in the Tsar's cavalry at the outbreak of war, and to all appearances twin brother to one of the minor characters in *Anna Karenina*, had risen by 1917 to the command of the Third Cavalry Corps stationed near Petrograd. After an unsuccessful bid to eject the newly-installed Soviet regime he fled south, was elected Ataman of the Don Cossacks with German support, and after the Civil War took refuge in Germany. His *Ot Dvuglavago Orla k Krasnomy Znamyeni, 1894–1921* was published in Berlin in, it seems, 1922. The 1552-page English version, *From the Two-Headed Eagle to the Red Flag, 1894–1921*, was published in Berlin in 1923, and an abridgement of the English text appeared in 1928. The earnestness of Krasnov's attempts to follow his great predecessor are evident throughout his book, as is his inability to sustain the effort. Only about a third of the novel deals with the First World War as such: *From the Two-Headed Eagle to the Red Flag* covers nearly four times the time-span of *War and Peace*. Krasnov also managed to live almost as long as Tolstoy and to die harder. In 1943 he undertook to raise and lead a Cossack army to help overthrow the Soviet government. After the defeat of Hitler he was tried by a Red Army tribunal, being then in his seventy-eighth year, and subsequently hanged. It does not seem that his authorship of *From the Two-Headed Eagle to the Red Flag was* an item in his indictment: perhaps the Soviet prosecutors had not been able to find a copy.[19]

Though Gilbert Frankau's *Peter Jackson: Cigar Merchant* was praised by The *Times Literary Supplement* as 'a novel of the old type ... it has "a beginning, a middle, and an end"', some writers felt that a story-line was not everything. This after all was the era of James Joyce, of whom Henry Williamson was briefly a disciple:

> Chaps going on forward. He was on his feet in the sissing criss-cross and stinking of smoking earth gaping – hullo, hullo, new shell-holes, this must be near the first objective. They had come three hundred yards already! Cushy! Nothing in going over the top! Then his heart instead of finishing its beat and pausing to beat again swelled out its beat into an ear-bursting agony and great lurid light that leapt out of his broken-apart body with a spinning shriek and the earth was in his eyes and up his nostrils and going away smaller and smaller into blackness
>
> and   tiny   far   away
>
> Rough and smooth. Rough was wide and large and tilting with sickness. He struggled and struggled to clutch smooth, and it slid away. Rough came back and washed harshly over him. He cried out between the receding of rough and the coming of smooth white, then rough and ...[20]

Another experimental work was Edlef Köppen's *Heeresbericht* (1929 – an English translation was published as *The Higher Command*), which interwove a fictional account of the experiences of a young artillerist with official communiqués, official letters, speeches, excerpts from newspapers and encyclopedias and apparently genuine (but actually fictional) extracts from private letters and diaries. In general however the prose writers who were caught up in the war were little more interested in experimentation than the poets. It was almost as if they felt their material was too serious, too important, for fancy footwork. Apart from *War and Peace*, it seems to have been Barbusse's *Le feu* which had the largest influence on later writers.

Before the war Henri Barbusse had been a writer in the French naturalist tradition. One of his earlier novels, *L'enfer*, is a study in depressingness and obsession which may, if one wishes, be taken as demonstrating that his naturalism had advanced significant stages beyond that of Flaubert or Zola; at any rate it certainly exhibits what one critic calls 'a Naturalist predilection for "unpleasant themes"', and Barbusse evidently found another such theme in the war. Contrary to what is sometimes claimed, he served several months as a rifleman in the trenches before being assigned to a first aid post. *Le feu: journal d'une escouade* was published in France in 1916 and in Britain, in Fitzwalter Wray's translation, with the title *Under Fire: the Story of a Squad*, during the following year. Its harrowing evocation of the meaningless sufferings of the frontline troops had the advantage of priority (though in fact conditions had become even worse since the period Barbusse described), but other writers, and painters like Georges Leroux, were already squaring up to the problem of showing the same thing. Barbusse's master-stroke was to seize on the small group drawn from different backgrounds, and the interaction of its members, as an expository model.[21]

Mulvaney, Ortheris and Learoyd in Kipling's *Soldiers Three* (1888) are merely a little clique within a unit stationed on Britain's imperial frontier. They are cross-sectional only in the same sense that Jamy, Macmorris, Gower and Fluellen, the Scots, Irish and Welsh officers in Shakespeare's *Henry* V are cross-sectional, and their sufferings together are much less in evidence than their united torturing of the English language. In *Le feu* the group is larger and it is experiencing the horrors of war as a complex entity. Siegfried Sassoon wrote that 'for an infantry subaltern the huge unhappy mechanism of the Western Front always narrowed down to the company he was in.' For the private soldier or lance-corporal it was not even the one hundred and fifty men of the company that provided the group one belonged to, it was one's platoon or even section:

> trench life is very domestic, highly atomic. Its atom, or unit, like that of slum life, is the jealously close, exclusive, contriving life of a family housed in an urban cellar. During the years of trench war a man seldom saw the whole of his company at

a time. Our total host might be two millions strong, or ten millions; whatever its size a man's world was that of his section – at most, his platoon; all that mattered much to him was the one little boatload of castaways with whom he was marooned on a desert island and making shift to keep off the weather and any sudden attack of wild beasts. Absorbed in the primitive job of keeping alive on earth naked except in the matter of food, they became, like other primitive men, family separatists.

After the war a few novels such as Josef Magnus Wehner's *Sieben vor Verdun* ('Seven before Verdun') dealt with the experiences of a number of soldiers who were in different units, but this approach was exceptional. First World War novels which were not fictionalized memoirs of individuals were most commonly novels about *groups*. Roland Dorgelès's *Les croix de bois* (1919; published in English as *Wooden Crosses* in 1920) was second only to *Le feu* as the best-known French novel of the war and followed Barbusse's format. Philip MacDonald's *Patrol* (1927), describing a cavalry patrol in Mesopotamia which becomes lost and is picked off one by one by hostile Arabs, Liam O'Flaherty's *Return of the Brute* (1929), in which a member of another patrol adds to the normal attrition of war by killing one of his comrades with a grenade and throttling the corporal before allowing himself to be mown down by a German machine gun, and Frederic Manning's *Her Privates We* (1931), which focuses on three friends in a section in a company in an unnamed battalion, are perhaps the most notable British instances of the same approach. American examples on the same model are James B. Wharton's *Squad* (1928) and William March's *Company K* (1930).[22]

The Germans showed a particular fondness for novels about groups of protagonists welded together by their shared experiences in the trenches. An early example was Fritz von Unruh's *Opfergang* ('Way of Sacrifice'), written at about the same time as *Le feu* but not published till 1919. Erich Maria Remarque's *Im Westen Nichts Neues*, published in book form in 1929, focuses on the experiences of four youths who had been in the same class in Gymnasium and had joined the army together as volunteers, and their trench-comrades Tjaden the locksmith, Haie Westhus the peat-digger, Detering the peasant, and Stanislaus Katczinsky the cobbler. The year 1929 also saw Karl Bröger's *Bunker 17: Geschichte einer Kameradschaft* (translated 1930 as *Pill Box 17: The Story of a Comradeship-in-Arms*); M.G.K. – i.e. 'Machine-Gun Company' – by Franz Seldte, who lost an arm in the war, became leader of the right-wing veterans' organization 'Stahlhelm', and, though never in Hitler's inner circle, minister of labour in the Nazi government, 1933–45; Ernst Johannsen's *Vier von der Infanterie* (published in English 1930 as *Four Infantrymen on the Western Front, 1918*), in which it was explained 'These four men – Job, Lornsen, Müller and the student – form a tiny comradeship within the greater one that takes in the whole front' – this was the book which was the basis for G.W. Pabst's unforgettable movie *Westfront 1918* – and Alfred Hein's *Ein Kompagnie Soldaten: In der Hölle von Verdun*, which, though largely from the point of view of Lindolf, the company runner, ends:

> Once more the company went forward in the winter night through the desolation of the front, their hearts illumined and purified by the still steady flame of human comradeship.

In 1930 appeared Werner Beumelburg's *Die Gruppe Bosemüller* ('Bosemüller's Squad') which, though only moderately successful in the last years of the Weimar Republic, became a million-seller after the Nazis came to power and banned Remarque's *Im Westen Nichts Neues* because of its negative attitude to war. The experiences of a squad were also described in Ernst Weichert's *Jedermann* of 1931, though with particular emphasis on the inner core of four soldiers: their representative status was of course sign-posted by the title, which means 'Everyman'.[23]

The group provided not merely a narrative device but a kind of symbol. Roland Dorgelès, for example, was fully aware of how the small group could serve to represent a whole army's whole experience of the war:

> I learnt to suffer, to bear witness in the name of those who have suffered so much ... Not for an instant did I think of keeping a diary of my regiment. I had a higher ambition – not to tell the story of *my* war but of *the* war. Throw out the dates, delete the names of the actors, forget the unit numbers, and draw from myself would-be memories so replete with truth that each ex-soldier would cry out, 'They're mine too.'

Symbolic representations of a more elaborate kind were rare: the influence of Franz Kafka, detectable in the fiction of the Second World War, only began to make itself felt during the late 1930s. In Remarque's *Im Westen Nichts Neues* the narrator becomes lost during a patrol, blunders into a French soldier in the dark, stabs him with 'my little dagger' and when daylight comes finds that his victim, a man with a small pointed beard', is still alive. Frantically, Remarque's narrator puts on field dressings, but by the middle of the afternoon the Frenchman is dead. It is too dangerous to leave the cover of the shell hole. 'Soon the silence is more unbearable than the groans. I wish the gurgling were there again, gasping, hoarse, now whistling softly and again hoarse and loud.' He begins to talk to the corpse. He takes out the Frenchman's wallet. 'It slips out of my hand and falls open. Some pictures and letters drop out.' He copies out the dead man's address. 'I have killed the printer, Gerard Duval. I must be a printer, I think confusedly, be a printer, printer ...' A shell hole also features in Vernon Bartlett's *No Man's Land* (1930), about a wounded soldier left to die in one, and in Hans Fallada's *Die Eiserne Gustav* (1938; translated as *Iron Gustav*, 1940), in which the protagonist Otto Hackendahl and a lieutenant from another unit engage in a pivotal dialogue while stranded together in a shell crater between the two front lines.[24]

The only First World War novelist who attempted to go much

further than this was another German, Arnold Zweig, in *Der Streit um den Sergeanten Grischa* (1928; English translation published in the same year under the title *The Case of Sergeant Grischa*) and *Erziehung vor Verdun* (published in exile, in Amsterdam, in 1935, and in English as *Education Before Verdun*, in 1936). In *Der Streit um den Sergeanten Grischa* an escaped Russian prisoner of war is sentenced to death as a result of a mix-up and is eventually executed because the attempts made to reverse the original error or to rescue him break down in the face of the German army's need to maintain discipline and his own resignation to fate. In *Erziehung vor Verdun* a young NCO objects to the other NCOs setting up their own kitchen and hogging the beer and the best food, and writes about it to an uncle, who is a senior officer. His letter is intercepted by the postal censors, who order that the young NCO should be court-martialled, but the trial is postponed, and the NCO is sent to a position of danger where he is conveniently killed. The novel functions quite well as a depiction of the Battle of Verdun from the sidelines, but the *cause célèbre* which is supposed to provide the essential narrative thread seems forced and scarcely capable of bearing the weight Zweig evidently wished to give it. The issue of German NCOs monopolizing the best sausages does not seem so very important in the context of the German army having violated Belgian neutrality, overrun almost the entire country, and laid waste half a dozen French *départements*; it is also curiously reminiscent of the picture conjured up by Charles Carrington's remark, half a dozen years earlier, 'No corrupt sergeant-majors stole my rations or accepted my bribes ... No casual staff officers ordered me to certain death, indifferent to my fate.'[25]

Zweig's own war experience perhaps explains both the symbolic ambitions and the failure of his novels. After thirteen months on the Verdun front, he was assigned to a department of the HQ on the Eastern Front responsible for producing German-language publications for circulation in the occupied areas of the Russian Empire. Zweig, himself Jewish, found himself amongst a group of assorted intellectuals – many also Jewish but including the

Expressionist painter Karl Schmidt-Rottluff – with access to censored books such as Barbusse's *Le feu*. One imagines that Zweig and his fellow members of the 'Intellectuals Club' at HQ looked increasingly askance at the activities of the General Staff officers – not all Prussians, of course, but mostly members of aristocratic, army-orientated families – whose policies they were employed to dress up in palatable form for public consumption. The Sergeant Grischa story-line seems to have been based on a real incident; at any rate the unsuccessful moral stands at the centre of the two novels tend to suggest that during his stint at HQ it had at least crossed Zweig's mind to take up similarly high-minded positions of principle. Even if this had not occurred to him at the time, the propaganda aspect of his employment would have given him good reason to reflect on the moral ambiguities that arise in wartime.[26]

Curiously enough, the best-known of all novels by a frontline veteran in which a much-put-upon individual is raised to symbolic status as the representative of his class, race, age group or whatever, actually had its genesis before the war. Jaroslav Hašek's classic piss-take *Osudy Dobrého Vojáka Švejka za Světové Války* ('The Fortunes of Good Soldier Svejk in the Great War', 1921–23, translated 1930 as *The Good Soldier Schweik)* is almost identical in tone to five stories Hašek wrote in 1911 about the idiotic Švejk's peacetime military service. Evidently for Hašek, as for Klee and Marinetti, the war was less of a surprise than it was for some other people: Clausewitz's famous dictum, that war is merely the continuation of politics with the admixture of other means is sometimes as applicable to literary studies as it is to military history.[27]

6

HEROES

The last four chapters have dealt with how writers and artists rose to the challenge of describing what they had experienced in the front line but there were other ways of responding creatively to the war besides writing and painting. An act of outstanding bravery might be just as much an assertion of human personality, just as much an exhibition of carefully nurtured skill or serendipity as an effective poem or a memorable canvas, and while most frontline combatants never found an opportunity to distinguish themselves others did so repeatedly. The coincidences of opportunity and chronology, and what Wilfred Owen called 'Chance's strange arithmetic' in the front line, operated not just for those who recorded the war for posterity but for their whole generation.[1]

In Ernest Raymond's *Tell England* the colonel says to the two newly commissioned teenage protagonists:

'Eighteen, confound it! It's a virtue to be your age, just as it's a crime to be mine ... Eighteen years ago you were born for this day. Through the last eighteen years you've been educated for it. Your birth and breeding were given you that you might officer England's youth in this hour. And now you enter upon your inheritance. Just as this is *the* day in the history of the world so yours is *the* generation. No other generation has been called to such grand things, and to such crowded, glorious living...'

Of course no one timed things that deliberately. Before August 1914 most of the men who fought in the First World War had had lives which they didn't think they were finished with, and many of them were still young enough to revert occasionally to childhood behaviour patterns. Here is one officer's diary account of a moment of relaxation:

> Lying here on the soft grass we ate our lunch, basking in the hot rays of the sun and finding life sweet. Then smoking and talking we made brooches and bows out of sedgegrass and tiny flowers. In order not to desecrate the happy little ruin we buried our sandwich paper and replaced the turf (though there were dozens of empty tins lying round). Then we threw our empty bottles into the stream and raced beside them, each cheering his own craft – TT versus Toper – until after about half a mile they were caught in the weeds and we lay down and panted on the bank.
>
> Strolling quietly back in silence, we found a dead pigeon and buried him, railing in his grave with little sticks and chains of plaited sedgegrass, and in his coverlet of pimpernels we erected a tiny white cross.
>
> Then we went out on to the hot white road where our troops lay under the hedge ...

Albert Ball, VC, DSO and two bars, MC, one of the great heroes of the war, seems to have regressed under the pressure of combat to the behaviour and language of an eight-year-old newly installed at his first boarding school: 'Oh, I am so poo-poo, for I do so want a rest', he wrote home; and on another occasion complained, 'really things are desperate just now, and my mind is full of poo-poo thoughts.' In July 1916 he wrote 'I am having a very poo time, but most interesting. On the 6th three topping chaps went off and never returned. Yesterday four of my best pals went off.' In fact he did not have any pals. Except at meals he avoided the other officers (who were all mostly bigger than him and no doubt inclined to be a little rowdy in their horseplay), and lived in a hut beside his aeroplane 'in solitary state with his violin and little garden – so much so that we called him the "Lonely Testicle, or Pill"'.[2]

It is remarkable how many of the outstanding writers of the war had had personal problems before August 1914. Ivor Gurney had shown symptoms of what may have been the psychiatric disorder which hospitalized him for the last part of his life. Rupert Brooke's unresolved bisexuality had brought him to the verge of a break-down. Wilfred Owen was homosexual, with the classic homosexual thing about his mother ('Love is not quenched, except the unenduring flickerings thereof. By your love, O Mother, O Home, I am protected from Fatigue of life and the keen spiritual Cold', he wrote to his 'own dear Mother' on 7 January 1917). Robert Graves was in love with a boy in a lower form at Charterhouse when he joined up. Sassoon, repressing his sexuality – also male-orientated – led a schizoid life before the war pretending simultaneously to be a man of letters and a fox-hunting squire, and covered this up not unsuccessfully in *Memoirs of a Fox-Hunting Man* and *Memoirs of an Infantry Officer* by presenting his narrator as a callow youth – admittedly twenty-eight but 'five years younger in looks' – from a modest county family, rather than the scion of a dynasty of wealthy Iraqi Jews. In 1921 he recalled his 'pre-war isolation from the people who can interest me', and the life he had lived amongst 'people who are definitely antipathetic to my career as an artist'. T.E. Lawrence also had a problem with his sexuality as he hinted, perhaps not inadvertently, in *Seven Pillars of Wisdom*:

The men were young and sturdy; and hot flesh and blood unconsciously claimed a right in them and tormented their bellies with strange longings. Our privations and dangers fanned this virile heat, in a climate as racking as can be conceived. We had no shut places to be alone in, no thick clothes to hide our nature. Man in all things lived candidly with man.

The Arab was by nature continent; and the use of universal marriage had nearly abolished irregular courses in his tribes. The public women of the rare settlements we encountered in our months of wandering would have been nothing to our numbers, even had their raddled meat been palatable to a man of healthy parts. In horror of such sordid commerce our youths began indifferently to slake one another's few needs in their own clean bodies – a cold convenience that, by comparison, seemed sexless and even pure. Later, some began to justify this sterile process, and swore that friends quivering together in the yielding sand with intimate hot limbs in supreme embrace, found there hidden in the darkness a sensual co-efficient of the mental passion which was welding our souls and spirits in one flaming effort. Several, thirsting to punish appetites they could not wholly prevent, took a savage pride in degrading the body, and offered themselves fiercely in any habit which promised physical pain or filth.

Ernest Raymond was less fussed by such issues, not even recognizing the connection between his older-brotherly interest in young officers and his sexual instincts till he re-read *Tell England* much later:

Another thing that is a cause of wonder to me as I re-read the book is the indubitable but wholly unconscious homosexuality in it. The earlier part was written when I was eighteen or nineteen; the latter part in my twenties, and in those far-off days 'homosexuality' was a word which – absurd as this may seem now – I had never heard. It was not then the daily topic in newspapers and converse that it is today ... I did not know that homosexuality could exist in embryo without even knowing itself for what it was, or desiring the least physical satisfaction, till the time came for it to die and be transcended by full and normal manhood. Its presence in the book is one more evidence of its author's unusually slow progress towards maturity. A fellow clubman, a witty Irishman, who, though fifty or sixty now, persists in loving *Tell England* always delights me when he says, as he has more than once, 'I have just read that damned book again, and as usual I've been surprised that your Radley [the hero schoolmaster in the first part] does not reappear in the Gallipoli chapters, but then, of course, I suddenly remember that he'd have been doing his five years in jug.'[3]

Not everybody was gay in the British army of course. Henry Lamont, alias Wilfred Saint-Mandé, had probably begun his career as a sex fantasist, if not his second career as a lady-killer, even before war broke out. Richard Aldington had already given himself up to the loathing of parents and the love of manipulative women which he was to write about so eloquently in *Death of a Hero*, in which George Winterbourne's wife is modelled on the poet Hilda Doolittle, whom Aldington had married in 1913, and George Winterbourne's useless father – 'an inadequate sentimentalist [who] messed up his children's lives by being weak and sentimentalist with them and by losing his money' – is a portrait of Albert E. Aldington, who in 1912 lost so much money in unlucky business speculation that poor Richard's university studies had to be curtailed and in 1915, though an official in the Ministry of Munitions, had insufficient pull to wangle Richard a commission, even though the latter had seen from the very beginning of the war that it was 'going to be the biggest thing in history'. (In the event he waited until military service became compulsory in 1916 and he was called up.) Mrs Winterbourne in *Death of a Hero* is May Aldington, though her son doesn't mention her status as the best-selling author of books such as *Love Letters that Caused a Divorce* and only in later life recorded his opinion of them as 'hideously vulgar and illiterate'. Parental problems may also have been behind eighteen-year-old Ernst Jünger's running away to join the French Foreign Legion in November 1913: bearing in mind that his father had formerly worked in a university laboratory, it is interesting to note that the official entry in Jünger's Foreign Legion pay book stated that he 'can neither read nor write'.[4]

So many of the best books about the First World War were written by misfits – people who were misfits before the war and remained misfits after it – that one tends to forget what a wonderfully successful time it was for some people: and not just armaments manufacturers. The war produced no heaven-born generals, except perhaps Paul von Lettow-Vorbeck in East Africa – one recent biographer describes the latter as 'the most successful guerilla leader in world history' – but it provided several young men with a connecting link between outstanding school careers and success in later life: men such as H.W. Yoxall, school captain at St Paul's, MC and bar during the war, later managing director of Condé Nast, and T.F. Tallents, head of school at Harrow, MC and bar, twice wounded in action, promoted major in the Guards Machine Gun Regiment at the age of twenty-three, later chairman and managing director of the New Zealand and Federal Shipping Company.[5]

Other men were unable to settle after the fighting ended, and at moments of stress might burst out with exclamations of incredulity at the post-war existences they had slipped into, like the preparatory school master recalled by Robin Maugham who would shout at unsatisfactory boys, 'Do you think I fought in the trenches of Flanders – *do* you think I waded through gore and mud in order to sit in a classroom teaching Latin to a little idiot like you?' Even Siegfried Sassoon, rereading his diary for June 1916 five years later, noted 'I wish I could "find a moral equivalent for war" ... I feel as if I were only half-alive'. Cyril McNeile's fictional Captain Hugh Drummond, DSO, MC, 'late of His Majesty's Royal Loamshires' placed an advert in the newspaper: 'Demobilised officer, finding peace incredibly tedious, would welcome diversion. Legitimate, if possible; but crime, if of a comparatively humorous description, no objection. Excitement essential.' Drummond's real-life counterparts joined organizations such as the *Freikorps* in Germany, or the Blackshirts in Italy, or the Auxiliary Division of the Royal Irish Constabulary, though George Stanley Brighten, a young solicitor who had been promoted to lieutenant colonel in command of a battalion less than three years after joining up, did indeed resort to crime of a comparatively humorous description, being named as a defaulter on the Stock Exchange six times between 1923 and 1930 before being sent to prison for fraudulent conversion of a cheque drawn on the casino at Deauvillle. Tim Birkin found a substitute for the war in driving racing cars:

> I was in the Air Force, and when Armistice came, found the view of my future life, as I then beheld it, a very dull and confined one ... I was lucky enough to have the money to look round for an occupation, and not accept the first that offered; and of all that I considered, motor racing provided the energy, adventures, and risks most like those of the battlefield. It had, moreover, the promise of a great future, and there was the same chance of unexpected disaster, the same need for perfect nerves, with a presence of mind that must never desert you, the same exhilaration of living in the shadow of death that often came so suddenly and gloriously, that it seemed to have no shadow. There was, besides, the peculiar delight of being responsible for your own calamities, since, once off the mark, you were at liberty to take risks or avoid them as you pleased, a state of independence few individuals enjoyed in the war.[6]

Other men had discovered a talent for homicide that could find no application in civilian life after 1918: men like Lance-Corporal Henry Norwest of the Canadian Expeditionary Force who obtained 115 observed 'kills' as a sniper on the Western Front; or Sergeant Alvin York of the American Expeditionary Force who won the Congressional Medal of Honour for killing twenty-eight Germans and capturing another 132, with thirty-five machine-guns, at the

Argonne on 8 October 1918; or Rittmeister Manfred *Freiherr* von
Richthofen, who with eighty victories in aerial combat was the
leading fighter pilot of the war and, of the millions of combatants,
probably the only one apart from Hitler and Churchill with much
chance of still being a household name in the twenty-second
century. The First World War sponsored new techniques, new
aesthetics in other areas besides literature and painting:

> Behind nearly every traverse we come on a dead body with the
> blood coming from numerous wounds caused by thin sharp
> splinters from hand grenades. It is a brief glance only, for our
> eyes are more in the air than on the ground. It is not a hard
> death: the force of the explosion takes life and consciousness
> away at once. It is a strange feeling to leap forward over these
> dead whom you have never seen alive. The satisfaction is a
> purely practical one, as though you saw before your eyes the
> expected result of an intelligent calculation and gave it a final
> assent. If it were oneself that was hit in such a moment, as I
> have been more than once, one would feel no more than the
> wonder of being so suddenly and incomprehensibly arrested,
> while the whole being was so bent on victorious activity that
> nothing else had any reality whatever.

Thus Ernst Jünger: and it seems that what was unusual about
Jünger was less his self-immersion in combat than the way he
wrote about it afterwards.[7]

It was one of the paradoxes of industrialization that, in
making it possible to bring unprecedented numbers of soldiers
to the battlefield, and by providing the technical means to fight
battles in an unprecedentedly complicated and investment-
intensive way, it also provided scope for new types of individual
skill. In 1930 Ernst Jünger edited a book entitled *Krieg und
Krieger* ('War and Warriors') which contained a '*Schöpferische
Kritik des Krieges*', a critique of the war from a creative point
of view, which argued:

War and the forms of war are a part of general cultural history. It is impossible to consider them outside their time and the intellectual currents of their time. Purely practical grounds have never produced wars or determined the nature and form of weapons, as the materialists used to believe; it is rather that in every period universal, not easily explicable, yet dominant intellectual forms, ideological entities exist, to which the style and forms of war conform. A history of style in war ought to be written: the form of combat and tactics, armaments and uniforms are just as revealing for the character of races and the intellectual content of different epochs as the corresponding sections of Art History: the changing history of the struggling human intellect is at least as evident in their symbolism, sometimes more so.

One may query the notion of 'dominant intellectual forms' ('*beherrschende Geistesformen*') in this context but, for example, it was not only the apparatus with which Norwest and Richthofen liquidated their victims that was characteristic of industrial era warfare, but also the number of their victims, and even the fact of their enumeration.[8]

It took over 2000 years of so-called civilization, in which wars were fought by literate and numerate combatants, for it to become established practice for the more successful practitioners to keep a running score of the enemies they had personally offed. In Roman times, as we now know from graffiti on the walls at Pompeii, the more successful gladiators fought and won more than fifty separate contests: 'Severus, freedman, fifty-five fights, has just won again'; 'Auctus of the Julian troop has won fifty times'; but these were sporting achievements, of interest only to people who frequented the amphitheatres and the betting booths, and the death of the losers, which was not automatic, was incidental and often subsequent to the applause. In the wars which the Romans fought, battles were too confused and crowded for anyone to think of keeping a score: it was in the nature of hand-to-hand (or spear-to-spear) combat involving men fighting in close ranks that when an adversary sank back under a blow, another one pushed forward. Some non-European cultures attempted to provide statistics for individual mayhem. In the Gempei War in twelfth-century Japan, the warrior monk Tsutsui Janyo Meishu distinguished himself defending a bridge across the River Uji, allegedly killing twelve enemy samurai and wounding eleven others with twenty (sic) arrows, cutting down five more with his *naginata* (pole-handled sword) and, when the blade of his *naginata* broke, felling eight others with his ordinary sword, before withdrawing with sixty-three arrows sticking in his armour, only five of which arrows had penetrated – which rather contradicts the account given both in this and other contemporary narratives of skewering two armoured men with the same arrow: but one can believe the bit about the *naginata* breaking.[9]

In Europe the appeal of knowing how many people one has personally butchered seems not to have occurred to the best-documented heroes of *arme blanche* warfare. William the Marshal (1146–1219) fought innumerable tournaments in the 1170s and 1180s but wasn't even interested in the injuries he caused, for the whole object of his fighting was to acquire his opponents' valuable equipment. On his death bed he was reported to have claimed

j'ai pris .v. cents chevaliers
Dont j'ai & armes & destriers
Et tot lor herneis retenu

('I have taken 500 knights whose arms and horses and all their armour I kept'). In the course of more than fifteen years of jousting it is more than likely that a couple of score men received fatal injuries as a result of losing a bout with William but that was not the aspect he chose to remember. Robert the Bruce (1274–1329), King of Scotland, was probably the most successful soldier of his day, but he is specifically recorded as having slain only two men:

John Comyn, stabbed treacherously in the Franciscan church at Dumfries (and even then it required a second dagger-thrust from Roger Kirkpatrick to finish him off); and Humphrey de Bohun, with an axe-blow to the head, in a preliminary skirmish just before the Battle of Bannockburn.

Much later, during the French Wars of 1793–1815, Robert Rollo Gillespie, the bravest man that ever wore a red coat, innumerable feats of heroism and was wounded countless times but the only men whom he is known for certain to have killed were the opposing principal in a duel in which he was a second – he was put on trial for this piece of bad sportsmanship but acquitted – and six West Indians who broke into his quarters with cutlasses and pistols one night when he was adjutant general at St Domingo in 1796. carried out Neither incident suggests that on the frequent occasions that he led his troops into action he stood and watched them do all the work.[10]

The actual collection of trophies that demonstrated that one has killed an enemy is – or used to be – characteristic of certain illiterate societies, notably the Sepik in New Guinea, the Dayaks in Borneo, the Jívaros and Mundurucù in Brazil. Amongst the Dayaks, a man could not marry, or wear a machete, unless he had been on a head-hunting expedition, and heads were also needed for important funerals and naming ceremonies. But the preparations for head-hunting expeditions took two or three months, so they cannot have been as frequent as one might suppose from travellers' tales. Among the Jívaro head-taking raids were organized by a *kakaram*, a 'powerful one', who had killed 'at least three or four persons', and most neighbourhoods had a couple of such heroes. After leading several head-taking raids a *kakaram* would become a *ti-kakaram*, a 'very powerful one' but by this stage he would already be quite elderly.

It is doubtful whether any individual Dayak or Jívaro ever killed as many as a dozen enemies, for both societies consisted of very small, demographically insecure populations. Even the famously warlike Maoris, at their peak, numbered fewer than 60,000.

Individuals with the desire and ability to kill twenty enemies in a day would hardly have fitted in.[11]

The blood-letting in European duels also seems to have been exaggerated. In March 1803 Captain J. of the British army and Lieutenant W. of the Royal Navy killed each other in a duel but, though the English custom of duelling with pistols was more likely to end in death than the continental fashion of duelling with swords, fatalities – or for that matter duels – were not especially common. In Britain duelling seems to have reached its peak between 1790 and 1830: two prime ministers of the day fought bloodless duels (Pitt in 1798, the Duke of Wellington in 1829) and in 1809 Viscount Castlereagh wounded George Canning in a duel shortly after they had both resigned from the cabinet. But in this period there is no authentic record of anyone killing more than one opponent in successive duels. The record number of duels fought in the British Isles by an individual – George Robert Fitzgerald – is twelve, in the course of which Fitzgerald was wounded twice, but that was mainly in Ireland, where duels were much commoner than in England. Later in the nineteenth century the O'Gorman Mahon was said to have fought thirteen duels, and to have a pistol bearing two notches, but there are no authentic details. The O'Gorman Mahon spent nearly thirty years abroad, rising (almost simultaneously) to the rank of general in the Uruguayan army, colonel in the Brazilian army and commodore in the Chilean navy, and his duels presumably occurred for the most part outside Europe. One of his contemporaries, Henry Ronald McIver, served in the British, Italian, American Confederate, Mexican, Brazilian, Argentine, Cretan, Cuban, French, Egyptian, Carlist, Herzegovinian and Serbian armies, finishing up as a general in the Greek army: He fought in six duels, three or four of which were fatal to his opponents: unusually he seems to have been more lethal with a sword than a pistol.[12]

If it is true that the O'Gorman Mahon cut notches in the butt of his pistol as a record of the men he had killed, he probably got the idea from the Wild West. The precise 'scores' of the most successful American gun-slingers are in fact rarely recorded. Wyatt Earp's total may have been as few as three, that of William Bonney, Billy the Kid, perhaps as many as twenty-one. Wild Bill Hickok, who owes his fame essentially to the fact that he was the first man to make a name for himself with a six-shooter, killed seven men (one by accident) before himself being gunned down in 1876: his preferred weapons incidentally were not Colt .45s in twin holsters, as in the movies, but two .36 Colt 1851 Navy revolvers which he carried butts forward tucked into a silk sash, an arrangement that was more practical for shooting people across a table during a poker game than the twin holsters worn high up on a belt shown in some of the photos taken of Hickok before his death. As it happened, it was the most successful gun-fighter of the West who was the only one of note to write his memoirs: John Wesley Hardin. He shot his first adversary in 1868 when nearer fifteen than sixteen years old. 'This was the first man I ever killed, and it nearly distracted my father and mother when I told them.' He went on the run and shot dead three soldiers who were hunting him. During the course of the next nine years he killed another forty men, always at more or less risk to his own life, but was arrested in 1877, tried and sentenced to twenty-five years' gaol for second-degree murder. Shortly after being released after serving two-thirds of his sentence, he was shot in the back by a policeman in El Paso.[13]

No doubt a considerable degree of skill was evinced by people like Bruno Lüdke, who murdered eighty-five women in various German towns between 1928 and 1943, but it was skill in catching people off guard, not the kind of face-to-face coolness of men like John Wesley Hardin: and no other criminal since Hardin has been so successful in disposing of other people while in immediate risk of his own life. Louis Buchalter alias Lepke (1897–1944), of Murder Incorporated, is said to have ordered the elimination of over seventy people, and international terrorist Ilich Ramírez Sanchez alias Carlos, on his arrest in August 1994, admitted responsibility for the deaths of eighty-three people, but in both cases someone else usually pulled the trigger. Vincenzo Gibaldi, alias Machine Gun Jack McGurn (1903–36), killed at least twenty-two people for reasons of private spite or at the behest of Al Capone; Abe Reles, who turned states evidence in the Murder Incorporated trial and was subsequently thrown from a window, is believed to have personally killed a dozen people. Dominic 'Mad Dog' McGlinchey of the Provisional IRA, later of the INLA, claimed to have killed over thirty policemen and soldiers in Ulster, though when he was eventually convicted of murder it was for killing an unarmed post-mistress: all pretty small beer compared to what law-abiding citizens showed themselves capable of when they put on their country's uniform.[14]

(Hector Grant Taylor, who wore uniform for almost two decades of his life, including the prison garb he had while serving fourteen months for bigamy in Wormwood Scrubs in the 1930s, is credited with shooting up to forty German and Italian personnel while acting as an assassin for the Special Operations Executive during the Second World War, but though he certainly served as a firearms instructor in both world wars the only other thing certain about him was that he had a tendency to indulge in fantasy.)[15]

Roughly contemporary with the career of the unfortunate John Wesley Hardin there occurred a development which contributed much more directly than the careers of Western gunslingers to making it socially acceptable to keep a score of the people one had killed. It had been customary since the eighteenth century – the period in which most English traditional sports became formalized – for men who indulged in the recreational slaughter of grouse and pheasant to keep a record of how many they had killed; but grouse and pheasant, though tricky to hit, were totally defenceless and fell out of the sky quite easily when winged, and with servants to provide a constant succession of loaded guns it was not impossible to massacre hundreds in one August or October day. Big-game hunting was much more of a challenge. It was physically demanding – big game wasn't available a pony-trap ride from the ducal castle – and it was dangerous. It provided the most extreme form of that strenuous sportiness which, with Britain in the lead, became an upper-class fashion in nineteenth-century Europe. Roualeyn Gordon Cumming's *Five Years in a Hunter's Life in the Far Interior of South Africa*, published in 1850 – third edition, under the title *The Lion Hunter of South Africa*, 1856 – was probably the first book to be devoted to the pleasures of pursuing animals dangerous enough to destroy human life. With the appearance of *The Hunting Grounds of the World* by 'The Old Shekarry' (i.e. Henry Astbury Leveson) in 1860 and William Charles Baldwin's *African Hunting from Natal to the Zambesi ... from 1852 to 1860* in 1862 the vogue of big-game hunting might already seem to have established itself, but in fact its real take-off depended on technical innovations.[16]

Loose powder-and-ball ammunition was not really suitable for rapid reloading in a tropical forest: brass cartridges loaded at the breech only became standard in the 1870s. Apart from the Winchester, which only fired pistol ammunition, magazine rifles were not generally available till the 1880s, and though Purdy had developed a high-velocity rifle in 1859, the 'express' was only widely available more than two decades later. Easy reloading and extra penetrative power were a *sine qua non* before amateurs were going to take on, alone or with a few companions, animals like elephants, rhinoceroses and African buffaloes. An early use of the term 'big game' was in Sir John Christopher Willoughby's *East Africa and its Big Game*, of 1889: it was followed by *American Big-Game Hunting* by Theodore Roosevelt and G.B. Grinnell, of 1893, and Clive Phillipps Wolley's *Big Game Shooting* of 1894. Rowland Ward's *Horn Measurements and Weights of the Great Game of the World: Being a Record for the Use of Sportsmen and Naturalists* came out in 1892; his earlier *The Sportsman's Handbook to Practical Collecting ... To Which is Added a Synoptical Guide to the Hunting Grounds of the World* had originally had 103 pages: the seventh edition of 1894 had

192 pages, which were increased to 303 in the tenth edition of 1911. The classic works of Roualeyn Gordon Cumming and William Charles Baldwin were also reprinted in the 1890s, as was E.C. Selous's *A Hunter's Wanderings in Africa*, which had first appeared in 1881 and had a fourth edition in 1895. Clearly big-game hunting was not simply a newly-created tradition, it was also an aspect of a newly-created *literary* tradition.[17]

Part of the point of big-game hunting was to bring home the trophies: the larger homes of Britain (and France and Germany) began to fill up with antlers and stuffed heads, and inscribing the details of when and where and by whom these melancholy objects had been collected provided a remunerative business for metal engravers. When, in 1915, the Big Game ethic transferred itself to aerial combat, successful fighter pilots often made a point of collecting trophies from aircraft they had brought down – propellers, rudders, national insignia – and hanging them on the walls of their quarters or unit mess. The hunting analogy was frankly confessed by Richthofen who, in an account he wrote of hunting aurochs, confessed 'in the moment when the bull advanced I had the same feeling, the same hunting fever, as seizes me if I sit in my aeroplane, see an Englishman, and have to fly for five minutes to come up with him.' William Avery Bishop, at one time acknowledged as the British Empire's leading ace, also insisted on the sporting analogy. In his war memoirs *Winged Warfare: Hunting the Huns in the Air* he wrote:

> The excitement of the chase had a tight hold on my heartstrings, and I felt that the only thing I wanted was to stay right at it and fight and fight and fight in the air. I don't think I was ever happier in my life. It seemed that I had found the one thing I loved above all others. To me it was not a business or a profession, but just a wonderful game. To bring down a machine did not seem to me to be killing a man; it was more as if I was just destroying a mechanical target, with no human being in it. Once or twice the idea that a live man had been piloting the machine would occur and recur to me, and

it would worry me a bit. My sleep would be spoiled perhaps for a night. I did not relish the idea even of killing Germans, yet, when in a combat in the air, it seemed more like any other kind of sport, and to shoot down a machine was very much the same as if one were shooting down clay pigeons. One had the great satisfaction of feeling that he had hit the target and brought it down; that one was victorious again.

On the other hand a member of the same flight as Albert Ball in No. 11 Squadron RFC noted, as if with surprise, 'There was in his attitude none of that sporting element which to a certain extent formed the basis of many scouts pilots' approach to air fighting.'[18]

It was no coincidence that though the most successful fighter pilots of the 1914–18 War were all brilliant marksmen, many of them were notably poor pilots. G.F. Smylie of the Royal Naval Air Service later remarked, 'The man who flew in a really finished manner, who was a joy to watch, was not usually the man to go into a fight. On the other hand the Hungetter was often a potential crash every time he landed.' A case in point was R.A. Little of the Royal Naval Air Service, with forty-seven 'kills' the top-scoring Australian pilot of the war: he was famous for his clumsy landings, though the crash that eventually killed him was caused by the fact that he was already bleeding to death from a bullet-wound in the groin. Even Albert Ball, who piloted his planes 'very safely and accurately' 'never flew for amusement'. It was not till after 1918 that skill in handling motor-driven machines came to be regarded as a manly accomplishment on a par with marksmanship.[19]

The Big Game Hunter approach did not manifest itself only in aerial combat: Richard Meinertzhagen, while a staff officer at the War Office in August 1918, took a trip to France and was very pleased with himself for having 'accounted for' twenty-three 'Huns' during a day spent operating a Hotchkiss gun in a Canadian armoured car. Some of the most lethal marksmen had been brought up in more plebeian traditions of sport. 'Every time a head come up I knocked it down', recalled Sergeant Alvin York of the day he killed twenty-eight German soldiers, no doubt thinking of a fair-ground booth: and describing how he used a pistol to dispose of a German officer and five men who charged him from twenty-five yards away, he explained:

> I teched off the sixth man first, then the fifth; then the fourth; then the third; and so on. That's the way we shoot wild turkey at home. You see we don't want the front ones to know that we're getting the back ones.[20]

Sergeant York's exploits were never equalled (or even approached) by anything known to have taken place in the Wild West, but were sometimes all but topped by other combatants on the Western Front. Captain Robert Gee of the Royal Fusiliers, having been taken prisoner, killed his guard with the spiked stick he carried in action, collected two revolvers from dead bodies and charged a machine-gun nest, killing eight Germans. Lieutenant Joseph Maxwell of the Australian Imperial Force shot three Germans with his revolver and took prisoner four others in a machine-gun nest, reloaded and shot dead five more Germans manning another machine gun. Then a German prisoner told him that some of the other men in his company were ready to surrender. With two other Australians Maxwell climbed down into the German trench and was immediately overpowered and disarmed. Having recovered his breath he produced an automatic pistol from his gas mask container, shot dead two more Germans and escaped with his companions in the resulting confusion.[21]

Twenty-two soldiers in the British and British Empire forces won the Victoria Cross by their prowess with the revolver or automatic pistol; ninety-seven won it by their skill with that coarsest of weapons, the hand grenade. (This doesn't include the nine men who won the VC by throwing themselves or stepping on grenades, or hurling one away at the last minute, to prevent their comrades being killed when it exploded). Invented in the sixteenth century the grenade had fallen out of favour by the mid-eighteenth, partly because there were fewer sieges than in the period of Louis XIV's wars, but chiefly because of the development of infantry tactics: whereas in the seventeenth century infantry formations combined a variety of weapons – pikes, muskets, grenades – eighteenth-century infantry were exclusively armed with muskets equipped with ring bayonets, thereby maximizing both fire-power and capacity for self-defence against attacking cavalry. A throwable missile charged with gunpowder was not sufficiently effective to be worth the diversion of man-power. The development of more powerful explosives in the second half of the nineteenth century, and the use of improvised grenades at the siege of Port Arthur during the Russo-Japanese War of 1904–5, caused the international military community to take a fresh look at this economical weapon. The British army's first modern hand grenade, a device with a sixteen-inch throwing handle designated Hand Grenade No. 1, was introduced in 1908. It was not till after the First World War had begun however that it was realised that the grenade was the perfect weapon for trench warfare – nobody had quite expected trench warfare anyway. Grenades also had the advantage of being relatively easy to manufacture: in the second half of 1914 only 2164 were made in Britain, but in the final quarter of 1915 output was 9,489,765.[22]

British army doctrine (which also emphasized the crucial importance of bayonet training at a time when the Germans were increasingly counter-attacking without fixed bayonets) tended to insist that the function of the grenade was 'solely to amplify and facilitate the use of the Rifle'. The rifle was far more accurate at a far longer range and it took far longer to use up one man's stock of rifle ammunition, but at short range, and especially in the confined space of a trench, the grenade was immeasurably more lethal. It was less effective against inanimate objects:

Another point to be borne in mind as regards the ordinary grenade is that it will *not* destroy doorways. There is a popular misconception among troops that the ordinary Mills hand grenade, if placed upon a doorstep and the pin withdrawn, will, when it explodes, burst open an ordinary door in such a manner as to allow troops to pass through. This is not so. The usual effect will merely be to make a number of shrapnel holes in the door, with probably a fairly large hole close to the spot where the bomb was placed.

But closed doors were not generally a problem on the Western Front, and till the deployment of the Bergmann sub-machine-gun by the German army in the last weeks of the war the grenade represented the only really satisfactory infantry assault weapon available: portable machine guns prior to the Bergmann were either too heavy, like the Lewis Gun or the German army's MG 08/15, or too slow-firing and unreliable, like the French Chauchat, or too rapid-firing and therefore needing constant reloading like the Italian Villar Perosa. The exploits with pistols mentioned previously were possible only for people with unusual innate skill or after arduous practice. The hand grenade of all weapons was the one that depended most on the man and least on his acquired military proficiency:

One of the men of my platoon was shot through the lungs, or some such place. He gasped terribly for breath, and fell behind me. Easing his head with my left hand, I threw bombs with the right, also saying a few cheering words to the boys. Presently I felt his head drop back – his fight was over. I was just preparing another bomb, with the upper part of my head and chest well above the parapet, when a German bomb burst near my neck, blowing away the left side of same and part of jaw, lower teeth and gum and upper teeth. Left arm was blown round my neck, and the biceps muscle was contracted like a ball on the top of left shoulder. Jugular vein, windpipe and carotid artery were fully exposed, and shoulder-blade badly out of place. My head lay helplessly on my arm, and sometimes almost rolled on my back. For a moment I was dazed, as I had already been hit three times with shrapnel in the early part of the morning while organising men of some other unit, who had lost their officers and NCOs, but I was soon clear again; still, what with loss of blood and almost blinded with it, I had to leave the boys, but I did not go far, only to the first line, where I lay in a shell-hole and watched how things progressed. But feeling myself becoming weaker and weaker, I set off to find a doctor. I had not gone far when I met the remnants of a carrying party. I wrote on a piece of paper asking for a dressing station, and they asked for the directions the boys had advanced. They were carrying bombs and the boys wanted them, so, staggering away, I took them up through the barrage. Five parties I led back, but the last one never got there, for a shell came over, killed three of them, and broke my jaw in another two places, so, almost blinded with blood and falling at every three or four steps, I left the field.

One suspects that the grenade's sheer nastiness as a weapon militated against its ever obtaining the publicity accorded aerial combat.[23]

John Buchan claimed, 'half the magic of our Flying Corps was its freedom from advertisement': but since Buchan had headed the Department of Information, responsible for propaganda, his remark may be taken with a pinch of salt. The Germans, French and Italians published the names of their aces in the regular army communiqués which were printed in the press, whereas the identity of their British counterparts only 'leaked out by way of the supplement to the *London Gazette*' when they were awarded decorations for gallantry. On the other hand, when Billy Bishop, supposedly the British Empire's top-scorer, appeared in the *London Gazette* as having been awarded the Military Cross on 26 May 1917, the Distinguished Service Order three weeks later, the Victoria Cross eight weeks after that, and a Bar to his DSO six weeks after his VC, people were likely to notice. In the early days shooting an enemy aeroplane down seemed so unusual and difficult that it received immediate recognition: Max Immelmann's first aerial victory on 1 August 1915 was followed by the award of the Iron Cross First Class within twenty-four hours, and French pilots were receiving the coveted *Médaille Militaire* for their first kill as late as August 1916. By the time of his death Immelmann, whose score of sixteen was soon to be vastly outdistanced, had been decorated with the Order *pour le mérite*, the Iron Cross First and Second Class, the Order of St Heinrich, the Albrecht Order with Swords, the Order of the House of Hohenzollern with Swords, the Bavarian Order of Merit, the Hanseatic Cross and the Turkish Iron Crescent. After his sixth kill he was summoned to dinner by his army commander, the Crown Prince of Bavaria: Immelmann's own King, Friedrich August III of Saxony, was among the other guests. Oswald Boelcke, on leave after receiving the Order *pour le mérite*, found himself the centre of attention wherever he went:

it is worse than having a warrant out against you. They stared at me all the time in the streets, both in Frankfurt and in Wiesbaden, where I was on Wednesday afternoon. Also the people in the Opera crowded round me in each interval – it was terrible.

But the worst was yet to come. When the opera-singer Schramm sang the well-known aria 'Father, Mother, Sisters, Brothers' he was loudly applauded and encored. At last he reappeared to start his encore. But just imagine – I could hardly believe my ears – the fellow did not sing the proper words but a verse in my honour which they had hastily strung together behind the scenes – it sounds like it. The singer himself sent me a copy round:

Listen friends, our brave airman
Lieutenant Boelcke is in the house!
Many times he's been the victor
Against the enemy in mighty struggle.
May he yet succeed

In vanquishing a hundred foes!
Oh how splendid and how nice,
If we see him again soon![24]

The deaths of the better-known aces were regarded as big news. When Albert Ball was killed in action at the age of twenty the *Nottingham Evening Post* printed his photograph and a column and three-quarters about him on the front page. The Lord Mayor of Nottingham had broken the story at that afternoon's council meeting:

> When the history of the war comes to be written no name will stand out more prominently than that of our gallant young citizen-airman, and I propose to immediately issue an appeal to the citizens of Nottingham and the country, and in fact to all his admirers, to subscribe to a fund to raise a statue to his memory in Nottingham.

When Richthofen was killed the *Berliner Lokal-Anzeiger of* 23 April 1918 gave half of its front page to the story, including a portrait drawing of *'Unser Fliegerheld Rittmeister v. Richthofen'*. When Georges Guynemer was reported dead the French Chamber of Deputies voted unanimously that his name should be inscribed on the walls of the Pantheon. His body was never recovered: Henri Lavedan of the *Académie Française* wrote, 'later on people will say: the ace of aces one day flew so high in combat that he never returned to earth.' In fact Guynemer (whose last victim – shot down in self-defence – was a British two-seater which persisted in firing at him) had crashed between the British and German lines, and before the Germans could do more than send out a medical team to examine his body *in situ*, the British began a bombardment of the entire sector which lasted fifteen days. At the end of two weeks there was no trace of the French air ace: it was thought advisable to conceal the role of *la perfide* Albion in his disappearance and pretend that he had simply vanished.[25]

But fame, like survival, could be something of a lottery. Edward Mannock, who is sometimes credited with shooting down even more planes than were claimed by Billy Bishop, and who certainly accounted for fifty-one German aircraft and a part-share of twenty-three others, was virtually unknown at the time of his death, his Victoria Cross being gazetted posthumously. And Manfred von Richthofen, though officially credited with the largest score, was by no means the most accomplished of these aerial serial killers. Richthofen once shot down four enemy planes in one day: two British and two Canadian pilots claimed to have shot down six aircraft in one day and the French ace René Fonck twice destroyed six – officially confirmed – in one day. On another occasion Fonck shot down three German aircraft in ten seconds: they all crashed within a 400 metre radius. '*Mon record,*' he noted modestly. Richthofen also had the advantage that he generally fought over his own lines, so that the aircraft he shot down landed in German-held territory; Allied fighter pilots, operating over the German lines, were not always able to obtain confirmation that the enemy plane they had fired at had crashed. René Fonck, who was officially credited with seventy-five victories, five less than Richthofen, also claimed a further fifty-one that could not be confirmed because they had fallen behind enemy lines.[26]

Sometimes the folks back home objected to their young men keeping scores:

In view of these many 'numbers' mother will be saying again that it is not right to number our victims in this unfeeling way. But we don't really do it – we do not number the victims who have fallen, but the machines we have brought down. That you can see from the fact that it only counts as one victory when two inmates are killed, but that it still remains a 'number' when both the inmates escape unhurt. We have nothing against the individual; we only fight to prevent him flying against us. So when we have eliminated an enemy force, we are pleased and book it as one up to us.

The convention however was to pretend that aerial combat was a revival of the values of medieval chivalry. Fighter pilots were frequently referred to as Knights of the Air. 'They are the knighthood of this War, without fear and without reproach,' said Lloyd George, the British prime minister. Though it was prohibited in the British service, pilots of other nations often adopted personal liveries for their aircraft. Manfred von Richthofen's all-red paint job earned him the posthumous soubriquet the 'Red Baron', but he seems to have copied it from the French pilot Jean Navarre's red Nieuport, which had become a familiar sight in the skies over Verdun during the spring and early summer of 1916. Godwin Brumowski, the leading Austrian fighter ace, also adopted a red livery; Josef Jakobs chose black; the Belgian André de Meulemeester had his Hanriot painted yellow but discovered that this 'set the British Flying Corps at his heels'. Interestingly enough one form of display that was to become customary in the Second World War was almost unknown in the 1914–18 period: painting rows of small symbols on one's plane to indicate how many of the enemy one had shot down. W.G. Barker seems to have pioneered this fashion by having white flashes painted on the struts of his Sopwith Camel at some point during 1918.[27]

Except in Italy, where torpedo-boat commander Luigi Rizzo won almost twice as many medals as leading air ace Franco Baracca, it was fighter pilots who held the record in the First World War for the largest number of decorations for gallantry awarded to an individual. René Fonck had, beside the *Medaille Militaire* and the *Croix de Chevalier de la Légion d'Honneur*, a *Croix de Guerre* with twenty-seven *palmes* (equivalent to bars) necessitating a remarkably extended ribbon. Mannock, McCudden and Barker each received six British decorations for gallantry. Though supposedly inclined to talk dismissively of medals coming up with the rations or of names being pulled out of a hat, recipients attached considerable importance to these awards. Siegfried Sassoon, who won the Military Cross (as did

Wilfred Owen, Edgell Rickword and a number of other writers who came to hate the war) felt entitled thereby to sneer in his poem 'A Last Word' at the cricket blue who had looked down at him before the war but had merely endured 'Four years' home service, twenty miles from home, / Drawing a Major's pay'. Oddly enough however three of the most impressive accumulations of gallantry awards in the British army were by men whose job did not involve shooting at other people. F.W. Lumsden of the Royal Marine Artillery won the Distinguished Service Order (at that time Britain's second highest gallantry award) with three bars as a staff officer and brigade commander plus the Victoria Cross during a brief interval commanding an infantry battalion: no doubt he brandished a revolver occasionally and after his death in action he was accused of having 'spent his time dancing about in No Man's Land', but his main business was organizing people under fire while keeping himself safe somewhere to the rear. Lance-Corporal W.H. Coltman, VC, DCM and bar, MM and bar, the most highly decorated British Other Rank did not carry a weapon of any sort: he was a stretcher-bearer. Captain Noel Chavasse, VC and bar, MC was a battalion medical officer.[28]

But perhaps the most eye-catching hero of the war was the Italian Enrico Toti, killed shortly after his thirty-fourth birthday on Hill 85, east of Monfalcone and posthumously awarded Italy's Gold Medal for Valour, and commemorated by a statue in the Pincio, in his native Rome. In his teens he had served in the Italian navy and had later become a fireman on the railways. His pre-war exploits as a cyclist – he had cycled to Lappland in 1911, to the Sudan in 1913 – enabled him to overcome official opposition and enlist in a Bersaglieri cyclist unit when Italy entered the war in 1915. Operating in rugged mountain terrain, the Italian army had little use for cycle troops, and it was as a simple soldier, albeit in a crack light infantry unit, steel helmet adorned with the famous Bersaglieri feathers, that Toti met his death, charging the enemy lines – despite having had one leg amputated, above the knee and too high up for an artificial limb to be fitted, as a result of a railway accident in 1908. (His statue shows him naked but waving a crutch.)[29]

By getting himself killed Toti at least solved the problem of what to do after the war. The British army's most decorated private, Henry 'Napper' Tandey, VC, DCM, MM, five times mentioned in despatches – in September 1918, it is said, Tandey took Adolf Hitler prisoner but he escaped back to the German lines – said of his war service, 'I went to be a soldier and did an ordinary soldier's job.' After leaving the army he worked as a commissionaire for the Triumph Motor Company in Coventry. Coltman became a municipal gardener. Perhaps they needed a quiet life after what they had experienced in uniform. The enduring psychological trauma of the war became one of the clichés of the 1920s. 'Why else, may I ask, should those who were once the flower of our youth form today so disproportionate a number of the down and out?' asked General Sir Ian Hamilton in 1929. In a prefatory note to *Im Westen Nichts Neues* Erich Maria Remarque claimed he was telling the story of 'a generation of men who, even though they may have escaped shells, were destroyed by the war'. Wilfred Saint-Mandé wrote a novel about 'how the War debased a young man, who subsequently failed to control his passions, until he came to a tragic and premature end'. In his 'Author's Foreword' he asked:

Since the War how many thousands of ex-soldiers have been sent to prison for crimes that would never have been committed had it not been for the atmosphere of bloodshed and rapine in which so many of my generation lived for over four years? There is at least one case on record of a man wounded in the head fighting for his country, and subsequently executed for a murder of which he almost certainly would not have been guilty had he not been taught to kill as a duty a few years previously. And a large proportion of those who came through the War with skins intact were wounded in more insidious ways.[30]

Of course there were some people who assessed what had happened from a completely opposite point of view:

> A particularly malignant falsehood is being propagated in the name of 'pacificism', to the effect that the wounds and nervous shock inflicted upon soldiers by the experience of war constituted an injury to racial qualities ... Let it at least be firmly understood by the noble women who choose to espouse these men that the injuries of war last but for one generation, and that their children will receive, as a natural dower, a constitution unimpaired, and the power to become all that their father might have been ...

The one thing that nobody doubted was that the war had changed both the men who had fought it and the national communities that had asked them to fight. The big question after 1918 was, what would this change lead to?[31]

7

LESSONS

Both a poem and an act of heroism might confer a kind of meaning on an aspect of the war but such a devastatingly total experience also demanded an explanation of what it meant as a whole.

During the war itself it was inevitable that a great deal of the rhetoric should have derived from pre-1914 expectations and pre-1914 cultural developments. The best-selling book by a frontline author in Germany during the war was Walter Flex's *Der Wanderer zwischen beiden Welten* (1917: 'The Wanderer between Two Worlds') in which the narrator encounters a young man who before the war had been a *Wandervögel*, one of the German youths who had spent their summers roaming the country, toughening themselves in the fresh air and communing with Nature. 'All that was bright and healthy in the German future seemed to him to come from the spirit of the *Wandervögel*, and if I were to think of him as embodying this spirit purely and clearly I would only be doing him justice ...' Flex himself told his brother:

I am inwardly as committed to the war as I was on the first day. I am not thus, and was not, like so many of my friends, from national but from moral fanaticism. It's not national but moral challenges that I hold up and represent. What I have written about the eternity of the German people and of the world-redeeming mission of German-ness has nothing to do with national egoism but is a moral belief which can realize itself in defeat, or as Ernst Wurche would have said, in the heroic death of a people ...

In *Der Wanderer zwischen beiden Welten* Flex wrote:

The thought of the heroic death of a people is not more terrible than the thought of the violent death of a man. Only dying is ugly for men and for peoples. But if a man receives a fatal shot which rips into his guts, then that's it. What follows is ugly and no longer belongs to him. The great and beautiful bit, the heroic life, is over. It must be the same if a people, in its honour and greatness, receive a death blow: what happens next should not be seen as part of its living, it has no part of it ...[1]

The same exhilarated sense of destiny that left no space for thoughts of tomorrow was later recalled by Ernst Jünger:

We had left lecture room, class room, and bench behind us. We had been welded by a few weeks' training into one corporate mass inspired by the enthusiasm of one thought... to carry forward the German ideals of '70. We had grown up in a material age, and in each one of us there was the yearning for great experience, such as we had never known. The war had entered into us like wine. We had set out in a rain of flowers to seek the death of heroes. The war was our dream of greatness, power, and glory. It was a man's work, a duel on fields whose flowers would be stained with blood. There is no lovelier death in the world ... anything rather than stay at home, anything to make one with the rest.

But when the war turned out to be so different from what had been expected and became a matter of enduring day after day, week after week, horrors which seemed certain to persist into a long futurity which one would not oneself live to see, perspectives began to change. Exhilaration gave way to the sternest determination to endure. Obliviousness of the morrow gave way to a resolute intention to survive, minute by minute, for as long as was necessary:

> a battle was no longer an episode that spent itself in blood and fire; it was a condition of things that dug itself in remorselessly week after week and even month after month. What was a man's life in this wilderness whose vapour was laden with the stench of thousands upon thousands of decaying bodies? Death lay in ambush for each one in every shell-hole, merciless, and making one merciless in return.[2]

During the war itself Otto Riebicke wrote:

> These German soldiers in their German Siegfried helmets with their fists on their hot rifles, with bronzed features of courage, love and horror, these heroes for whom mines and shell-fire again and again flatten out and fill up everything so that they have to lie out in the open, with only a couple of handfuls of sand in front of them, and the enemy beating at them from stronger positions and hurling ten thousand tons of High Explosive in clattering trench-mortar bombs so that the sky is full of razor-sharp slashing, rotating knives and the earth spurts as high as houses against the sky – these men on the Somme are the barrier against the monstrous hurricane of the war, behind which the homeland goes on to the harvest carefree and full of confidence.

Perspectives rooted in pre-war notions began to be replaced by a sense of novelties that were at once horrifying and thought-provoking. 'The Europe of to-day appeared here for the first time on the field of battle', wrote Jünger later:

> all the frightfulness that the mind of man could devise was brought into the field; and there, where lately there had

been the idyllic picture of rural peace, there was as faithful a picture of the soul of scientific war. In earlier wars, certainly, towns and villages had been burned, but what was that compared with this sea of craters dug out by machines? For even in this fantastic desert there was the sameness of the machine-made article. A shell-hole strewn with bully-tins, broken weapons, fragments of uniform, and dud shells, with one or two dead bodies on its edge ... this was the never-changing scene that surrounded each one of all these hundreds of thousands of men. And it seemed that man, on this landscape he had himself created, became different, more mysterious and hardy and callous than in any previous battle. The spirit and the tempo of the fighting altered, and after the battle of the Somme the war had its own peculiar impress that distinguished it from all other wars. After this battle the German soldier wore the steel helmet, and in his features there were chiselled the lines of an energy stretched to the utmost pitch, lines that future generations will perhaps find as fascinating and imposing as those of many heads of classical or Renaissance times.

There was even a kind of exhilaration in the sheer awfulness of it all:

Hellrot fällt Mondlicht auf meinen harten Helm. Der Schatten wird matt, zerstirbt im Phantastischen.

Ich klettere durch einen Granattrichter hoch – in die Sommeschlacht.

Weit hinten stirbt Bapaume in Pulver, Rauch und Qualm.

In tausendjährigen Katakomben harren deutsche Soldaten des Rufes zum Sturm, Männer mit Siegfriedhelmen und Siegfriedstreue.

Darauf hämmern Englands schwere Granaten ihren brüllenden Zorn.

('Blood-red falls the moonlight on my hard helmet. The shadows become faint, fading into the fantastic. I clamber up through a shell hole – into the Battle of the Somme. Far in the rear Bapaume dies in dust, fumes and smoke. In thousand-year-old catacombs German soldiers await the signal for the assault, men with the helmets of Siegfried and the loyalty of Siegfried. On them England's heavy shells pound their bellowing anger.')[3]

For Jünger and Riebicke the real meaning of what they had endured was revealed in November 1918 when they discovered that their four-year ordeal, and the deaths of more than a million and a half of their comrades in arms, had been in vain – worse than in vain, the prelude and pretext for disgrace, loss of territory, humiliating restrictions. (Flex had succumbed to wounds in October 1917.) Someone like Ezra Pound who was on the winning side – even if inadvertently – could write of myriads dying

> For an old bitch gone in the teeth
> For a botched civilization

but those who had risked all and lost did not even have the old bitch for comfort. Yet with final defeat Jünger reconsidered his experiences and thought he began to understand:

> Now I looked back: four years of development in the midst of a generation predestined to death, spent in caves, smoke-filled trenches, and shell-illumined wastes ... in short, a monotonous calendar full of hardships and privation, divided by the red-letter days of battles. And almost without any thought of mine, the idea of the Fatherland had been distilled from all these afflictions in a clearer and brighter essence. That was the final winnings in a game on which so often all had been staked: the nation was no longer for me an empty thought veiled in symbols; and how could it have been otherwise when I had seen so many die for its sake, and been

schooled myself to stake my life for its credit every minute, day and night, without a thought? And so, strange as it may sound, I learned from this very four years' schooling in force and in all the fantastic extravagance of material warfare that life has no depth of meaning except when it is pledged for an ideal, and that there are ideals in comparison with which the life of an individual and even of a people has no weight. And though the aim for which I fought as an individual, as an atom in the whole body of the army, was not to be achieved, though material force cast us, apparently, to the earth, yet we learned once and for all to stand for a cause and if necessary to fall as befitted men ...

And if it be objected that we belong to a time of crude force our answer is: we stood with our feet in mud and blood, yet our faces were turned to things of exalted worth. And not one of that countless number who fell in our attacks fell for nothing. Each one fulfilled his own purpose.[4]

Ernst Jünger's account of his First World War experiences, *In Stahlgewittern: aus dem Tagebuch eines Stosstruppführers* (1920; translated into English as *The Storm of Steel*, 1929) was a best-seller in Germany during the 1920s. Joseph Goebbels, later Hitler's propaganda minister, was a keen admirer, calling it '*Das Evangelium des Krieges. Grausamgross!*' (The gospel of the war. Grisly-great!). Nevertheless it did nothing like as well as Gunther Plüschow's cheerful narrative of how he outwitted and escaped from the English in *Die Abenteuer des Fliegers von Tsingtau* ('The Adventures of the Airman of Tsingtao') which sold over 600,000 copies between 1923 and 1927. Walter Flex's *Der Wanderer zwischen beiden Welten* also continued to sell well; even Barbusse's *Le feu*, published in German translation in Zurich in 1918 as *Das Feuer* and on sale in Germany after the Armistice, seems also to have kept ahead of the sales of *In Stahlgewittern* till the time of Hitler's coming to power in 1933. Jünger's version of the war may be seen indeed as one of several rival versions which were in competition during the period of the Weimar Republic. The publication in the late 1920s of Georg von der Vring's unheroic *Soldat Suhren*, which deals mainly with training and life in a quiet section of the front, with battle and wounds only at the end, Ludwig Renn's *Krieg*, Moritz Frey's *Die Pflasterkästen*, a medical orderly's worm's eye view of life behind the lines – the author was attached to the same regimental headquarters as Hitler – and Erich Maria Remarque's *Im Westen Nichts Neues* might even suggest that the Jünger version of the war was finally swamped by that of his rivals, especially in view of the huge success of Remarque's novel, sales of which approached one million by the time Jünger was at the 100,000 mark. In reality *In Stahlgewittern* was one of those books which influenced other writers and intellectuals as much, or more, than publications that enjoyed considerably larger sales. In particular it was calculated to have much more appeal than, for example, Barbusse's novel to those who remembered the war but had been too young to fight in it – a group prominent in the Nazi party in the late 1920s. By the end of the 1920s moreover its message was taking on a new topicality.[5]

Having survived open civil war, attempted coups and the collapse of the currency, the Weimar Republic was by the beginning of 1929 at least as firmly established as the Third Republic in France. The latter had been born in comparable circumstances of defeat and national humiliation and still, after nearly sixty years, had all the glamour and convincingness of the botched-up temporary compromise that it was, but had demonstrated that it was not necessary that the citizenry should believe in it, so long as there was no agreement on how to replace it. The world economic recession of 1929 threw all the governments of Europe into crisis, and the Weimar regime was not particularly less capable of dealing with the economic catastrophe than the governments of other European states. As elsewhere, rocketing unemployment provided recruits for extremist parties which had first flourished during the years just after the war and which had been perfecting their organization and techniques, though with little chance of seizing power, during the relatively affluent mid-1920s.

The economic and social crisis of 1929 seems also to have fostered a revaluation of the world war: this was perhaps the one phenomenon of the time that was more marked in Germany than elsewhere. In the foreword of his popular history of the war, *Sperrfeuer um Deutschland* (1929), Werner Beumelburg wrote of wanting to 'fuse together the military events with the spiritual events. In this way a picture will be produced that, based on the results of reliable research, places on record the living face of the war.' *Sperrfeuer um Deutschland* ('Artillery Barrage around Germany') attempted to present the whole nation as the protagonist in the war: a similar message was embodied in the various novels of the period dealing with groups of frontline soldiers. Both Communists and Nazis held up the common man, the common soldier, as the embodiment of the corporate ideal: 'Don't ask yourself what this war did for me, for you, for anybody in particular', wrote Erwin Zindler, 'rather ask what this war meant for the great Unknown Soldier. We are all merely a part of him. But he is the visible, willing, self-sacrificing Germany, which lives through his dying.' Ulrich Sander claimed, 'It was the war that first brought us into touch with the common man. It was through the war that we first found the sources of our race.' Among the critically acclaimed novels of the period was one by Franz Schauwecker, who during the 1920s had been associated with Jünger in the Stahlhelm, the right-wing veterans' organization. In its English translation it is called *The Furnace* but the original German title – *Aufbruch der Nation* – means something like 'The Departure of the Nation' or 'The Setting Out of the Nation'. The novel ends with the end of the war: the two protagonists sit in a café and discuss why it is that no one from the front line does anything to oppose the revolution that is sweeping through Germany's cities. One of them concludes that they should discover why Germany lost the war: 'We had to lose the war, in order to win the nation.' 'And with that they left the room and went to the station. Nobody observed them. No-one knew them.' They were, in fact, part of the great Unknown Soldier, setting out to survive the Weimar Republic and to prepare the way for rebirth.[6]

German academics – much more responsive to contemporary literature than British academics, especially at this period – observed literary developments with not entirely disinterested attention. Ernst Jünger himself appeared in the 1931 edition of *Brockhaus* – the standard German-language encyclopedia – as 'opposing to Pacifism a "heroic realism" which decisively affirms the idea of the nation and raises military spirit above bourgeois security: he is one of the most influential representatives of the "new nationalism"'. Not bad for a man still aged only thirty-six. In the same year Herbert Cysarz published his *Zur Geistesgeschichte des Weltkriegs: die dichterischen Wandlungen des deutschen Kriegsbilds, 1910–1930* ('Towards an intellectual history of the world war: the literary transformation of the German view of the war.') This argued against the existence of any essentially new intellectual current, claiming that Expressionism, the movement to which, for example, the painter Ludwig Meidner had belonged, had been 'from 1910 to 1914 a prophet of the war, from 1914 to 1918 a measure of the war and its cultural crisis, from 1918 to 1923 the after-tremor of the war'. But political developments in Germany soon made it unfashionable to trace anything of significance in contemporary life back beyond 1914. Hitler's accession to power in 1933 (officially known as the *seizure* of power) made the correct attitude to First World War literature *de rigueur*. After the first celebrated public book burnings in May 1933, Propaganda Minister Joseph Goebbels issued a list of authors, including Erich Maria Remarque and Arnold Zweig, whose works were to be withdrawn from all bookstores and libraries. The ban extended even to Ernst Glaeser's somewhat mawkish account of the impact of the war on youngsters on the Home Front, *Jahrgang 1902*, which had sold 100,000 between 1929 and 1931, and was to be popular enough when reprinted after the Second World War. Importations of Barbusse's *Das Feuer* from Switzerland were stopped. Arnold Zweig fled abroad: his manuscript of *Erziehung vor Verdun* was confiscated. Before 1933 the war had been presented by German writers from at least as many different points of view as in other countries: after 1933 only the pro-war point of view was permitted. And not merely permitted: it is difficult to understand how Werner Beumelburg's dull and creakingly ironic *Die Gruppe Bosemüller* sold a million copies in the Nazi period unless it was officially promoted, and Franz Schauwecker's appearance in *Brockhaus* as standing 'next to Ernst Jünger' as amongst 'the leading writers of militarism' had little to do either with his prose style or his mediocre sales, for *Aufbruch der Nation* was evidently too heavy-going to qualify for the popular-classic status enjoyed by *Die Gruppe Bosemüller.*[7]

In academic circles the question of 'Leader and Led' (*'Führer und Geführte'*) quickly established itself as one of the key issues of literary criticism. Even before Hitler had come to power Heinz Grothe had announced, 'The Führer is the mirror of his men ... For as the Führer is, so is his unit ... The most beautiful thing is of course when the leaders somehow feel an inner call to take their place at the head of their troops'. Herbert Weyand's dismissive *Der Englische Kriegsroman (Strukturprobleme)* (1933), 'The English War Novel (Problems of Structure)' found that the question of 'Leader and Led' was discussed by British writers only from a negative point of view, and only with regard to the higher national level: the reason for this, in Weyand's view, was that 'The English spirit draws its nourishment from the English soil. Its realm is reality ... It sees in the first instance facts ... The Englishman limits himself to the appearance of facts'. The following year Hermann Pongs, Professor at Stuttgart Technical University, published an article on 'War as National Destiny in German Writing' in the periodical *Dichtung und Volkstum*, and later issued the same piece as a pamphlet. He gave special emphasis to 'the structure of the whole: men and officers, people and Führer': he began by quoting a recent speech by Dr Goebbels. Walther Linden meanwhile contributed an article on 'Popular Literature of the World War and Post-War Period' to *Zeitschrift für Deutschkunde* ('Journal of German Studies') of which he was co-editor: he wrote of 'the comradeship of a nation's frontline soldiers forged in blood and suffering' and of how 'A new manhood was forged in the fire of the front'. He complained that for Remarque war was only cruelty, meaningless murder, spiritual destruction, and that the huge sales of a work so nihilistic as *Im Westen Nichts Neues* 'will for ever remain a disgrace'. He did not approve of Ernst Glaeser or Arnold Zweig either, but concluded 'German war literature is in the truest sense one of the most valuable constituents of contemporary literature in Germany ... It is a people's literature [*völkische Dichtung*] which bears witness to the German collectivity's immense experience of destiny ...' From the war, he claimed, 'a new Man was born, who demanded quite different life structures and political structures from the pre-war, bourgeois ones. This is the inward transition which led from the Second Reich [1871–1918] to the Third Reich'.[8]

Somewhat less overtly political was Privy Councillor Dr Ernst Volkmann's anthology *Deutsche Dichtung im Weltkrieg, 1914–1918* (1934), which even included a selection from Georg Trakl, though care was taken to mention the failure of Trakl, '*dieses dem Kriege seelisch nicht gewachsener und am 3. November 1914 im Garnisonsspital in Krakau aus dem Leben geschiedenen Dichters*', to develop spiritually in step with the war. Volkmann approvingly quoted Hitler's *Mein Kampf* in his introduction and employed an interesting piece of phrasing, not elaborated but soon to be taken up by younger critics: 'The longer the troops lay before the enemy and under fire, the stronger grew the spiritual value of Leadership and Followership [*Führertum und Gefolgschaft*] as also of true comradeship for man and society'.[9]

A caveat has to be entered here. Having their origin in a common language spoken thousands of years ago, and to some extent modified with reference to one another during more recent centuries, most European languages resemble each other relatively closely in sentence structure and in distinctions between concepts – certainly much more closely than they resemble Chinese or Inuit or Zulu. But the words of one language are rarely absolutely and unambiguously the same in meaning and resonance as words in another language, and peculiarities of syntax mean that a sentence in one language will have a different emphasis from a sentence in another language with the same general meaning. I have for example quoted Walther Linden as writing of 'the comradeship of a nation's soldiers forged in blood and suffering', which might be a rendering of 'die in Blut und Leiden zusammengeschmiedete Kameradschaft der Frontkämpfer eines Volkes' but is actually meant to be a translation of 'die Kameradschaft der in Blut und Leiden zusammengeschmiedeten Frontkämpfer eines Volkes'. It is not the comradeship but the frontline soldiers that have been forged together in blood and suffering, which sounds slightly odd in English: and the word 'forged', though better than 'welded' (for Linden doesn't use the normal word for 'welded,' implying use of a welding torch) is very weak compared to *zusammengeschmiedeten*, which suggests having been hammered together at an anvil by a blacksmith while red hot. Similarly I have had to translate *völkische Dichtung* as 'a people's literature' and *Volksgemeinschaft* as 'collectivity' and *Volksschicksal* as 'national destiny' but the word *Volk* has a resonance in German that cannot be represented in English – certainly not by using the cognate form 'folk'. The Nazis in any case had a quite distinct concept of *das Volk* which, since they only needed to express themselves in their own language, does not mitigate the problems of translation: for example they regarded *Volk*, as a natural, organic collective, as quite distinct from *Nation*, an artificial collective. Hermann Pongs seems to have had a special fondness for compounds using the root *volk*: he appears to have been responsible for changing the name of the journal *Euphorion* to *Dichtung und Volkstum*, of which the only non-risible translation is *Literature and Nationhood* though its implication is closer to *Poetry and Peoplishness* or even more *Poesy and Peopledom*. When he wrote, for example, 'Hier ist Volkszusammenhang, zwischen Führer und Mann' he obviously pretended to mean more than the mere connection, hanging together *(Zusammenhang)* of *Führer* and Man.[10]

Amongst the most problematic words is *Führer*. When Mussolini established his dictatorship in Italy he revived an archaic word to describe his office: *Duce*. Hitler did not revive an archaic word: he expropriated one of the commonest nouns in the German language. Before 1914 *Führer* was in everyday use to mean a driver, a guide, a guidebook, a person who steers something or someone somewhere. During the 1914–18 war the word came to take on an almost mystical import. A senior commander was a *Befehlshaber*, a command-haver; a lower level commander with a substantive appointment was a *Kommandeur*, but an officer with only a temporary, acting command was a *Führer*: and in practice all junior frontline commanders, the men who actually led troops into battle and got shot at while doing so, were *Führer*. The word took on as much importance as one's nominal rank in the army, as one can still see from the memorials to fallen officers in German civic cemeteries: Erwin Müller *Leutnant u. Kompagnieführer*, Rudolf Hartmann *Major u. Bataillonsführer*, and so on. Jünger's *In Stahlgewittern* is sub-titled *Aus dem Tagebuch eines Stosstruppführers*, from the diary of a shock-troop commander. The fighter ace Ernst Udet, when commanding a fighter squadron on the Western Front in 1918, signed himself 'Udet *Oberlt d. R. und Führer*'. Even the future communist Vieth von Golssenau ('Ludwig Renn') had for a period been referred to by hundreds of men under his command simply as 'Der Führer'. It was the natural word for an ex-soldier leading a para-military organization to adopt, though one cannot help wondering if Hitler, amongst the many chips on his shoulder, did not have a particular chip about not having been in a position to lead anyone in the war, for though a *Gefreiter* (something like a Private First Class in the U.S. Army) he was a regimental messenger rather than in charge of a section.[11]

'That was perhaps the most important thing for us, the emergence of a Führer to whom one paid unconditional allegiance.' (Another attempt to translate the untranslatable: '*dies Herauschristallisieren eines Führers, dem man unbedingte Gefolgschaft zollte*'). So wrote

Fritz Baur, in a book published in Vienna in 1929. From the time and place of publication it is not clear that this had any reference at all to Hitler, but Erhard Wittek's *Durchbruch Anno Achtzehn: ein Fronterlebnis* ('Breakthrough AD 1918: A Frontline Experience'), published in the autumn of 1933 and announcing itself as a book about '*Führertum* and nothing else', though dedicated to the heroic battalion commander (*Bataillonsführer*) who had inspired and guided the author in 1918, was professedly written by way of penance for not having sooner embraced the irresistible greatness of Adolf Hitler and his National Socialist movement. Nor can there be any doubt as to where Otto Paust's exaggeratedly heroic novel *Volk im Feuer* (1935) stood: the four syllables of just the title ('Folk in the Fire' or perhaps rather 'A People in the Flames') are a miracle of compressed Nazi rhetoric. The novel is a hymn to comradeship:

Comradeship is stronger than dying
Comradeship is bigger than death
Comradeship is something supernatural
In it glows the spark of eternity.

It is also a hymn to collectivity:

We are all only trustees of our blood, the Fatherland has us at its disposal. We are all merely tools, means to an end. But this end is so holy, that dying ennobles each and every one of us. In our death lies the fulfilment of an Idea called Freedom.

The one thing needed to pull all this together, the one thing lacking in 1918, was someone like Adolf Hitler: 'The Fatherland lacked a Führer, who stands above all, to whom the military and civil authorities are subordinated.'[12]

Next year, 1936, there appeared Sigmund Graff's *Unvergesslicher Krieg: ein Buch vom deutschen Schicksal* ('Unforgettable War: a Book of the German Destiny'), another popular history of the war which, like Beumelburg's *Sperrfeuer um Deutschland*, attempted to present the People as a single protagonist:

> Out of a people whose every member had believed himself entitled to something different, there grows – in the tattered garb of the frontline fighter in storms and battles – an idea that now all are under obligations to each other. This is the new thing, the overwhelming experience. The world changes and is transformed. From this new spiritual viewpoint, gained in the mud of the shell hole and at the bottom of the deepest dugout, a new order of things results, determined by necessity. The discovery of the Great War, the only discovery which made the war worth while for us, was the German human being *[der deutsche Mensch]*. Within the German community he and he alone must be in all the future the goal and starting point of all truly German politics, the object and centre of all internal struggles and discussions. This is the new achievement, overwhelming, unforgettable, and ever secure. For the sake of this one new thing two millions have died. And not one too many.

Another work which appeared in 1936 was the first part of an anthology entitled *Die Mannschaft: Frontsoldaten erzählen vom Front-Alltag* ('The Men: Frontline Soldiers tell of everyday life at the Front'). The editor, Jürgen Hahn-Butry, used his introduction to stress the importance of comradeship:

> The comradeship of men!
> That was our most abiding memory of this frightful yet beautiful war: that we had learnt to live together!
> Thus this holy comradeship forged something whole out of single men.
> One of the old force, Adolf Hitler ...[13]

It was of course Hitler's share in 'this frightful yet beautiful war' which qualified him, a man who was not even a German citizen by birth, to lead this nation of ex-soldiers. And not only ex-soldiers. Both Graff's *Unvergesslicher Krieg* and Hahn-Butry's *Die Mannschaft* were aimed at a popular readership, but 1936 also saw the appearance of a Greifswald university doctoral dissertation by Günther Lutz, one of the post-war generation that had grown up in the shadow of the Treaty of Versailles and saw in the Nazi regime an escape from the communal frustrations and contracted horizons that had hemmed in their adolescence. Lutz's dissertation, which was dedicated to Reinhard Heydrich, Himmler's second-in-command in the SS, was entitled *Die Front-Gemeinschaft: das Gemeinschaftserlebnis in der Kriegsliteratur*. This word *Gemeinschaft* means an organic as distinct from an artificial collectivity or community, a distinction originating with the nineteenth-century social theorist Ferdinand Tönnies but much favoured by the Nazis. Lutz wrote that comradeship was the fulfilment of a Community of Sacrifice (*Opfergemeinschaft*). He adopted Volkmann's pairing of *Führer* and *Gefolgschaft*, discussing their mutual effect on one another and asserted that '*Gemeinschaft* is not equality but unity in spite of and through difference'. In his section on *Frontgemeinschaft* and *Volksgemeinschaft* he claimed that 'in the trenches and scattered holes, in filth and necessity [*in Dreck und Not*], there arose a new nucleus of true *Volksgemeinschaft*'. It was these new spiritual factors, he wrote, that Adolf Hitler had used as the basis for the Nazi movement:

> Thus the sacrifice and the legacy of the front and its two million dead is fulfilled, and an unshakable foundation laid for all political, social and spiritual life in future centuries and millennia.[14]

No doubt his 1936-vintage political correctness was regarded by the examiners of Lutz's dissertation as making up for a certain tendency towards over-simplification:

Leadership is directly connected to the trust, love and loyalty of the followers [*Gefolgschaft*], yes, ultimately can only stem from community *[Gemeinschaft]* ... In this double relationship of comradeship amongst the men, of trust and loyalty of the followers for the Führer, as in the solidarity of the Führer with his followers, lies the ultimate unity and wholeness [and] reciprocal solidarity.

Since Lutz says nothing of inspiration or exhortation or of officers setting a good example to their men, it all seems pretty mystical, and the ordinary constraints of military hierarchy, backed up by courts-martial, seem rather to have become lost from view. Nor is this merely the verdict of hindsight. Till Kalkschmidt, author of an equally abstract thesis presented at Marburg University, *Der deutsche Frontsoldat: Mythos und Gestalt* (1938), reviewed Lutz's opus dismissively in *Dichtung und Volkstum*, mentioning the crudity of Lutz's ideas and his failure to recognize the *Führer's* creative role and his essential superiority to his followers, and assessing the 'literary-historical level' as 'lower than that of Cysarz, Pongs and Linden'.[15]

In his own Ph.D. dissertation Kalkschmidt had suggested that a distinction should be made between the literature of comradeship, exemplified by Beumelburg's *Die Gruppe Bosemüller*, and the literature of the *Führergestalt*, represented by Jünger's *In Stahlgewittern*, and also a distinction between the 'more human-natural action of the comrade-experience and the more spiritual-moral action of the follower experience'. Jünger himself, who, of course, unlike Lutz and Kalkschmidt, had actually lived through the worst awfulness of the frontline experience, was less concerned with abstract formula, and was still open to reconsidering the implications of what he had gone through. In 1925 he had written:

To have to crouch under fire without cover, belaboured without a pause by shells of a calibre sufficient each one to lay a fair-sized village in ruins, without any distraction beyond counting the hits mechanically in a half-dazed condition, is an experience that almost passes the limits of human endurance. For this reason the men who issued the order, and threw hundreds of thousands naked and defenceless into the fire, took on themselves one of the heaviest responsibilities the mind can conceive. And yet, even though I may be one of the victims, I can but admit they were right. Time works with heavy tools, and in the battle for some slag-heap of horror, over whose wreathed smoke rival conceptions of the world's future are locked in demoniac strife, it is not a question of the few thousand men who may perhaps be rescued from destruction, but of the dozen or two survivors who are there in the nick of time to turn the scales with their machine guns or their bombs. That is a view of the world's destiny which few have the iron nerve and masculine force to bear, and yet one may be proud to live in a time when such a spirit has shaped events to its mould of tempered steel. Though few may emerge from these flaming plains that offer no shelter but the mettle in a man's own heart, and though these few, resolute in aim and act, may still find fate turn against them and deny them their goal, yet I feel as surely as I feel anything at all that a gain will be scored that can never be scored out. For they who can come through this – and, as I say, there can only be a few – what can there be that they could not come through? And so I see in old Europe a new and commanding breed rising up, fearless and fabulous, unsparing of blood and sparing of pity, inured to suffering the worst and to inflicting it and ready to stake all to attain their ends – a race that builds machines and trusts to machines, to whom machines are not soulless iron, but engines of might which it controls with cold reason and hot blood.

In 1929, in the Preface he wrote for the English edition of *In Stahlgewittern*, Jünger announced, 'Time only strengthens my conviction that it was a good and strenuous life, and that war, for all its destructiveness, was an incomparable schooling of the heart.' But as another war approached he began to turn things round in his mind and to have increasing reservations about the new Germany which had grounded itself, in part, on his rhetoric. He may have recognized earlier than his readers that his glorification of survivordom was given a worrying new emphasis by Goebbels's claim that 'it is all right to use up one youthful generation if by so doing you open paths to life for a new one.' Mobilized at the outbreak of the Second World War, and awarded the Iron Cross Second Class for rescuing a man under fire on the Siegfried Line early in 1940, by 1943 he was on the fringes of the military conspiracy to overthrow Hitler: but his failure to capitalize on his status as the leading ideologue of military enthusiasm during the mid-1930s suggests that his essential disenchantment dated from much earlier in the regime. By the mid-1930s however German literature was well on the way to becoming simply a component of an integrated political culture and so long as Jünger wished to stay in Germany he could not recant.[16]

Another contribution to the science of war literature by Günther Lutz was an article in *Dichtung und Volkstum* analysing non-German accounts of the war. Lutz decided that a characteristic of French writing about the war was that the war itself was not conceived as something experienced corporately, but only as something affecting individuals. 'In the foreground ... stands not the crisis of the *Gemeinschaft*, not the crisis of the whole race, but the quite personal fate of the individual.' *Führer-Gefolgschaft* relationships were depicted, he claimed, simply as logical, intellectual, coloured by the ever-present fear of one's individuality being crushed in the military machine. As for English war literature, 'it was defined not by the War but by the *Zeitgeist*, and concerned not war as an inner experience ... but as a literary "Destiny" of Mankind ... as merely a *leit-motiv* or chance topic ... War appeared only as an episode, through which the participant in the war passed as through one period of a lifetime.' Only the Italians, Lutz thought, recognized the *Führer-Gefolgschaft* issue and showed an 'emphasis on the Will as the source of power to overcome Fate'.[17]

This of course misrepresented just about everybody, even the Italians. There were in fact relatively fewer personal memoirs of the war published in Italy than elsewhere, as if the establishment of Mussolini's dictatorship had obviated the psychological need for such books, or else shifted people's attention from the past to the future: writing in exile in 1937 Emilio Lussu even claimed 'There do not exist in Italy, as in France, in Germany, or in England, books about the war.' What books there were represented, according to one officially-sponsored critic, 'the discovery of the people, of the mass, with its virtues and its blemishes ... a precious experience which was to enter into the political action of the party which took power in 1922'. Even while the war was still in progress Michele Campana had written:

> The war has taught that in the gravest hour of communal life, the collective replaces the middlemen, abolishes the social classes, destroys the concept of property, provides directly for the life and work of millions and millions of men.

A little later, after the final victory over the Austrians at Vittorio Veneto, Enrico Corradini claimed:

> Our race which is in every one of us, in our flesh and in our soul, identified with our soil and our sky, with our language and with the structure of our cities, in each one of us from the least citizen to the head of state, from the obscurest private to General Diaz, from the factory worker to the boss, from the humblest pleb to His Majesty the King, our race, so ancient and always renewed and inexhaustibly everlasting, our race, without which we have no awareness, is already working in its depths on the victory of Vittorio Veneto in order to transform it into new life force, new power of will and capacity, new strength to do and suffer, to transmit and distribute to

the generations that will come. Rivers of blood from the mountains and the plains, five million soldiers holding out in the trenches for three and a half years, three and a half years of national unity and solidarity and effort by every arm and every mind, three and a half years of fervour and passion in every heart, fourteen battles, every miracle of ancient times surpassed on land, at sea and in the air, an immense weeping in every city, village and hovel, and the hymn to victory sung by forty million Italians, that's what our generation offers to the race, to future generations, to the Fatherland.[18]

Of course, if one thinks about it, the winning side had much better reason to be conscious of itself as a successful community than those who, like the Germans, had been defeated and had thereupon collapsed into revolution and civil strife. Again, soldiers in the French and British armies were as fully aware of comradeship as their German counterparts:

There is a very fine feeling of comradeship out here, both amongst the men and officers, and one really feels quite a little touch of pride every time one slides round these bally old trenches. Damn funny thing, patriotism, isn't it! Did I tell you of that most pathetic and touching incident of the aged French woman who strewed the road with flowers and sweet herbs for our fellows to march on when we had that long trek?

Cyril McNeile wrote of wartime comradeship in almost Germanic terms: 'One hoped so much that it would endure: that out of the furnace a permanent welding might emerge.' He concluded sadly that it had not: but one reason why the British did not need to insist upon it so much was that, whereas in Britain's 1926 General Strike strikers played football with the police, the more serious-minded Germans, seven years earlier, fresh from fighting the enemy shoulder to shoulder, started shooting each other in the streets of their cities. Nevertheless it is possible to see in the paternalistic and sometimes admiring relationship with the working classes that was forced on middle-class officers in the British Army in the 1914–18 war a half-way stage towards left-wing intellectuals' accepting commissions in the 1939–45 war so that they 'would be able to do something for the men', itself a preliminary to the condescensions and careerisms and the discreet fascism of the post-1945 Welfare State.[19]

One aspect of the new sense of national community based on frontline comradeship was the mingling of individuals from different social classes and different geographical regions, and this was something which received relatively less emphasis in German writing than in the literature of other countries. Most Italian regiments were composed of men from different regions. In the French and British armies, for reasons relating to class structure and social geography, the officers who made up the majority of frontline commanders did not usually come from the same area as the rank and file. In the German army the strong regional basis of regimental organization meant that the junior officers usually came from the same district as their men, had mostly gone to the same schools (as was certainly not the case in the British army) and, in a culture which tolerated regional variations of language even amongst the educated classes, usually spoke, or at least understood, the same dialect. The use of sub-Kiplingesque soldier-cockney in, for example, Vernon Bartlett's *Mud and Khaki* (1917) or Cyril McNeile's *Shorty Bill* (1926), though well-intended seems condescending and inauthentic whereas the use of dialect by Piero Jahier in *Con me e con gli alpini* (1919) and Paolo Monelli in *Le scarpe al sole* (1921) seems to refer to an interesting personal discovery and a new awareness of the complexities of national identity and also appears deliberately researched, the dialects in question being recognizably parallel derivatives of Latin, to which Jahier and Monelli attempt to give the orthographically correct form. Other than a few poems written entirely in dialect, published for strictly local consumption, this sort of thing had no counterpart in German war literature.

The different social backgrounds of men in the same section is referred to in Remarque's *Im Westen Nichts Neues*, though half the protagonist's group are schoolmates who had volunteered at the same time as himself, and in Johannsen's *Vier von der Infanterie*, and the theme of Benno von Mechow's *Das Abenteuer: ein Reiterroman aus dem grossen Krieg* (1930) is the student-protagonist's difficulties in fitting in with his plebeian fellow soldiers, but there is nothing in German as self-consciously elaborate as the pop sociology which Barbusse established as the tradition amongst French and Anglo-American writers of war novels:

what were we? Sons of the soil and artisans mostly. Lamuse was a farm servant, Paradis a carter. Cadilhac, whose helmet rides loosely on his pointed head, though it is a juvenile size – like a dome on a steeple, says Tirette – owns land. Papa Blaire was a small farmer in La Brie. Barque, porter and messenger, performed acrobatic tricks with his carrier-tricycle among the trams and taxis of Paris, with solemn abuse (so they say) for the pedestrians, fleeing like bewildered hens across the big streets and squares. Corporal Bertrand, who keeps himself always a little aloof, correct, erect, and silent, with a strong and handsome face and forthright gaze, was foreman in a case-factory. Tirloir daubed carts with paint – and without grumbling, they say. Tulacque was barman at the Throne Tavern in the suburbs; and Eudore of the pale and pleasant face kept a roadside café not very far from the front lines. It has been ill-used by the shells – naturally, for we all know that Eudore has no luck. Mesnil André, who still retains a trace of well-kept distinction, sold bicarbonate and infallible remedies at his pharmacy in a *Grande Place*. His brother Joseph was selling papers and illustrated story-books in a station on the State Railways at the same time that, in far-off Lyons, Cocon, the man of spectacles and statistics, dressed in a black smock, busied himself behind the counters of an ironmongery, his hands glittering with plumbago; while the lamps of Bécuwe

Adolphe and Poterloo, risen with the dawn, trailed about the coal-pits of the North like weakling will-o'-th'-wisps.

And there are others amongst us whose occupations one can never recall, whom one confuses with one another; and the rural nondescripts who peddled ten trades at once in their packs, without counting the dubious Pepin, who can have had none at all.[20]

An early imitator of this was Patrick MacGill in *Red Horizon:*

Who were we? Why were we there? Goliath, the junior clerk, who loved Tennyson; Pryor, the draughtsman, who doted on Omar; Kore, who read Fanny Eden's penny stories, and never disclosed his profession; Mervin, the traveller, educated for the Church but schooled in romance; Stoner, the clerk, who reads my books and says he never read better; and Bill, newsboy, street-arab, and Lord knows what, who reads *The Police News*, plays innumerable tricks with cards, and gambles and never wins.

The British in any case had Fluellen, Macmorris and Jamy in Shakespeare's *Henry V*, plus all those there-was-an-Englishman-an-Irishman-and-a-Scotsman jokes:

Grouped some few paces off three men are conversing. The first by his black hair, thick and hatchet face is Irish, the second red-headed, thick necked, with twisted smile a Lowland Scot, the third extraordinarily weedy, alert, a consumer of many cigarettes, a master of nick-names bestowed in a moment, is probably a Cockney.

In *Return of the Brute* (1929) Liam O'Flaherty (founder of the Irish Communist Party) devoted a whole chapter to describing his nine protagonists and their original civilian employments, which were:

grocer's assistant
labourer in a chocolate factory
policeman
officer in the Army Service Corps (cashiered)
farm labourer
drunken good-for-nothing 'a tout for a street book-maker ...
chucker out in ... a brothel': enlisted prior to 1914
general labourer
student [named, by coincidence (?), Louis Lamont]
excise officer, but enlisted before 1914

J.B. Priestley, who did not write a war novel, used the same formula in his best-selling *The Good Companions*, in which a Yorkshire mill-worker, a colonel's daughter from Gloucestershire and a Cambridge-educated prep school master from a concert group to tour England in the depths of the depression. Similarly, at the beginning of his novel *Squad* the American writer James B. Wharton listed the squad's members as:

Ole Anderson, a Swedish-American rancher from the Texas Panhandle.
Stanley G. Allen, American, a high school youth from San Francisco.
James Marzulak, Serb, a miner from Coal Valley, Pennsylvania.
Harvey Whittaker, American, from Oklahoma City, Oklahoma.
Emmanuel Waglith, Jewish proprietor of a shoe store in the Bronx, New York.
Giuseppe Novelli, from "Little Italy," South Eighth Street, Philadelphia.
Michael O'Connors, itinerant Irish-American worker.
Hugh Gray, American, graduate of Center High School, Columbus, Ohio.

Even non-fiction writers insisted on the varied backgrounds of the men in some units of the American Expeditionary Force:

In the big war companies, 250 strong, you could find every sort of man, from every sort of calling. There were Northwesterners with straw-colored hair that looked white against their tanned skins, and delicately spoken chaps with the stamp of the Eastern universities on them. There were large-boned fellows from Pacific-coast lumber camps, and tall, lean Southerners who swore amazingly in gentle, drawling voices. There were husky farmers from the corn-belt, and youngsters who had sprung, as it were, to arms from the necktie counter. And there were also a number of diverse people who ran curiously to type, with drilled shoulders and a bone-deep sunburn, and a tolerant scorn of nearly everything on earth.[21]

Regional differences were perhaps less striking, in the long run, than differences of social class which, in the French and Italian armies especially, came as a moral as well as a political revelation. The artist Fernand Léger recalled, nearly forty years later:

It's in the war that I got my feet on the ground ... I found myself on the same level as the entire French people; as I was assigned to the Engineering Corps my new comrades were miners, ditch-diggers, artisans who worked wood or iron ... The coarseness, variety, humour, perfection of certain types of men around me, their concrete understanding of practical things and of their practical applications to this drama of life and death into which we had been thrown ... Even more, they were poets, inventors of everyday poetic images – I mean of slang, so mobile and colourful ...

During the war itself an anonymous contributor to a French soldiers' newspaper wrote:

The lesson to be learnt by us thinking men from this war is a lesson in humility. Our brethren in glory and pain are unsophisticated ... Our comrades of the great war surround us with ignorance and intellectual tranquillity ... When our exhausted nerves and painful muscles let the pick fall, their strong arms continue to dig the trench with the same strong, regular rhythm; because our jerky efforts were slower and less skilled they had to do part of our work for us. Often during night fatigues they helped us carry the beam under which we would march at first, bending painfully down into the mud, and under which we soon staggered; they took our place and, still carrying their own burden, they helped us at the same time. It was they who pitied us, and our souls which were full of gratitude and prayer, humility and shame; for we were ashamed of our white hands and our feeble arms. And we were ashamed sometimes of our excessive sensitivity. On days when the prolonged and violent bombardment brought our poor nerves to their limit, their calm and balanced temperament endured without impatience, without restiveness, all the emotions of the pounding, of that waiting below ground, in the shadow where death hovers, in the face of the terrible unknown ... When we had to brave the open ground swept by shot they faced the fire with a broader and stronger breast, with stronger arms, with more skilful movements, more simple and more sure. Better than us at labouring, they were often better at fighting too, better shots, better runners, more dextrous with their bayonets. At rest, they slept more easily than those of us whose brains persisted in thinking. They soon forgot their weariness. And, although sometimes they would admire us in turn when our knowledge was apparent, although we would then feel their slightly superstitious schoolboy respect for us as for a schoolmaster, we remained humble before them because we felt keenly how much we lacked their strength and physical skills, how much our over-sensitive nervous system was something inferior, almost a handicap. We understood that there is no need to be a philosopher to be great when faced with the greatest of all things, to face up to danger despite the shrinking back of the flesh, to understand and perform all one's duty, to approach death proudly, 'stoically' – that death before whom we are all equal and which lays side by side these bodies of ours, similar and equal in value when the unequal flame of intelligence leaves them.[22]

The soldiers of other belligerent nations were also at least as conscious as the Germans that the trenches in some indefinable way strengthened those who were able to survive. Even in his anti-war tirade *Death of a Hero* Richard Aldington could write of the faces of veterans returning to the Front after leave in Britain:

They were lean and still curiously drawn although the men had been out of the line for a fortnight; the eyes had a peculiar look. They seemed strangely worn and mature, but filled with energy, a kind of slow, enduring energy. In comparison the fresh faces of the new drafts seemed babyish – rounded and rather feminine.

Frederic Manning saw something similar:

It may have been a merely subjective impression, but it seemed that once they were in the front line, men lost a great deal of their individuality; their characters, even their faces, seemed to become more uniform; they worked better, the work seeming to take some of the strain off their minds, the strain of waiting. It was, perhaps, that they withdrew more into themselves, and became a little more diffident in the matter of showing their feelings. Actually, though the pressure of external circumstances seemed to wipe out individuality, leaving little if any distinction between man and man, in himself each man became conscious of his own personality as of something very hard, and sharply defined against a background of other men, who remained merely generalised as 'the others'. The mystery of his own being increased for him enormously; and he had to explore that doubtful darkness alone ... If a man could not be certain of himself, he could be certain of nothing. The problem which confronted them all equally, though some were unable or unwilling to define it, did not concern death so much as the affirmation of their own will in the face of death; and once the nature of the problem was clearly stated, they realized that its solution was continuous, and could never be final. Death set a limit to the continuance of one factor in the problem, and peace to that of another, but neither of them really affected the nature of the problem itself.[23]

As in the German army, head-gear provided an outward symbol of inward militancy. The French were the first to introduce shrapnel-proof steel helmets – or almost shrapnel-proof, for Apollinaire was wearing one when wounded in the head – and their generals were regularly photographed wearing these medieval-looking casques, as was King Ferdinand of Rumania, who, commanding his army in the field though in little personal danger of being brained by shrapnel, evidently recognized that a helmet concealed his unusually prominent ears.

There is also a famous photo of King Albert of the Belgians in a helmet but this appears to have been a studio portrait. As a symbol the helmet was much easier to depict in drawings or photographs than key concepts like the Front, the Trenches, *Führertum*. The English pudding-basin/shaving-bowl helmet was less photogenic than either the French or the German model but prior to its introduction frontline troops had adopted the habit of removing the wire stiffeners in the caps worn by both officers and men, altering the angular flat-topped appearance to one of unkempt bagginess; this was known as a 'Gorblimey Hat' and was important as distinguishing frontline troops from staff and base personnel.

There were also numerous non-German writers who rivalled Ernst Jünger's dizzy pass-me-another-hand-grenade enthusiasm for the war: the problem was they were not generally such good writers as Jünger:

A moment only – and we were right up against the enemy …

I turn a corner quickly – two grey Germans stand straight in front of me … Two red flashes straight into my face – done for already! – but they haven't hit me, so now it is my turn. A snap-shot at one of the two, and the other disappears round a corner. The road is free! 'Come on boys, give them hell!' At the next corner a shower of rifle-bullets and 'sticks' whizz past my head from a machine-gun post … I fire away madly till my magazine is empty; then I fling down the rifle and hurl my bombs at them – the trench is chockfull of dust and smoke. Mac has come up close behind me, his shots thunder right into my ears … From behind they are throwing bombs by the dozen, without minding in the least who and what they are hitting. They shout and yell: 'Give them hell, boys!' The German dynamite-bombs are bursting everywhere around Mac and I; in the trench and on the parapet. We throw ourselves flat at the bottom of the trench and are not even hit by an explosion three yards away, though a cartload of rubbish descends on our backs. Jack comes up from behind with a fresh supply of Mills bombs. … 'Here you are, Fritzie boy, damn you! … and here is another!' Ah, they have had enough, they are done for, the bastards! A couple of survivors dash off from the post, and we rush after them, tear our hands and kilts on the wire, jumping across the overturned machine-gun and the dead or dying gunners, running panting and perspiring along the dry, hard trench, corner by corner … and then we reach the next machine-gun post and throw ourselves against it, yelling and roaring, with bombs and bayonets, battle-mad – regardless of everything in the world, our whole being intent on one thing alone: to force our way ahead and kill!

The writer just quoted also tried to find socio-cultural reasons to explain how men could persist and endure under such awful conditions:

What is it that gives them their courage? Is it their religious faith, their trust in God's Will and Providence, their belief in a life after death? I myself do not believe in or take count of another life after this, and death has therefore no fear or hope for me; but nearly all of the others believe certainly in eternal life – many of them even feel sure that he who gives up his life on the battlefield will be admitted at once into paradise. Or is it confidence they have in their righteous cause, their love for their country, their hatred of the Huns? I don't think so.

Such acquired dogmas and theoretical reflections may certainly help people to do their duty, to go voluntarily to their death if need be, but they do not free them from fear.

But for hundreds of years the spirit of the British race has striven towards one ideal, has valued one thing above everything else in the world: to be men – strong, inflexible, fearless. They have reached their goal: the old curse, the dread of death, has been defeated; they have learned to meet suffering and death with open, steady eyes – and they have gained the mastery of the world.

This reads like a fairly routine piece of patriotic tub-thumping but is worth quoting because it is not the author's own words but a paraphrase. This is how the last paragraph quoted appears in the author's own words:

Jeg tror, det er den britiske nations århundredgamle, klippefaste vilje til, fremfor alt andet i verden, at være mænd, stærke, ubøjelige, frygtløse mænd, som har undrettet vidunderet, har hævet den ældgamle forbandelse, dødsfrygten, lært dem at gå mod lidelser og død med åbne, rolige øjne, – og gjort deres race til verdens herre.

The author was Thomas Dinesen VC, one of several Danes who

volunteered – and overcame various obstacles – to fight in a war in which their own country was neutral.[24]

Jünger himself fully recognized that even in Germany his attitude to the war had not been shared by every soldier:

We, too, have no lack of those who, like the Frenchman, Barbusse, regard war as a material affair and, turning its negative side outwards, endeavour to run up on the other a temple of peace and happiness. They give as their reasons devastated towns and frightful sufferings – as though our highest duty was the avoidance of pain. They have no mind to accept the responsibilities that demand sacrifice of such corruptible treasures as life and property when a nation's greatness and its ideas are at stake.

On the other hand he was pretty sure which attitude he himself wished to be identified with:

One man has a mind for adventure and is thrown like a modern Sindbad from one danger to another. Another sees only the sanguinary glare on the face of events and is petrified as by the sight of a Gorgon's head. Another goes with the stream because he feels that fate is stronger than he is. He takes his quarters as they come; trusts to his star in battle; and even in the drear monotony finds his little pleasures growing like the bright lichens on a bare stone. Others again are soldiers first and last. Their eyes are hard and cold beneath the rim of the helmet. They are centres of energy about whom the wavering lines rally in the battle. In them the will-power of a nation at war seems to be most clearly and terribly expressed.[25]

In his Introduction to the English edition of *In Stahlgewittern* R.H. Mottram wrote that Jünger 'seems to imagine that a sort of Nietzschean-Wagnerian atmosphere of heroics translated into terms of gas and tanks can be re-created out of the wreckage of empire', and it is worth asking how far is it true that only a German writer could have mixed violence and philosophizing in the way Jünger did. It seems obvious that people living in a different culture, reading different books, educated at schools organized according to different principles, governed according to different political traditions *must* to a large extent think differently. The following can only have been written by a Briton because it refers to a uniquely British institution and assumes that the reader shares prejudices that are specifically bred in such an institution:

> Bedwell had just left a public school sixth form and carried the *Iliad* about with him. What a magnificent type of man compared with the officers we got later from secondary schools or from the ranks. Nor was he the only example of the superiority of the public school boy – and of the public school boys the quiet scholarly type were the best. The smart young men and the athletes would throw their weight about behind the lines but they were not chosen for a nasty job and after a few months' real war they were likely to crack up. The middle-aged married men and the quiet young men were the war's heroes – and how much harder it was for them too.

The particular pitch and tone of British writers when they draw attention to the tinniness of tin gods is also hard to mistake:

> The Brigadier wore a mackintosh jacket over his uniform, a pair of mackintosh trousers over his breeches, and a steel helmet that tended to slide over his left ear. There was no visible mark of rank at first, but later he fixed on his helmet the crossed sword and baton. His real badge of office was a wooden staff exactly four feet six inches long, and with this he tested the height of the top layer of sandbags on the parapet over the fire-step. It was decreed that this height of four feet six inches must never be exceeded – there was

little danger of any shortage, but a tall man standing on the fire-step felt acutely conscious of his upper eighteen inches. This mackintoshed figure, with boyish face and pouting expression, conscientiously measuring his staff against the trench wall, and finding a quiet satisfaction in the rare tallying of the two heights, commanded a force of three thousand men.[26]

The different religious traditions of foreign countries might give a peculiarly alien quality to even their secular rhetoric:

Men of my country, I learn to know you better each day, and it is from having contemplated your face in the depths of suffering that I have shaped a religious faith in the future of our race. Above all it is from having admired your resignation, your native goodness, your serene confidence in the best times, that I believe in the moral future of the world. Even when the most natural instinct taught ferocity to the world, you retained on your beds of pain, a beauty, a purity of look which in themselves redeemed the great crime. Men of France, your naive greatness of soul exculpates all humanity of its greatest crime and its deepest fall.

The different historical mythology of different communities inevitably led to emphases that might seem strange and even disgraceful to readers educated in another country:

Avant cette guerre on respirait un air impur ...
Dans l'histoire on ne parlera pas de nos pères vaincus, on dira
    que nous fûmes des hommes neufs nés des pères obscurs ...
Nous engendrons dans la douleur de cette guerre notre joie.
La joie de notre force, la joie de notre triomphe ...
Entre autres choses, nous avons fait La Marne and Verdun.
Nos pères firent Sedan puis y pensèrent sans en parler
Par delà des générations souillées nous réclamons comme

immédiats géniteurs ceux de 93 et tous ceux de nos ancêtres
qui furent vainquers

('Before this war we breathed impure air ... In history they won't
talk of our defeated fathers, they'll say we were new men born from
obscure fathers ... In the pain of this war we give birth to our joy, the
joy of our strength, the joy of our triumph ... Amongst other things,
we achieved the Marne and Verdun, our fathers achieved Sedan so
they think about it without saying anything. By-passing the sullied
generations we claim as our immediate forebears the men of 1793
and all those of our ancestors who were conquerors.') But of course
both the vaingloriousness of the words just quoted from Drieu
La Rochelle and the mawkishness of the preceding passage from
Duhamel came out of the same national culture: however uniform
and stereotypical a national culture may appear to foreigners,
the writers who partly embody it are nonetheless individuals
speaking with their own personal voices even though obliged to
use the language of their community. This of course was as true
of Jünger as of anyone else. His philosophizing has its parallels in
books by writers who served in the armies opposed to Germany,
as do his scenes of violence and horror: it is the combination of
disparate elements that is perhaps the most distinctive feature of
In Stahlgewittern but this combination surely has less to do with
German-ness than with the fact that a man who was at the forefront
of so many battles survived to write it all down.[27]

Nevertheless, the mere fact of Jünger's survival had an important
influence on German literature in the inter-war years. There was
a psychological need in Germany for someone like Ernst Jünger
that did not exist in France or Britain because, quite simply, they
had not lost the war. *In Stahlgewittern* was not a phenomenon
that, if it had not existed, would have had to have been invented.
It was something that could only have been produced by a gifted
author like Ernst Jünger, and if he had not been born, or had been
killed in the war like so many others, no conceivable substitute
or replacement could have had the same impact. Beumelburg,

despite his subsequent huge sales, or Otto Paust were not in the same league as writers. (This is a good illustration of the way in which the qualitative aspects of literature are as much a factor in its impact on society as its timeliness or subject-matter; the writings of Paust and Schauwecker grew out of the war just as much as those of Jünger, but their growth was simply of a different, and much smaller, order. One may wonder what might have happened in Britain if Rupert Brooke had emerged from four years in the trenches as a lieutenant-colonel with a Victoria Cross: or Charles Sorley; or even Edward Mannock, a man of distinctly fascistic leanings remembered by his fellow officers as an electrifying public speaker.) There were however two peculiarly German factors which reinforced Jünger's influence. One was the particular conditions of German academe; a number of British writers on the war found at least temporary refuge in university literature departments – Blunden, Graves, Nichols, Lamont – though only Blunden, appointed a Fellow of Merton College, Oxford in 1931, attained a position of much eminence – but their teaching obligations within the British university curriculum required them to turn their backs on the twentieth century. There were also fewer so-called scholarly journals in Britain and France than in Germany (though perhaps after all they were more scholarly than *Dichtung und Volkstum*); thesis writing was much less established in Britain, whereas in France university *thèses* needed to be much longer than German Ph.D.s and necessarily took much longer to appear. Neither Britain nor France had the kind of regime in 1936 which made it a smart move to dedicate one's Ph.D. thesis to the man in charge of the secret police. The scholarly debate in Germany on 1914–18 literature was thus a phenomenon without real parallel in other countries. Even more important was the way the Nazi regime simply eliminated half of the discordant voices amongst the chorus of war writers. The reason why Beumelburg replaced Remarque as the author of Germany's best-selling war novel, and the reason why Jünger's sales finally overtook those of the German translation of Barbusse's *Le feu*, was that the Nazi regime, as well as creating a climate favourable to the works of Beumelburg and Jünger, banned those of Remarque and Barbusse. If the Communists had gained power instead of the Nazis (not that there was ever much possibility of this) it would have been Ludwig Renn and perhaps Arnold Zweig who would have benefited from official controls and official sponsorship.[28]

Germany of course was not the only country to be defeated in the First World War. It is only in the last twenty years or so that first-hand accounts by Turkish frontline combatants have begun to make a posthumous appearance in print though this may have less to do with the backwardness of Turkish literature than with the radical restructuring of public life in Turkey in the early 1920s. Developments partly analogous to those in Asia Minor seem also to have cut off the flow of writing about the war in Italy and Portugal in the 1920s, which suggests that the important factor was not victory or defeat in the actual fighting but rather what happened afterwards. In Austria, defeated and dismembered, the most striking literary response to the war was an extravaganza on the theme of its monstrous, destructive stupidity: Karl Kraus's satirical, apocalyptic and (as it unfortunately transpired) prophetic drama *Die letzten Tage der Menschheit* (1922: 'The Last Days of Mankind'). Kraus, a journalist, had been exempted from call-up on health grounds in 1915 and the two most notable works inspired by the war by Austrians who had served in the firing line, Joseph Roth's *Radetzkymarsch* (1932) and Robert Musil's *Der Mann ohne Eigenschaften* (1930–43; translated eventually as *The Man without Qualities)*, both deal with the period before hostilities, and end before, or in Roth's case, quite soon after the shelling starts, an idea possibly borrowed from Zola's *La bête humaine* of 1890. (Roth's Polish friend Józef Wittlin unintentionally managed the same effect with *Sol Ziemi*, 1935 – translated into English as *Salt of the Earth*, 1939 – which was the first part of a planned trilogy, of which the final third was never written and the middle section was lost when the author fled for his life during the German invasion of France in 1940; the published text ends as the recruits are given uniforms and sworn in.) In his Introduction to the first volume of the official history of the Austro-Hungarian army's part in the First World War, Carl Vaugoin, vice-chancellor and army minister in the Austrian government, announced the book as 'a last memorial of the gigantic battle of heroes which for more than four years the Austro-Hungarian army fought till, still everywhere on enemy soil, it fell victim to an inexorable fate ...', but the prevailing attitude in post-1918 Austria to the war and the old Habsburg Empire seems to have been one of cynical bemusement.[29]

Hungary had officially enjoyed equal status with Austria within the Habsburg Empire in 1914 and was thus in theory equally responsible for the Empire's participation in the war. There was certainly not the same undercurrent of resentment at being dragged into Vienna's war that was evident in the Slav territories. The most widely-read anti-Empire text by a soldier in a nominally 'Hungarian' unit, Miroslav Krleža's *Hrvatski Bog Mars* (1922: 'The Croatian God Mars') was by a Croat; a harsh and sombrely ironic treatment of the theme of Slavs dying for the Habsburgs, it reads like a sourer-toned continuation of Hašek's unfinished *Šveik* or Wittlin's truncated *Sol Ziemi*. (It was probably no coincidence that Krleža, Hašek and Wittlin all chose to write about fictional protagonists much less well-educated than themselves, as if to emphasize the distance between the Habsburg Empire's privileged classes and its Slav subjects.) In 1917 Andreas Latzko produced a collection of anti-war, though not specifically anti-Habsburg, stories which became an international best-seller during the last months of the conflict. In English it may be found both under the title *Men in Battle* and as *Men in War*, and there were also wartime translations into French, Swedish and Dutch; but though Latzko had written in Hungarian at the outset of his career, this particular book was composed in German, and was only published in Hungarian after the Austro-Hungarian capitulation.[30]

The characteristic Magyar literature of the war – Géza Gyóni's collection of poems *Levelek a Kálváriáról* (1916: 'Letters from

Calvary') and his posthumous collection *Rabságban* (1919: 'In Captivity'), Lajos Zilahy's novel *Két fogoly* (1927: translated into English as *Two Prisoners*, 1931) and Rodion Markovits *Szibériai garnizon* (1929: translated as *Siberian Garrison* in the same year) – dealt with the experience of being a prisoner of war in Siberia; Aladár Kuncz's *Fekete kolostor* (1931: *The Black Monastery*, 1934) was based on the author's experiences as a civilian internee in France. Hungary had obtained complete independence after the Habsburg collapse, so that the Hungarians, though defeated on the battlefield, had come out of the war as a kind of winner. The theme of military imprisonment – embracing defeat, suffering, survival and self-vindication – could not have been more appropriate; though it was perhaps not entirely a coincidence that a generation later the greatest Hungarian writer of the Second World War, Miklós Radnóti, also a prisoner, ended up being shot by guards who were just as Hungarian as he was.[31]

It is arguable that the most interesting Portuguese writing about the Great War was also by prisoners of war – for example Alexandre Malheiro's *Da Flandres ao Hanover e Mecklenburg (Notas d'um Prisoneiro)* and Carlos Olavo's *Journal d'um prisoneiro de Guerra na Alemanha*, both published Lisbon 1919 – but that was because captivity represented such a large proportion of Portuguese contact with the enemy. This was not the case with Hungary: in a couple of Hungarian counties one in five of the male population of military age were killed in the war. (There were also of course numerous British memoirs describing life in prisoner of war camps – including accounts of successful escapes – but by the end of the war there were nearly fifteen times more British personnel in enemy hands as Portuguese.)[32]

The history that we struggle to understand can only be seen through the distorting lens of hindsight. A generation of young men who had read Jünger as schoolboys became officers in an army that overran practically the whole of Europe. France, psychologically prepared, one might say, by the mawkishness of Duhamel and the hysterical rant of Drieu la Rochelle, was one of Germany's earlier victims; the Italians, coming into the war on Germany's side, staggered from blunder to blunder. One question to be answered here is whether any of this had to do with the books about the 1914–18 war published in the inter-war period: and the answer has to be *no*.

A possible formulation would be that for the French the First World War was something they survived, for the British something they handled, for the Italians something they proved themselves at, for the Austrians something they lost, for the Hungarians something the Austrians lost, for the Germans something that taught them to be stronger. Yet there seem to have been no gradations of difference in the lack of enthusiasm with which the general population of the belligerent nations entered the war in September 1939. After the collapse of France in June 1940 stories multiplied about French defeatism: in reality of course defeated armies always do have a defeated appearance, and there were no convincing signs of French defeatism before the Germans attacked, other than those recalled after the event. It is true that Alan Brooke, later Chief of the Imperial General Staff and Britain's senior army officer, was astonished by the demeanour of French troops at a parade he attended two months after the declaration of war:

> Seldom have I seen anything more slovenly and badly turned out. Men unshaven, horses ungroomed, clothes and saddlery that did not fit, vehicles dirty, and complete lack of pride in themselves or their units. What shook me most, however, was the look in the men's faces, disgruntled and insubordinate looks, and, although ordered to give 'Eyes left', hardly a man bothered to do so.

But Brooke, like most British professional officers of his generation, was a spit and polish man, out of sympathy with the casualness of continental armies. One might wonder what he would have made of the turn-out of the rank and file of the Soviet divisions that poured into Germany in 1945. Most scholars who have examined the evidence agree that the true explanation for the French defeat is to be found in the strategic and tactical rather than the psychological sphere. They had more and better tanks than the Germans, though an inferior doctrine of employment, as many and almost as good fighter planes, good bombers even if too few of them owing to units being in the throes of re-equipment (though lack of numbers was less crucial than the poor use made of what was available): they were defeated quite simply because the Germans struck where least expected and having broken through pushed forward their armoured spearheads with a boldness that made even Hitler nervous. The French High Command's inability to respond effectively was not owing to the senility of senior generals, the rigidity of command structures or the defeatism of majors, but owing to the way the army had been deployed. The Belgians had seen they were done for by 28 May, the nineteenth day of the German offensive: the French struggled on gallantly for almost another three weeks. The army that most disappointed expectations in the Second World War was the Italian one, trained up and equipped under the ostentatiously invigorating influence of Fascism: but the cause of the failure of the Italians could not have been Fascism as such, since it was the newer Fascist regime in Greece that first defeated it. The likeliest explanation lies in the emphasis on cosmetic appearances at the expense of underlying realities which characterized almost every part of Mussolini's administration but which cannot be regarded as an altogether inevitable feature of right-wing dictatorship. Meanwhile the British army, led by officers who in the 1914–18 war had been repeatedly decorated for gallantry and had in some cases risen while still in their twenties to the command of battalions and even brigades, was consistently wrong-footed by German generals who in many cases had only had desk jobs in the First World War.[33]

Nothing in pre-1939 literature caused or foreshadowed or represented tendencies parallel to any of this. The last two chapters have suggested that literature – in the sense of literature as understood in university literature departments – was not the only intellectual response to the war, and much of what happened on the military side in the years 1939–1945 may be attributed to military professionals misreading of what they themselves had experienced in the previous conflict. But that of course is another story. Here it should be enough to say that it was not the course of the Second World War but the literary response to it which was most influenced by the writers of the 1914–18 generation.[34]

CONCLUSION

Actually this section isn't really a conclusion because I don't believe one is possible. I make a number of statements in this book, for example that writing about war in the modern sense did not exist before the nineteenth century, that developments pre-1914 in literature and art were of less assistance to writers than to painters when it came to evoking the awfulness of the Western Front, and that elaborate symbolism is not generally a feature of First World War fiction, but these statements do not add up to a thesis that can be neatly summarized here. In fact I have been moving away during the past forty-five years from the notion of theses that can be neatly summarized in order to pad out undergraduate survey courses.

It is not simply that all writing about history is necessarily only a work in progress, with each successive generation asking new questions and exploiting new sources of information: I increasingly believe that the accumulation of questions and information during the past couple of centuries has not brought us much closer to any real understanding of our past. We know a lot about fragmentary aspects of our past but if anything our emphasis on individual fragments has got in the way of comprehending how they fit together. I have spent four decades trying to fit things together and have come to the conclusion that until we know much more and understand much more than we already do an integrated overall

picture of the past simply won't be possible. Along the way I
have produced a number of fragments, including eight scholarly
monographs, more than thirty articles on different aspects of
military history, twenty articles on poetry and the novel, plus
contributions to *The Journal of Legal History, Journal of the
Royal Anthropological Institute* and *Transactions of the London
and Middlesex Archaeological Society*, and a mass of unpublished
notes that will presumably go in a dustbin at some point in the
next twenty years.

I was originally a student of early nineteenth-century British
politics, the politics of aristocratic cousinages and party factions,
but in my second year of research for my doctorate I became
interested in the overlap between academic history and the
study of English literature, and in the possibility of studying the
literature of past periods as an essentially historical phenomenon,
like the politics or social structure of past societies, rather than as
something organized round a canon of professorially approved
texts that speak to our current preoccupations and contemporary
sensibilities out of a professorially garbled past: not Shakespeare
our contemporary, not Shakespeare with his enduringly relevant
insight into the the complexity and drama of human ineraction but
Shakespeare dead and buried (along with everyone he had intended
to address) four centuries ago, but still uniquely illuminating
from the historical point of view for what he tells us about the
intellectual and psychological dimensions of an era separated from
ours by four hundred years of wars, civil wars, rise and decline,
exponential population growth and technological change.[1]

My first literary studies, an article on English epic poetry
in the romantic period in *Philological Quarterly* vol.55, 1976
and a book *English Poetry in a Changing Society, 1780–1825*
(published in 1980) went little further than identifying phenomena
and suggesting that they might have some sort of cause. Then,
having had five perhaps more conventional studies of the novel
published in refereed journals, I had an article in that rather
eccentric publication *The Cambridge Quarterly* (vol. 12, 1984)

entitled 'English and History: Yet another Plea for Correlation', in which I argued (pseudonymously) for a set of questions, regarding what I called 'exterior relationships' such as literary marketing at the time of a work's publication and the social and ideological background, and 'interior characteristics' such as style and genre, together providing a kind of analytical paradigm, which needed to be applied in any investigation of literature as a historical entity. I thought it might be possible to establish a new synthesis of history and literary studies that would go beyond the cherry-picking by professors of English of whatever isolated bits of historiography suited their particular view of a particular author, and would examine writers, and the texts they produced at different stages of their careers, as contextualized historical actors and as individuals acted upon by the events of their lifetime, in the same way as historians looked at cabinet ministers or working-class rebels.

Three years divided between Italy and Germany caused me to extend my scope from English literature to European literature and also European art, and colleagues in Italy encouraged me to take a more elaborately theoretical approach to the history-literature overlap than I had attempted previously, with the result that my next book, *Literature into History* (1988), put forward a somewhat cumbersome neo-Marxian causal model encompassing art as well as literature in Britain, France, Germany and Italy. My research for *Literature into History* led me to see that visual art and literature do not necessarily develop step by step and along parallel lines, an insight to some extent incorporated in this present book. It also enabled me to see the fatuity of the academic specialism known as comparative literature, in which one or two authors from one national literary culture are compared with one or two authors from other national literary cultures, with only the most cursory of polite nods to the notion that the literary culture of one society is something that might be compared, as perhaps a historian might, with the literary culture of another society on the basis of the recognition that literary culture does not consist of one or two authors, but of all those authors' predecessors and contemporaries, as seen in the light of their successors' careers. *Literature into History* obtained even less attention than my two previous monographs: Post-modernist History, in which there was no such thing as history, only historians, and Deconstructionism, in which there was no such thing as literature, only writing, were becoming the fashion, along with the notion that there was no such thing as scholarship, only people paid above average salaries to carry it out.

After returning from Italy I embarked on a comparative study of world war, which resulted not only in my longest book, *Collision of Empires: Britain In Three World Wars, 1793–1945* (1992) but also in a series of essays on military technique and technology and aspects of military organization which appeared in respectable periodicals like *Air Power History*, *British Army Review*, *Journal of the Society for Army Historical Research*, *The RUSI Journal* and *War in History*. My immersement in details apparently unconnected with literary history made it increasingly clear to me that a kind of questionnaire like the one I had proposed in *The Cambridge Quarterly* simply got in the way of recognizing phenomena when and where they present themselves, and without reference to *a priori* assumptions about cause and effect, causation and outcome. I began to see that any attempt to suggest a paradigm tends to withdraw attention from the possibility (and desirability) of making types of cross-connection that no one has ever made before, cross-connections that might eventually *in the future* lead to a scientifically rigorous approach to the underlying mechanisms of history.[2]

This present book only has the simplest of paradigms, being divided up mainly according to the questions Who? What? How? (and also So What?). I deal less with causes than with effects. I don't see that the literature of the First World War was an effect determined by the First World War as a cause: Wilhelm Lamszus's wartime best-seller *The Human Slaughterhouse* came out *before* the war, as did the first of Jaroslav Hašek's Šveik stories: but I have tried to concentrate on *what* was written and have scarcely gone into the question of *why* it was written other than to adopt the rather banal assumption that the writers had experiences or perceptions that they felt impelled or at least encouraged to write down. Obviously there are certain preconditions (one might call them external factors or even adopt the terminology I used in the 1980s, exterior relationships) affecting literary production: these include, though relevant chiefly to a period much earlier than the one discussed here, levels of literacy and the existence of a publishing industry and a market for books. But preconditions of this sort, though they may represent an opportunity, are not in themselves motives or – given the variety of texts available in modern society – even main determinants in choice of subject. Basically, it is very questionable whether historical phenomena – including literature – can usefully be seen as the effect of determinable causes. We are now accustomed to think of the 1914–1918 as a great turning point, involving the destruction of old certainties, the inauguration of new instabilities. But one might well question whether the Austro-Hungarian, Russian and Ottoman empires or even the federated German monarchies, would have survived indefinitely if had not been for the war and whether the disruption of the war was the precondition for the rise of ideologically assertive dictatorships after he war. Portugal had actually thrown out its king and commenced the slide into half a century of one-party rule before the war began; of the European states that remained neutral in the war, Spain experienced dictatorship, the expulsion of its royal family and civil war during the years that followed, whereas Sweden, not a conspicuously progressive polity in 1914, moved in the opposite direction, towards a prosperous social democracy.

It is a mistake to look for the meaning of events in their supposed consequences: we do not actually know that what occurs after an event, or a conglomeration of events *is* a consequence, or *if* it is a consequence, what it is a consequence of; and of course the notion that the Great War was a great turning point, a great divide between a settled world that existed before 1914 and the instability that followed after 1919, begs the question of how far the Great War itself was a consequence of earlier developments.

History does not progress in stops and starts but moves on continuously, with every generation experiencing what it thinks is a great divide. 'Who that contemplated the character of the late war could for a moment think of comparing the events of that war and the state of things growing out of it with the events and effects of any former war?' asked one statesman, a man who himself had served as Britain's prime minister in wartime – but he was speaking not in 1922 but in 1822 and was referring to what was then called the Great War with France.[3]

I have suggested some of the patterns and parallels to be seen in writing in different countries about the war, and some of the structural – one might even say *sociological* factors – that may have been involved in divergences but not for a moment have I thought any of this represents a near approach to the kind of scientific history that might one day be possible, or constitutes even to a limited extent an explanation or an understanding in terms of cause and effect that goes beyond the obvious statement that there was a great war and that people who lived through it found it so important an experience that they wished to write about it. What after all *is* there to understand or explain in the literature of a world war, that is to say, what sort of formal, structured explanation of readable length *could* be offered for the literature of a war involving millions of participants, thousands of writers or would-be writers? Perhaps the question is *where do you begin?* Each one of the books I discuss may indeed be a part, a strand, a component of a communal expression of a shared trauma. We might even want to read them simply as the expression of a shared experience. But in the end the poems and the memoirs are simply records of single individuals' encounter with the dehumanizing face of communal action, records of single individuals' realization, reiterated in different languages and in different tones, that any one of us might 'know himself utterly powerless against death and destruction and yet discover in himself the invincible resistance of an animal or an insect, and an endurance which he might, in after days, forget or disbelieve.' We read these writers because what they lived through challenges comprehension and explanation and yet teaches us something about the potentialities of our own existence. To see their work as components of a communal whole, as a sociological phenomenon requiring a sociological explanation, is to deny its most insistent feature, its authors' clinging to their own individualities.[4]

In the end the distinction I thought I recognized decades ago between the academic historian's approach to the past as something to be understood according to criteria that emphasized the past's difference from the present, and the professor of literature's approach to the past as offering texts that speak to our current preoccupations is just another of those *a priori* categorizations that get in the way of understanding. We cannot really understand literature, whether published four hundred years ago or four minutes ago, without understanding that we ourselves are living in a historical moment, with a culture inherited from a historical past and a psychology shaped by our own individual private histories and, in ways so subtly pervasive that we tend to discount them, by the biological history of our species. We cannot understand history, even areas like economic history that deal not with individuals but with human aggregates, without acknowledging that it involves factors such as, for example, consumer demand, social inequality, emulation, that have a role in our own lives as individuals. We cannot understand literature as a historical product without acknowledging that the difference in quality of different novels and poems, which still determines the *choice* of texts studied by students of literature, and conventional distinctions between first-rate and fourth-rate, relates to differences in the intensity and scope of authors' responses to what is now for us a distant historical conjuncture. And having understood that much, we have to understand that we do not yet know enough to understand the whole of what was going on. I hope in this book I have helped readers to have a better appreciation of various aspects of the literature produced by those who attempted to share their experience of the First World War, but I will have only succeeded in what I have tried to do if I have helped convince a few people that the overall picture of the 1914–1918 conflict defies scholarly attempts at analysis and that to expect anything like an explanation or a conclusion is impiety towards the dead, fatuity with regards to the present and presumption, even hubris, in the face of possible futures.

NOTES

Introduction

1. The passage from Laurence Binyon's 'To the Fallen' is quoted on p.47
2. Louis Untermeyer, *Robert Frost* (1964), p.18
3. James Campbell. 'Combat Gnosticism: The Ideology of First World War Poetry Criticism; *New Literary History*, 30 (1999), pp.203-15, at p.204. The books by Lloyd George and Churchill referred to are David Lloyd George, *War Memoirs* (6 vols. 1933-6) and Winston S. Churchill, *The World Crisis* (6 vols. 1923-31), and cf. p.250 below, note 20. Churchill was at the front for about ten weeks January-May 1916, his battalion alternating between the front line and rest positions, with his battalion headquarters being shelled on a number of occasions: an account of how he seemed to one of his officers is provided by 'Captain X.' [A.D. Gibb], *With Winston Churchill at the Front* (1924). Roder Martin du Gard, who also won the Nobel Prize for Literature, was in the French Army but in a supply column.
4. For Radnóti see Zsuzsanna Ozsváth and Frederick Turner, *Foamy Sky: The Major Poems of Miklós Radnóti: a Bilingual Edition* (Budapest, 2000), in which, however, the English translations seem distinctly clumsy.

1 Before 1914

1. J. R. Hale, *Artists and Warfare in the Renaissance* (New Haven, 1990), p. 169 for the quotation from Dürer.
2. William Shakespeare, *Henry V*, Act III, scene 6, lines 66 foll; [W. Scott ed.], *Memoirs of Robert Carey, Earl of Monmouth*, written by himself (Edinburgh, 1808).
3. George Wither, *Campo-Musae, or the Field Musings of Captain George Wither* (1643), p.16; John Dryden, *Essay of Dramatic Poesie* (1668), third paragraph: *The Works of John Dryden* (20 vols. Berkeley, 1956-89), xviii, pp. 8-9; John Dryden, *Annus Mirabilis: the Year of Wonders MDCLXVI* (1667), stanzas 64 and 131: *The Works of John Dryden*, i, pp.69 and 79.

4. Joseph Addison, *The Campaign* (1704), lines 350-53; 'Samuel Johnson, *Lives of the English Poets*, ed. George Birkbeck Hill (3 vols, Oxford, 1905), ii, pp. 186-7 (Life of Prior): a well-known newspaper of the period was the *Gazetteer and Daily Advertiser*, founded in 1756, but Johnson was probably using 'Gazetteers' as a generic term of abuse, cf. his *Dictionary of the English Language* (1755): 'Gazetteer: A writer of news. It was lately a term of the utmost infamy, being usually applied to wretches who were hired to vindicate the court.'

5. Laurence Sterne, *The Life and Opinions of Tristram Shandy*, i (1760), chapter 26.

6. The etchings of Goya's *The Disasters of War* were completed some time between 1810 and 1820 but not published till 1863. For Gros see *Saur: Allegemeines Kunstler-Lexikon* (still in process of publication, Munich 1992-), lxiii, pp. 64-9; for West see *Oxford Dictionary of National Biography* (60 vols. Oxford 2004), lviii, pp.212-6.

7. William Napier, *The Life and Opinions of General Sir C.J. Napier* (4 vols. 1857), i, pp. 94-110, at pp. 99-100; Mrs H. Baring, ed., *The Diary of the Right Hon. William Windham, 1784 to 1810* (1866), p. 282, 17 July 1793.

8. *Quarterly Review*, 2 (1809), pp. 426-7, in an anonymous review (actually by Walter Scott) of John Wilson Croker's poem *The Battle of Talavera*. W.R.Inge, *The Victorian Age*, Cambridge, 1920, p.14.

9. The quotation is from Charles Loftus, *My Youth by Sea and Land* (2 vols. 1876), i, p. 4. The later careers of men who were undergraduates in this period can be traced in the published registers of the different colleges

10. The only reference to Grigby's resignation in the records of his college is in connection with the election of his replacement: Gonville and Caius College Archive, Gesta, 30 October 1804 (GOV 03/07). I am grateful to Dr R.B. Outhwaite and to Ellie Clewlow, archivist of Gonville and Caius, for supplying me with information on this point.

11. Stendhal, *The Life of Henry Brulard*, trans. John Sturrock (1995), p. 462 (originally written 1836); Stendhal, *The Charterhouse of Parma* (Everyman 1992 ed.), pp. 46-7.

12. Walter Scott, *The Field of Waterloo* (Edinburgh, 1815), p. 22 (stanza 11); Robert Southey, 'The Battle Blenheim', first published in *The Morning Post*, 9 August 1798, first four stanzas.

13. C.C. Southey, *The Life and Correspondence of Robert Southey* (6 vols. 1850), iv, pp. 134-5, Southey to John May, 6 October 1815; Robert Southey, *The Poet's Pilgrimage to Waterloo* (1816) pp. 68 and 73 stanzas 39 and 48. For the picnic on Skiddaw, see *Life and Correspondence of Southey*, iv, pp. 121-2, Robert Southey to Henry Southey, 23 August 1815. Other Waterloo poems include *Wellington's Triumph, or the Battle of Waterloo*, by William Thomas Fitzgerald (1815, second edition as *The Battle of Waterloo* 1825); *The Battle of Waterloo*, by George Walker (1815); *The Battle of Waterloo*, by David Home Buchan (1816); *Waterloo*, by Henry Davidson (1816); *Mont St Jean*, by William Liddiard (1816); the anonymous *The Campaign of One Day* (1816) and *A Ballad of Waterloo* (1817); *The Battle of Waterloo*, by C. F. Warden (1817) *Waterloo: a poem* by George Erving Scott, [Cambridge, 1820]; *A Poem on the Battle of Waterloo*, by William

Whitehead (1820) The Battle of Waterloo: 'A Poem in Two Cantos. Written between Fourteen and Fifteen' [i.e. 1817-1818] in Edward George Lytton Bulwer, *Ismael; an Oriental Tale, with Other Poems* (1821), p.143-98 and 'Waterloo' in Chauncy Hare Townshend, *Poems* (1821), pp.337-60 There are doubtless others that appeared only in newspapers. George Erving Scott's poem won the Chancellor's Medal at Cambridge in 1820, Chauncy Hare Townshend's poem was a runner up in the same competition. Byron went to Waterloo in May 1816 and noted, 'The Plain of Waterloo is a fine one – but not much after Marathon & Troy.': Leslie A. Marchand, ed., *Byron's Letters and Journals* (12 vols. 1973-82), v, p. 76. See also Byron's *Childe Harold's Pilgrimage*, canto III (1816) stanzas 17-30 and note to stanza 30.

14. *The Diary of Sir Moore*, edited by Sir J. F. Maurice, was published in two volumes in 1904. The paucity – as it then seemed – of military memoirs and the predominance of those by 'persons in the *inferior ranks* of the army' was commented on by J.C. Mämpel, *The Young Rifleman's Comrade: A Narrative of his Military Adventures, Captivity, and Shipwreck* (1826), p. xiv.

15. *Memoirs of the Late War: Comprising the Personal Narrative of Captain Cooke ...* (2 vols. 1831), i, p. 129; Cavalié Mercer, *Journal of the Waterloo Campaign* (2 vols, Edinburgh, 1870), i, pp. 318-9. The wound described by Cooke was most probably caused by a small cannon ball or a grape-shot scraping the top of the soldier's skull. The passage of a musket ball would not have exerted sufficient suction to remove the brain tissue, and a large cannon ball would have taken away more of the skull.

16. Hallam Tennyson, *Alfred Lord Tennyson: A Memoir* (2 vols. 1898-9 edn.), ii, p. 215-6. This occurred in the 1850s.

17. The *Athenaeum*, 9 December 1843, p. 1092b, described *The Post-Captain* as 'the parent of all our nautical novels', but this is too generous. There were seven editions between 1806 and 1815, the third and fourth of which attributed the authorship to Dr John Moore, the novelist father of Sir John Moore of La Coruña fame. Charles Laughton recorded in *Notes and Queries* (fifth series, 10, p. 239) that Davis was said to have been 'a purser in the navy', but since he was only eighteen when he joined the Royal Navy in 1793 and twenty-three when he left the service to go to America, his position was probably one of less responsibility. For Trelawny and the cremation of Shelley see E.J. Trelawny, *Recollections of the Last Days of Shelley and Byron* (1858), pp. 132-5; for his inspection of Byron's feet, ibid., p.224. For Michael Scott see Mowbray Morris's introduction to the 1895 edition of *Tom Cringle's Log*, pp. viii-xii.

18. William Henry Dillon, *A Narrative of My Professional Adventures* (1790-1839), ed. Michael A. Lewis (2 vols. 1953, 1956), i, p. 130. For Lockhart's admiration for Goethe see Andrew Lang, *The Life and Letters of John Gibson Lockhart* (2 vols. 1897), i, p. 219, ii, p. 273: Lockhart was a friend of Thomas Hamilton and, as a young man, had visited Weimar with Hamilton's elder brother, Sir William Hamilton the metaphysician.

19. Ian Parsons, ed. *The Collected Works of Isaac Rosenberg* (1979), p. 237, Rosenberg to Mrs Herbert Cohen [July 1916?]. Willard Glazier, *The Capture, the Prison-Pen and the Escape* (New York, 1865) can claim to be

the first mass-selling war book, with sales of over 400,000, which according to John Algernon Owen, *Sword and Pen; or Ventures and Adventures of Willard Glazier (The Soldier Author) in War and Literature* (New York, 1880), pp. 309-10, was 'larger by many thousand that that most extensively circulated and deservedly popular book *Uncle Tom's Cabin*' ever attained. The first anthology of war poetry seems to have been William Gilmore Simms ed., *War Poetry of the South* (New York, 1867).

20. Joshua Chamberlain, *The Passing of the Armies*, (New York, 1915) pp.18, 19 – 20. Edmond Wilson, *Patriotic Gore: Studies in the Literature of the American Civil War* (1962) employs the term 'Literature' in the broadest sense, with 154 pages devoted to the memoirs of Generals Grant, Sherman, Lee and other senior commanders as compared to 22 pages on Ambrose Bierce: most of the rest of this 794-page book deals with civilians. Joshua Chamberlain, author of far and away the most interesting book about the war to be written by an active participant, is not mentioned. Of course any general's memoirs, since they consist of words, might be counted as Literature: but so might a drill manual considered on the same basis.

21. Ethel Lynn Beers, 'All Quiet Along the Potomac', first stanza. According to John Wood Davidson, *The Living Writers of the South* (New York, 1869), p. 194, this poem, originally published in *Harper's Weekly*, 30 November 1861, was claimed by six poets, the most vociferous of whom, Major Lamar Fontaine, stated in 1868, 'I wrote it, and the world knows it; and they may howl over it and give it to as many authors as they pleased. I wrote it, and I am Southern man, and am proud of the title.' (ibid., p. 197). Ethel Lynn Beers does not appear in the authoritative 2241-page *American Women Writers: A Critical Reference Guide from Colonial Times to the Present* (4 vols. New York, 1979-82), edited by Lina Mainiero.

22. 'Walter Bloem, *The Advance from Mons* (1930; originally published as *Vormarsch*, Leipzig, 1916), p. 68; other well-known German writers dealing with the 1870 war included Carl Bleibtreu and Detlev von Liliencron: the latter had fought as a Prussian officer against Austria in 1866, as well as against France in 1870, but his volume *Kriegsnovellen* (1895) seems to have been quickly outsold by Bloem's novels on their appearance: see Scott D. Denham, *Visions of War: Ideologies and Images of War in German Literature Before and After the Great War* (Bern, 1992), pp.23-41. For the French poetry of the war of 1870 see *Times Literary Supplement*, 10 September 1914, p. 416a-c.

23. Barrie Rose, 'The Volunteers of 1859', *Journal of the Society for Army Historical Research*, 37 (1959), pp. 97-110 at p. 102-3; *Encyclopaedia Britannica*, 11th edit., xxviii, p. 209.

24. Charles Carrington ('Charles Edmonds'), *A Subaltern's War* (1929), p. 63; I.F. Clarke, *Voices Prophesying War: Future Wars, 1763-3749* (Oxford, 1992), p. 333-6 for the success of *The Battle of Dorking*, The National Archives, IR 59/207, note by J.E. Chapman, 5 May 1903, for Henty's income 'as Author and Journalist'.

25. Alfred Tennyson, *Maud* part III, stanza 4; Mark Girouard, *The Return to Camelot: Chivalry and the English Gentleman* (New Haven, 1981), especially pp. 220-30 and 275-93: there was a parallel development on the Continent,

especially in Germany, but this still awaits its historian; William Morris to
Fred Henderson, quoted in E.P. Thompson, *William Morris: Romantic to
Revolutionary* (1977 edn.), p. 14: see also Thompson's discussion of Keats's
disgusted turning away from actuality, ibid., p. 10-21; Herbert Asquith, *The
Volunteer and Other Poems* (1917), p. 9 – first published December 1915.
*Record of the Expedition to Abyssinia: Compiled by Order of the Secretary
of State for War by Major Trevenen J. Holland ... and Captain Henry M.
Hozier ... under the Direction of Colonel Sir Henry James ... Director of
the Topographical and Statistical Department* was issued by the War Office
in two volumes in 1870. Separate accounts of the operations of the Royal
Artillery and of the Royal Engineers at the siege of Sevastopol had been
published in 1859 but no official account was provided of the operations of
the infantry and cavalry in the Crimea.

26. See Joseph Conrad, *Notes on Life and Letters* (1921), p. 111-151, 'Autocracy
    and War', originally published in *Fortnightly Review* in 1905. The Battle of
    Mukden, fought 20 February to 10 March 1905, resulted in a Russian army
    of 343,000 men suffering 88,352 casualties; the victorious Japanese, initially
    numbering 281,000, had 15,892 dead and 59,612 wounded.

27. *War and Peace* appeared in French translation in 1879, in German translation
    in 1885-6 and in English translation (from a French version) in 1886.
    An English translation from the original Russian appeared in 1889, but
    Constance Garnett's classic rendering appeared only in 1904. The Louise and
    Aylmer Maude version was published in 1922-3.

28. Romain Rolland, *Tolstoy* (1911). p. 85 n. 1; R.F. Christian, ed., *Tolstoy's
    Diaries* (1994 edn.), p. 89, 13 April 1855, but cf. Rolland, *Tolstoy*. p. 57 n. 1
    for the account of his feelings on the Crimean War which he gave after he had
    taken to religion; 'Sevastopol: In December 1854', dated 25 April 1855 (Old
    Style); *War and Peace*, x. ch. 39 (1933 World's Classics three volume edn. of
    Louise and Aylmer Maude's translation, ii. p. 543); ibid., x, ch. 37 (World's
    Classics, ii. p. 536); *Tolstoy's Diaries*. p.85, 7 December 1854.

29. Paul Boyer, *Chez Tolstoï; entretiens à Iasnaia Poliana* (Paris, 1950), p. 40.

2 Poets

1. Léon Riegel, *Guerre et littérature: le bouleversement des consciences dans la
   littérature romanesque inspirée par la Grande Guerre (littératures française,
   anglo-saxonne et allemande), 1910-1930* (Nancy, 1978), p. 559; Edmund
   Gosse, *Some Diversions of a Man of letters* (1919), p. 264; *Whitaker's
   Almanack*, 1913, p. 764; William Hudson, *Wilhelm and His Gods: and
   Other War Sonnets* [1917], p. 47; William S. Murphy, *The Genesis of British
   War Poetry* (1918), p. 13; Maurice d'Hartoy, *Au front* (Paris. 1916), p. vii,
   preface by the Marquis de Ségur; Jan Bernaerts, Hendrik Heyman, eds.,
   Oorlogspoëzie: verschenen in 1914 en 1915 en onuitgegeven gedichten (Port
   Villez, 1916); Ernst Volkmann. *Deutsche Dichtung im Weltkrieg, 1914-1918*
   (Leipzig, 1934). p. 8, cf. W.G. Randall. 'The German War and the German
   Poets', *Contemporary Review*, 111 (June 1917), pp. 747-53, at p. 748. See
   also Elizabeth A Marsland, *The Nations Cause: French, English and German
   Poetry of the First World War* (1991), p. 2.

2. Siegfried Sassoon, 'Base Details', in *Counter-Attack and Other Poems* (1918), p. 25 – see also Osbert Sitwell's 'Armchair', in *Argonaut and Juggernaut* (1919), pp. 116-8; Herbert Blenheim [pseud.], 'Song in Wartime', *The Egoist*, 1, no. 23 (1 December 1914), p. 446b; John Moorcroft Wilson, *I Was an English Poet: A Critical Biography of Sir William Watson (1858-1936)* (1981), p. 188; David Newsome, *On the Edge of Paradise: A.C. Benson the Diarist* (1980), p. 312. The earliest instance I know – pointed out to me by Martin Ceadel – of a contrast being drawn between the horrors of life in the trenches (in this case in the Crimean War) and the complacency of those who advocated the war, 'comfortably snoring in their beds' at home, is in a letter Cobden wrote to Bright on 15 August 1855, British Library, Add. MS 43650, fos. 125-6. When Britain went to war with France in 1793 both prime minister and foreign secretary were thirty-three and the man nominated to command the troops sent to the Continent was twenty-nine – i.e. they were much the same age as men serving in the ranks; in 1914 both the prime minister and the commander of the British Expeditionary Force were sixty-two.

3. J. Heylen, 'Brief van den soldaat', in Bernaerts and Heyman eds., *Oorlogspoëzie*, p. 38; F.S. Flint, 'Zeppelins', in *Other World: Cadences* (1920), p. 54; Giovanni Scarabello, *Il martirio di Venezia durante la grande guerra e l'opera di difesa della marina italiana* (2 vols, Venice, 1933), i, p. 59; A.D. Harvey, *Collision of Empires: Britain in Three World Wars, 1793-1945* (1992), pp. 392, 394, 396. One can still see damage to the front leg of one of the bronze sphinxes alongside Cleopatra's Needle on the Embankment in London, and to the corner of the sphinx's plinth, resulting from a bomb dropped in the roadway that killed three people on 4 September 1917.

4. Henry Head, 'To Courage, Seated', in *Destroyers and Other Verses* (1919), p. 14; Harvey, *Collision of Empires,* p. 396; The National Archives, WO 95/922, 15th Corps General Staff War Diary, 27 June 1917; H.W. Miller, *The Paris Gun: The Bombardment of Paris by the German Long-Distance Guns and the Great Offensives of 1918* (1930), passim.

5. Wilfred Gibson, 'Breakfast', published in his collection *Battle* (1916): Gibson joined the army in 1917; The Marquess of Crewe, 'A Grave in Flanders', originally published *The Harrovian: War Supplement*, 3 (February 1915), p. 1; The National Archives, AIR 1/1567/204/80/54, and AIR 1 /1575/204/80/76: the family tradition that Robert Gregory was shot down in error by an Italian plane (see A. Norman Jeffares, *W.B. Yeats: A New Biography* (1988), p. 236) is not confirmed by official records: the weather conditions were so bad that an aerial interception would have been unlikely; Laurence Binyon 'For the Fallen', stanza 4, originally printed in *The Times*, 21 September 1914, p. 9c-d.

6. Johan Daisne 'Zur Geschichte von Lili Marleen', in *Hans Leip: Leben und Werke* (Hamburg, 1958), pp. 69-71.

7. John Masefield, 'August 1914', last stanza; Maurice V. Brett and Lionel Viscount Esher, eds, *Journals and Letters of Reginald Viscount Esher* (4 vols. 1934-8), iv, p. 57, Esher to John Charteris, 16 October 1916; John Masefield, *Gallipoli* (1916), pp. 7-8. 34-5.

8. René Hugues, *Dans La Guerre* (Paris, 1918), p.13; Roland Dorgelès, *Souvenirs sur les croix de bois* (Paris. 1929), p. 39; Patrick MacGill, *The Great Push* (1916), pp. vii-viii, 50-51, 58.

9. Anthony Trollope, *An Autobiography* [1883], pp. 88-9; manuscript inscription to Gerald Kelly by Hugh Walpole, June 1922, in a copy of Hugh Walpole, *The Dark Forest* (1916) in the British Library, c. 134 c.9; Walpole's novel does not, in fact, provide much description of events on the Eastern Front; Richard Aldington 'Living Sepulchres', in *Collected Poems* (1929), p. 75: the *haiku*, a poem of seventeen syllables, originally a Japanese form, had enjoyed a minor vogue in England since the late 1890s; Giuseppe Ungaretti 'Veglia' ('Vigil') in *Allegria di naufragi* (Florence [1919]), pp. 62-3, originally published in *Il porto sepulto* (Udine, 1916): Ungaretti dated this poem 'Cima 4 il 23 dicembre 1915' – Peak 4 23 December 1915; August Stramm, 'Wunde' ('Wound'), August Stramm, *Das Werk* (Wiesbaden, 1963), p. 69, originally published in *Der Sturm*, Jahrgang 5, no. 19/20 (January 1915). If one reads for content rather than style one may also find a parallel between Ungaretti's 'Veglia' and Géza Gyóni's 'Őrségen' ('On Guard Duty'), the second stanza of which may be rendered:

> Death lurks beyond this bridge
> Drizzle falls from swirling clouds–
> And on the Vistula bridge
> The soldier thinks of a fairy-tale woman:

Lengyel Mezőkön: Tábortűz Mellett (Przemysl, 1914), p. 11.

10. André Charpentier, *Feuilles bleu horizon*, 1914-1918 (Paris, 1935),p. 377; Stephane Audoin-Rouzeau, *Men at War, 1914-1918: National Sentiment and Trench Journalism in France during the First World War* (Providence, Rhode Island, 1992), pp. 8-9; J.G. Fuller, *Troop Morale and Popular Culture in the British Armies, 1914–1918* (Oxford, 1990), pp. 7, 9; Patrick Beaver, ed., *The Wipers Times: A Complete Facsimile etc.* (1973), pp. xi, xiii; for *The Cambridge Magazine*, see A.D. Harvey, 'Jaw, Jaw about the War, War', *Times Higher Education Supplement*, 4 October 1991, p. 19a-f; for Second World War British Army papers, see *Union Jack: A Scrapbook. British Forces' Newspapers, 1939-1945* (1989), pp. 7-9, 251-54; Karl Corino, *Robert Musil: Leben und Werk in Bildern und Texten* (Reinbek bei Hamburg, 1988), pp. 245-46; Karl Kurth, *Die deutschen Feld und Schützengrabenzeitungen des Weltkrieges* (Leipzig, 1937), pp. 88-92, 133, 207. See also Mario Isenghi *Giornali di trincea, 1915-1918* (Turin, 1977). For a rare example of a diary kept by an ordinary soldier – not an officer – while at the front see *Harry's War: the Great War Diary of Harry Drinkwater* ed.Jon Cooksey and David Griffiths (2013).

11. Julie Vogelstein, ed., *The Diary of Otto Braun: With Selections from his Letters and Poems* (1924), p. 139, Braun to Julie Vogelstein, 20 March 1915; Julien Hervier, *Entretiens avec Ernst Jünger* (Paris, 1986), pp. 24-25; Edmund Blunden, *Undertones of War* (1982, Penguin edn), p. 217; ibid., p. 78; Osbert Sitwell *Laughter in the Next Room: Being the Fourth Volume of Left Hand, Right Hand!* (1949), p. 83-84; Lacy

Collison-Morley, *Shakespeare in Italy* (Stratford, 1916), Dedication; David Jones, *In Parenthesis* (1963 edn.), p. 196, notes to part 3; Siegfried Sassoon, *Memoirs of an Infantry Officer* (1930), pp. 65-66, 110; Wilfrid Ewart, *Scots Guard* (1934), p. 91; Edgell Rickword, 'Trench Poet', in *Behind the Eyes* (1921), p. 44: 'What needst thou have more covering than a man?' is the last line of John Donne's Elegie XIX 'To His Mistris Going to Bed'. See also Paul Fussell, *The Great War and Modem Memory* (1975), pp. 161-9.

12. Donald E. Stanford, *British Poets. 1914–1945* (Detroit. 1983), p. 307; Blunden, *Undertones of War*, p. 196; Klaus Lankheit, Uwe Steffen, eds. *Franz Marc: Letters from the War* (New York, 1992), p. 66. to Maria Marc, 23 September 1915; Jean Norton Cru, *Témoins* (Paris, 1929), p. 4; Jean Vic, *La littérature de la guerre: manuel méthodique et critique des publications de langue française* (5 vols. Paris, 1918-23), iii, p. 257; Siegfried Sassoon, *Siegfried's Jouney* (1945), p. 60; Cru, *Témoins*, pp. 557-65; ibid., p. 565.

13. André Bridoux, *Souvenirs du temps des morts* (Paris, 1930), p. 9; F.W. Harvey, *A Gloucestershire Lad: At Home and Abroad* (1916), p. viii, preface by Colonel J.H. Collett; Siegfried Sassoon, 'Dreamers', in *Counter-Attack and Other Poems* (1918), p. 19; Ivor Gurney, 'De Profundis', in PJ. Kavanagh, ed., *Collected Poems of Ivor Gurney* (Oxford, 1982), p. 41; Ford Madox Hueffer, 'The Iron Music', in *On Heaven: and Poems Written on Active Service* (1918), p. 36.

14. John Bell, ed., *Wilfred Owen: Selected Letters* (Oxford, 1985), p. 210, Wilfred Owen to his mother Susan Owen, 7 January 1917; Alun R. Jones, *The Life and Opinions of T.E. Hulme* (1960), p. 182, 'TEH Poem'; Abbreviated from the Conversation of Mr T.E.H.: Trenches St Eloi'; Paul O'Prey, ed., *In Broken Images: Selected letters of Robert Graves, 1914-1946* (1982), p. 32, Graves to Eddie Marsh, 22 May 1915; Geoffrey Keynes, ed., *The Letters of Rupert Brooke* (1968), p. 654, Brooke to John Drinkwater, 18-25 January 1915; Rupert Hart-Davis, ed., *Siegfried Sassoon: Diaries, 1915-1918* (1983), p. 96. 19 July 1916; Siegfried Sassoon, *Memoirs of an Infantry Officer* (1930), p. 216.

15. *Wilfred Owen: Selected Letters*, pp. 243-4, Wilfred Owen to Colin Owen, 14 May 1917; R.H. Tawney, *The Attack and Other Papers* (1953), pp. 13-14 (originally printed in *The Westminster Gazette*, August 1916).

16. Ivor Gurney, 'On Somme', in PJ. Kavanagh, ed., *Collected, Poems of Ivor Gurney*, p. 157; Max Deauville [Maurice Duvez], *La boue des Flandres* (1964 edn), p. 10 (Avant- propos); Vivian Gilbert, *The Romance of the Last Crusade: With Allenby to Jerusalem* (New York, 1923), pp. 43-4; Herbert Buckmaster, *Buck's Book: Ventures - Adventures and Misadventures* (1933), p. 146; A. D. Gristwood, *The Somme* (1917 – but quoting 2006 Columbia S.C. edit.), p. 18; Michael and Eleanor Brock, eds., *Margot Asquith's Great War Diaries 1914-1916: the View from Downing Street* (Oxford, 2014), p.277, Raymond Asquith to Margot Asquith, 6 July 1916; *Wilfred Owen: Selected letters*, p. 217-18, to Susan Owen, 4 February 1917; Paul Nash, *Outline: An Autobiography and Other Writings* (1949), pp. 195-6, Paul Nash to Margaret Nash, 6 April 1917, cf. Gristwood, *Somme*, p. 21 for the sinister beauty of Verey lights.

17. A.D. Harvey, 'Robert Nichols on the Western Front', *Notes and Queries;* 260 (2015), pp. 445-6; The National Archives, WO 334/18193 (personal file of Robert Nichols): Proceedings Of A Medical Board 12 Jan. 1916; R.K.R. Thornton, ed., *Ivor Gurney: War Letters* (Ashington, 1983), p. 207, Ivor Gurney to Marion Scott, 26 September 1917; Michael Hurd, *The Ordeal of Ivor Gurney* (Oxford, 1978), pp. 121, 123, 195-8; H.C. Marr, *Psychoses of the War: Including Neurasthenia and Shell Shock* (1919), p. 48; W. Johnson and R.G. Rous 'Neurasthenia and War Neuroses', in W.G. Macpherson et al., *Medical Services: Diseases of the War* (2 vols, 1923), ii, pp. 1-67 at p. 41, 44: the text on p. 44 is ambiguous but it seems that it was not 10 per cent of total shellshock cases that were sent home but 10 per cent of neurasthenia cases at base hospitals, i.e. 1.2 per cent of the total, though, the figure would rise if the base hospital became overcrowded; Norman Fenton, *Shell Shock and its Aftermath* (1926), p. 23 figure 2, p. 28 figure 6 and p. 29: despite its London imprint this is the main authority for shell shock in the American Expeditionary Force; Johnson and Rous 'Neurasthenia and War Neuroses', p. 4, table III, and cf. *Statistics of the Military Effort of the British Empire during the Great War, 1914-1920* (1922), pp. 263-4; Johnson and Rous, 'Neurasthenia and War Neuroses', pp. 7, 8, cf. *Statistics of the Military Effort*, p. 249; William Linton Andrews, *Haunting Years: The Commentaries of a War Territorial* [1930], p. 5; *The Guinness Book of Records* [1958], p. 221.

18. Charles S. Myers, *Shell Shock in France, 1914-18* (Cambridge, 1940), pp. 73-5. For a general discussion of war neurosis during the First World War, see Eric J. Leed, *No Man's Land: Combat and Identity in World War I* (Cambridge 1979), pp. 163-92; and for three recent accounts see Leo van Bergen, *Before My Helpless Sight; Suffering, Dying and Military Medicine on the Western Front, 1914-1918* (Farnham, 2009) pp. 206-64, Fiona Reid, *Broken Men: Shell Shock, Treatment and Recovery 1914-1930* (2010) and Stefanie Linden, T*hey Called it Shell Shock; Combat Stress in the First World War* (Solihull, 2016); for its occurrence in earlier wars see John Talbott, 'Combat Trauma in the American Civil War', *History Today*, 46, March 1996, pp. 41-7, Anthony Babington, *Shell Shock: A History of the Changing Attitudes to War Neurosis* (1997), pp. 13-20, and R.L. Richards 'Mental and Nervous Diseases during the Russo Japanese War', *Military Surgeon*, 26 (1910), p. 177-93. See also Peter Hodgkinson, *Glum Heroes: Hardship, Fear and Death: Resilience and Coping in the British Army on the Western Front 1914-1918* (Solihull, 2016) and Suzie Grogan, *Shell-Shocked Britain: the First World War's Legacy to Britain's Mental Health* (Barnsley, 2014).

19. Mark VII [Max Plowman], *A Subaltern on the Somme in 1916* (1927). p. 23: letters in *The Times* from Brigadier General Robert Pigot, General Sir Ivor Maxse and Lieutenant Colonel Graham Seton-Hutchison, *The Times*, 16 April 1930, p. 10e, and 17 April 1930, p. 17e; Robert Graves, *Goodbye To All That*, p. 144; *Times Literary Supplement*, 12 June 1930, p. 485d; *Statistics of the Military Effort of the British Empire*, p. 660: in the year ending 30 September 1918 there were 980 trials of officers by court martial outside the UK, of which 387 were for drunkenness, and in the year ending 30 September 1919, 1001 trials of officers by court martial, of which 293

were for drunkenness. Robert Graves's 'two-bottle company commander' is identified as 'Jack Greaves', i.e. Captain R.C.J. Greaves, in a copy of *Good-Bye to All That* formerly owned and annotated by Captain J.C. Dunn (the medical officer in Graves's battalion) now in the possession of the Royal Welch Fusiliers – see Robert Graves, *Good-Bye to All That*, ed. Richard Percival Graves (Oxford 1995), p. 345, note to p. 158 line 12e. Greaves's personal file in The National Archives, WO 339/45704 however provides no indication of any alcohol problem – unlike that of, for example, Frederic Manning, WO 339/88843.

20. Wyndham Lewis, *Blasting and Bombardiering* (1937), p. 119; Charles Carrington ('Charles Edmonds'), *A Subaltern's War* (1929), pp. 20 and 195; A.W. Smith, *A Captain Departed* (1934), p. 44.

21. John Joliffe, ed., *Raymond Asquith: Life and letters* (1980), p. 277, Raymond Asquith to Lady Diana Manners, 21 July 1916; Sitwell, *Laughter in the Next Room*, p. 80; letter from an Old Etonian in the 2nd Battalion Warwickshire Regiment, printed in *The Zeppelin: Piloted by Present Etonians*, 26 March 1915; letter from an Old Etonian in the 2nd Battalion Coldstream Guards, printed in the same issue; *The Radleian*, no. 402, 9 March 1915; Max Egremont, *Siegfried Sassoon: A Biography* (2005), p. 91 quoting a letter of Sassoon to Hamo Thornycroft, 18 May 1916; George Thomas, ed., *Edward Thomas: Selected Letters* (Oxford, 1995), to Julian Thomas, 30 March 1917.

22. Cyril McNeile, *Sapper's War Stories: Collected in One Volume* [1930], pp. 9-10 (Foreword); Carrington, *A Subaltern's War*, p. 195; Siegfried Sassoon, *Memoirs of an Infantry Officer* (1930), p. 277.

23. Graham H. Greenwell, *An Infant in Arms: War Letters of a Company Officer 1914-1918* (1935), p. ix; ibid., p. 305, Greenwell to his mother, 26 December 1918. See also Adrian Carton de Wiart, *Happy Odyssey* (1950), p.89: 'I had enjoyed the war; it had given me many bad times, lots of good ones, plenty of excitement, and with everything found for us.' Carton de Wiart's bad times included being wounded eight times.

24. *Colfensia: The Chronicles of Colfe Grammar School*, no. 19 (1913) p. 21-2, shows that Yeates, in Form VA, was a vice-captain for sport in Buff House while Williamson, a sixth former, was captain of the Buff House harrier team: Douglas Herbert Bell, author of *A Soldiers' Diary of the Great War* (1929) had also been at Colfe, but was a few years older; Eugen Marinescu, *Cîntăretul Luptelor Şi Al Biruinţelor: căpitanul-poet Nicolae Vulovici* (Bucharest, 1977), p. 107-10 (the other two poets were Mihail Săulescu and Constantin Stoika); Leonid I. Strakhovsky, *Craftsman of the Word: Three Poets of Russia* (Cambridge, Massachusetts, 1949), p. 31; Christopher Barnes, *Boris Pasternak: A Literary Biography* (2 vols., 1989-98), pp. 179, 182; Wiktor Woroszylsk, *The Life of Mayakovsky,* (1972), p 141: Avril Pyman, *The Life of Aleksandr Blok* (2 vols. Oxford, 1979-80), ii, pp. 234-35: Gordon McVay, *Esenin: A Life* (1976), pp. 73-77; Charlotte Douglas, ed., *Collected Works of Velimir Khlebnikov,* (2 vols., Cambridge, Massachusetts, 1987-9), i, p. 106 and, especially, p. 116 letter 91.

25. Osbert Sitwell, 'Sheep-Song', in *Argonaut and Juggernaut* (1919), pp. 97-8 (dated September 1918); for the petty persecution of *The Cambridge Magazine* by the authorities see A.D. Harvey, 'Watching the Intellectuals: The Government

and *The Cambridge Magazine* in 1916', *Cambridge Review*, 112, no. 2315 (December 1991), pp. 184-6; for wartime censorship in Germany, see John D. Halliday, *Karl Kraus, Franz Pfemfert and the First World War* (Passau, 1986), pp. 169, 172-3. It is true that Brigadier General G. K. Cockerill, Director of Special Intelligence at the War Office, took an interest in Sassoon's war poems (see Sassoon's army personal file, The National Archives, WO 339/51440) but in all probability this was not because Sassoon was regarded as subversive and a security risk but because Cockerill was himself a published poet. As for Ford Madox Hueffer, though he might not have become an officer in the German Army, his army personal file indicates that he was in fact a German rather than a British citizen, and was investigated as such by MI5. His first CO in France reported 'very adversely on him as wholly unfitted to lead men', but the commander of another battalion in his regiment admired his 'considerable powers of organization', and he was allowed to continue serving at the front: The National Archives, WO 339/37369.

26. Verna Coleman, *The last Exquisite: A Portrait of Frederic Manning* (Melbourne. 1990), p. 118, quoting Aldington to Harriet Monroe, 7 August 1914; Gordon Martel, 'The Origins of the Chatham House Version', in Edward Ingram, ed., *National and International Politics in the Middle East: Essays in Honour of Elie Kedourie* (1986), pp. 66-88, at p. 74, quoting Arnold Toynbee's letter to his mother of 12 November 1914. The classic brief statement regarding future war poets enlisting for reasons of high idealism and suffering traumatic disillusion as a result of their involvement 'in stupid battles' is probably in Samuel Hynes, *A War Imagined: the First World War and English Culture* (1990), p. x, but of course the attitude of writers like Siegfried Sassoon was not necessarily typical of all officers commissioned from civilian life during the war: for every doleful poet there was at least one man who abandoned a successful career when his country called and, like the clergyman schoolmaster the Rev. Bernard Vann VC, MC and bar or the chartered accountant Silas Danby DSO and bar, MC, became so focused on the demands of their new vocation that they rose to the command of battalions in less than three years. The possible differences between the attitude of professional soldiers and those with war-only commissions was however later curiously demonstrated in Japan, in last letters home written by suicide pilots: '[Navy] Academy graduates ... wrote very little ... It was the reserve officers from civilian colleges and universities, who had only a hasty military training before receiving their assignments, who wrote the most': Rikihei Inoguchi, Tadashi Nakajima, with Roger Pineau, *The Divine Wind: Japans Kamikaze Force in World War Two* (1959), p. 180.

27. The phrase 'lost voices' was coined, or at least given bibliographical form, by Tim Cross in *Lost Voices of the First World War* (1987).

3 Artists

1. *La bataille de Tripoli, 26 octobre 1911, vécue et chantée par F.T. Marinetti* (Paris, 1912) and F.T. Marinetti; *Zang Tumb Tuum: Adrianopoli Ottobre 1912: Parola in Libertà* (Milan, 1914) passim; for Ludwig Meidner, see Richard Cork, *A Bitter Truth: Avant-Garde Art and the Great War* (New Haven, 1994), pp. 13-15. Cork's book is probably the best general study of

the visual art of the First World War but see also Peter Thurmann et al. *Sterne Fallen: von Boccioni bis Schiele. Der Erste Weltkrieg als Ende Europäischer Kunstlerwge/Fallen Stars: Disrupted Lives from Boccioni to Schiele* (Kiel, 2014)

2. William Rothenstein, *Men and Memories* (2 vols. 1931-2), ii, p. 350; Max Ernst, *Écritures* (Paris, 1970), pp. 24-5.

3. William A.Camfield, *Max Ernst: Dada and the Dawn of Surrealism* (Munich, 1993), p. 41, quoting Ernst, 'Some Data', *View* (April, 1942), p. 30 and catalogue, Musée National d'Art Moderne, Paris 13 Nov – 31 Dec. 1959; Max Ernst, *Écritures* (Paris, 1970), pp. 24-25; Lothar Brieger, *Ludwig Meidner: mit einer Selbstbiographie* (Leipzig, 1919), p. 13; Otto Griebel, *Ich war ein Mann der Strasse: Lebenserinnerungen eines Dresdner Malers* (Halle, 1986), p. 59; Oskar Schlemmer, *Idealist der Form: Briefe, Tagebücher, Schriften, 1912-1943* (Leipzig, 1990), pp. 20-21; Felix Klee, ed., *The Diaries of Paul Klee, 1898-1918 (1965)*, p. 355 no. 1026a, 6 December 1916; ibid., p. 313, nos. 951 and 952, 1915. Though brought up in Switzerland, Klee was regarded by both the Swiss and the German authorities as a German national, his father having come from Hesse.

4. *Blast*, 2 (July 1915), pp. 33-4.

5. Kenneth E. Silver, *Esprit de Corps: The Art of the Parisian Avant-Garde and the First World War, 1914-1925* (Princeton, 1989), pp. 79-80, 85: *Fernand Léger 1881-1955* (Catalogue of Exhibition at the Palais de Beaux Arts, Brussels, October-November 1956), p. 30; Maurice Vlaminck, ed., *André Derain, Lettres à Vlaminck* (Paris, 1955), p. 221, 227; ibid., pp. 221, 224, 225; Paul Maze, *A Frenchman in Khaki* (1934), p. 145. For Dix's wartime pictures see Eva Karcher, *Otto Dix: 1891-1969* (Cologne, 1992), pp. 28-39 and Birgit Dalbajewa, Simone Fleischer, Olaf Peters, *Otto Dix: Der Krieg – Das Dresdner Triptychon*, (Dresden, 2014), p. 46-66. Edward Rydz, who before the war had studied art in Krakow, Vienna and Munich, made a living as an artist and refused a commission in the Austrian army, later painted, sketched fellow officers and exhibited in a gallery back home while serving as a colonel in the Polish Legions operating on the Eastern Front; but he was actually a quite mediocre artist whose paintings and sketches would not be remembered today if it had not been for the fact that later, as Marshal Śmigły-Rydz, he was commander-in-chief of the Polish army and in effect head of the ruling clique in Poland at the time of the German invasion in 1939: see Wiesław Jan Wysocki, *Edward Śmigły-Rydz: malarz i poeta* (Warsaw, 1997), pp. 104-5 for his work in oil and aquarelle, *Poległy Legionista* ('Fallen Legionary'), and Wiesław Jan Wysocki, *Marszałek Edward Śmigły-Rydz: Portret Naczelnego Wodza* (Warsaw, 2009), p. 42 for sketches of his fellow officers.

6. Theodor Rocholl had been born in 1854, Wilhelm Schreuer in 1866: see *Kriegsfahrten deutscher Maler: Selbsterlebtes im Weltkrieg, 1914-1915* (Bielefeld, 1915), pp. 9-84 for Rocholl, pp. 87-106 for Schreuer. Albin Egger-Lienz, born in 1868, was called up for service in a territorial defence unit in 1915 but was later discharged and became a civilian war artist in 1916: his wartime work is largely an adaptation of the maneristic Post-Impressionism of his pre-war career, cf. his *Haspinger Anno Neun* of 1908-9 and his wartime masterpiece *Den Namenlosen 1914* of 1916. Rocholl and Schreuer were simply representational in their war art, rather in the style of depictions

of military action in late-nineteenth-century illustrated weekly papers. Emil Eber – later calling himself Elk Eber – became a war artist after being buried by a shell and left unfit for further combatant service, but it is unclear how much time he spent at the front after he resumed his artistic work. The first ever official war artist was probably Jan Cornelisz Vermeyen, whom the Emperor Charles V took on his expedition to Tunis in 1535: the sketches he made were the basis for tapestries now in the Kunsthistorisches Museum in Vienna.

7. Campbell Dodgson quoted in Cork, *A Bitter Truth*, p. 197; *Illustrated London News*, 8 May 1915, p. 592, and *Sketch*, 12 May 1915, p. iv, both quoted in Peter Harrington, *British Artists and War: The Face of Battle in Painting and Prints, 1700-1914* (1993),p. 306.

8. John Lavery, *The Life of a Painter* (1940), p. 148; Wyndham Lewis, *Blasting and Bombardiering* (1937), p. 180; for Orpen's war paintings see reproductions in Robert Upstone and Angela Weight, *An Onlooker in* France (2008); for 'Realismo magico' see *Grande Dizionario Enciclopedico UTET* (20 vols. Turin, 1984-91), xvii, p. 119, and cf. Franz Roth, *Nach-Expressionismus-Magischer Realismus: Probleme der neuesten europäische Malerei* (Leipzig, 1925).

9. Nevinson in the *Daily Express,* quoted Cork, *A Bitter Truth*, p. 71; Ester Coen, *Umberto Boccioni* (New York), pp. 244, 246 (text originally published in *La fiera letteraria*, 10 July 1927); John Rothenstein, *Modern English Painters* (3 vols. 1984 edn.), ii, p. 51 – first published 1956; Campbell Dodgson and C.E. Montague, *British Artists at the Front*, i, *C.R.W. Nevinson* (1918), p. 3; *Westminster Gazette*, 2 October 1916, p. 7; *Times Literary Supplement*, 5 October 1916, p. 469b: Samuel Butler's notion that machines would ultimately come to rule the human race was first published in a New Zealand paper, *The Press*, 13 June 1863, under the heading 'Darwin Amongst the Machines' and elaborated in chapters XIII to XV of his book *Erewhon* (1872).

10. *Times Literary Supplement*, p. 469d; C.R.W. Nevinson, *Paint and Prejudice* (1937), p. 110; Osbert Sitwell, 'The Modern Abraham' – dated 1917 – in *Argonaut and Juggernaut* (1919), p. 106.

11. Paul Nash *Outline: An Autobiography and Other Writings* (1949). pp. 210-11 Nash to Margaret Nash, 6 Nov. 1917 and cf. his letter to same, 6 April 1917, ibid. pp. 195-6 quoted on p. above; Wyndham Lewis, *Rude Assignment: A Narrative of My Career Up-to-Date* [1950]. p. 128.

4 Truth

1. Sven Hedin, *With the German Armies in the West* (1915), pp. 9-14, 45-6 – first published as *Från Fronten i Väster: September-November 1914* (Stockholm, 1915): Hedin, who as a young man had known Ibsen, later became an admirer and personal friend of Adolf Hitler; see also Karl Hildebrand, *Ett starkt folk* and *Donaumonarkien i krig* (both published Stockholm, 1915, and quickly translated into German); Scott D. Denham, *Visions of War: Ideologies and Images of War in German Literature Before and After the Great War* (Bern, 1992), p. 73, cf. Stefan Zweig, *The World of Yesterday* (1943), p. 178. The National Archives, FO 395/222/46969

contains the draft of the first two chapters of Nichols's projected book on the Royal Engineers: judging by the quality, he was probably advised not to continue: see A.D. Harvey, 'Robert Nichols in the Public Record Office', *PN Review*, 91 (May-June 1993), pp. 10-11; The National Archives, FO 395/221/242479/41719 and FO 395/227/241379/241379.

2. E.P. [Ezra Pound], *Hugh Selwyn Mauberley* (1920), p. 12, 'Ode pour l'élection de son sépulchre', part IV; Stéphane Audoin-Rouzeau, *Men at War, 1914-1918: National Sentiment and Trench Journalism in France during the First World War* (Providence, Rhode Island, 1992), p. 60, quoting *On progresse*, 1 April 1917; *The Dud* (11th Kings Shropshire Light Infantry), June 1916, p. 1; 'Mother in the Trenches', *The Dud* (14th Argyll and Sutherland Highlanders), November 1916, p. 21 – this and the previous item are bound together in the British Library, call mark PP 4039 wba.

3. See for example Captain Gerard Orby Sloper's account of being captured on 16 June 1915 in The National Archives, WO 339/6118, printed in A.D. Harvey, 'How I Fell Captive To The Germans', *BBC History Magazine*, February 2015, pp. 36-9, at p. 37; Michele Campana, *Perchè ho ucciso* (Florence. [1918]), p. 153, '*congeda*', dated 10 October 1918, written in hospital in Florence.

4. Wilfred Owen, *Poems* (1920), Preface; Wilfred Owen, 'Dulce Et Decorum Est'.

5. For Anton Schnack see Patrick Bridgwater, *The German Poets of the First World War* (1985), pp. 96-119; Harold Owen and John Bell eds., *Wilfred Owen: Collected Letters* (1967), p. 55 fn. 1, jotting 5 May 1918 regarding future projects; Paul O'Prey, ed., *Robert Graves: In Broken Images. Selected Correspondence* (New York, 1988), p. 113, Graves to Blunden, 2 July 1919.

6. Ernest Richards suggested as early as 1931, in the preface to his schools anthology *Tales of the Great War*, that 'the bonds of memory were suddenly loosed' in 1928; Godfrey Winn, *PQ* 17 (1947), p. 8 – Lord Beaverbrook is not actually named but his identity is sufficiently obvious from the context; Ernest Raymond, *The Story of My Days: An Autobiography, 1888-1922* (1968), pp. 132-3; Stephen Graham, *Life and Last Words of Wilfrid Ewart* (1924), pp.257-8, and The National Archives, FO 369/1837, p. 130, Mexico City Legation to Foreign Office, 15 January 1923: see also his army personal file, The National Archives, WO 339/27180; for Marinetti's diaries for 1917 and 1918 see Filippo Tommaso Marinetti, *Taccuini: 1915-1921* (Bologna, 1987) pp. 43-402: Marinetti was an artillery officer during the war; Ernst Jünger, *Feuer und Blut: einer kleiner Auschnitt aus einer grossen Schlacht* (2nd edn. Berlin 1926), Preface. The two Portuguese books referred to are Albino Forjaz de Sampaio's *A Avalanche* (1918) and the anonymous *A Sinfonia Macabra* (1920). One might also mention *Cursed Epic*, by António de Cértima (1924), which sounds better in the original Portuguese: *Epopeia Maldita*. There is a serviceable bibliography of Portuguese writing about the First World War in *Grande Enciclopédia Portuguesa e Brasiliera* (40 vols, Lisbon and Rio de Janeiro [1936-60]), vol. xviii pp. 149b-151a.

7. C.M. Grieve ['Hugh MacDiarmid'], 'A Four Years' Harvest', in *Annals of the Five Senses* (Montrose, 1923), pp. 59-121, at p. 65; Heimo Schwilk, ed., *Ernst Jünger: Leben und Werk in Bildern und Texten* [Stuttgart, 1988], p. 89; Hans-Harald Müller, *Der Krieg und die Schriftsteller: Der Kriegsroman*

der Weimarer Republik (Stuttgart, 1986), pp. 101-2; Edmund Blunden, *Undertones of War* (1982, Penguin edn), p. 7; Charles Carrington ('Charles Edmonds'), *A Subaltern's War* (1929), p. 7; J.B. Priestley, *Margin Released: A Writer's Reminiscences and Reflections* (1962), p. 89, see p. 139 for his explanation of why he did not write a war novel; Vincent Brome, *J.B. Priestley* (1988), p. 48. Priestley's army file, The National Archives WO 339/106913, suggests that he may have been less than impressive as a soldier: more than two and a half years after he enlisted he was still only a lance-corporal.

8. Rupert Hart-Davis, ed., *Siegfried Sassoon: Diaries, 1920-1922* (1981), p. 100, 7 February 1922.

9. Burke Davis, *War Bird: The Life and Times of Elliott White Springs* (Chapel Hill, North Carolina, 1987), p. 23; ibid., pp. 78-79; Elliott White Springs, *Nocturne Militaire* [1927], p. 250-51.

10. Vernon Bartlett, *Mud and Khaki: Sketches from Flanders and France* (1917), p. 11; Ernst Jünger, *In Stahlgewittern* (1920), Preface; [Cyril McNeile], *Shorty Bill* [1926], Preface, dated February 1925; T.W. White, *Guests of the Unspeakable: The Odyssey of an Australian Airman – Being a Record of Captivity and Escape in Turkey* (1928), p. 7, 'Apologia'.

11. József Lengyel, *Prenn Drifting* (1966), p. 292 – originally published as *Prenn Ferenc hányatott élete* (Budapest, 1959); V.M. Yeates, *Winged Victory* (1961 edn.), p. 6, note by Yeates written on the flyleaf of Henry Williamson's copy of the first edition; John Gibbons, *Roll On, Next War! The Common Man's Guide to Army Life* (1935), p. 3; The National Archives, AIR 1/2386/228/11/26, staff college essay by K.L. Harris: W.E. Theak in the 1931 intake was of the same opinion, cf. AIR 1/2392/228/11/185; Carrington, *A Subaltern's War*, p. 9. See also Michael Roper, 'Re-remembering the Soldier Hero: the Psychic and Social Construction of Memory in Personal Narratives of the Great War', *History Workshop Journal*, 50 (Autumn 2000), pp. 181-204.

12. Paolo Monelli, *Toes Up* (1930), p. 220 – for the original Italian text of this see pp. viii-ix of the 1928 (4th) edition of *Scarpe al sole*. Monelli's comparison of his memories of battle with the 'vain images' of silent cinema parallels Winston Churchill's account of the Battle of Omdurman, in *The River War: an Historical Account of the Conquest of the Sudan* (2 vols.1899) vol.2 p.142: 'The whole scene flickered exactly like a cinematograph picture; and, besides, I remember no sound.' This passage does not appear in the shorter 'New and Revised Edition' of 1902, which subsequently became the standard version, frequently reissued.

13. A.D Harvey, 'Hugh Kingsmill on the Western Front', *Notes and Queries*, 257, p. 413-6, at p. 415 cf. The National Archives, WO 374/31691, and F.W Harvey, *Comrades in Captivity: A Record of Life in Seven German Prison Camps* (1920, pp. 3-7. At least thirteen officers whose confidential statements regarding the circumstance of their becoming prisoners of war are preserved in The National Archives also published accounts after the war: see A.D. Harvey, 'Differing Versions: Official Accounts and Published Accounts of Being Taken Prisoner in the Great War,' *Critical Quarterly*, forthcoming.

14. Jean Norton Cru, *Témoins: essai d'analyse et de critique des souvenirs de combattants édités en français de 1915 à 1918* (Paris, 1929), pp. 559, 563, 588-93, 631 etc.; ibid., p. 592; André Bridoux, *Souvenirs du temps des*

morts (Paris, 1930), pp. 10-11; Edmund Blunden, *Undertones of War* (1982, Penguin edn.), p. 182.

15. Bridoux, *Souvenirs du temps des morts*, p. 12; 'Ex-Private X' [A. McLellan-Burrage] expressed a similar view in *War is War* (1930), p. 5; 'Ludwig Renn' (Arnold Vieth von Golssenau), *Anstösse in meinem Leben* (Berlin, 1980), p. 70.

16. For Williamson during the war see Anne Williamson, *A Patriots Progress: Henry Williamson and the First World War* (Stroud, 1998).

17. Cf. J. Galtier-Boissière and Daniel de Ferdan, *Les fusillés pour exemple*, special number of *Le crapouillot*, August 1934, based on proceedings leading to the rehabilitation of soldiers unjustly executed during the war, which Cobb cites in a 'Note' at the end of his novel.

18. Jeffrey Meyers, *Hemingway: A Biography* (1985), p. 29-31, and Michael S. Reynolds, *Hemingways's First War; The Making of Farewell to Arms* (Princeton, 1976), pp. 123-8, 134; Carlos Baker, ed., *Ernest Hemingway: Selected Letters, 1917-1961* (1985, paperback edn.), p. 12, Hemingway to his family, 21 July 1918.

19. *Times Literary Supplement*, 26 June 1930, p. 534b: in fact two frontline diaries were printed after the war with the title *A Soldier's Diary of the Great War*, one by G.A. Prideaux (Chiswick, 1918) and one by D.H. Bell (1929), and the same words appear on the sub-title of John Glubb's war diaries *Into Battle* (1978; and see also *Harry's War: the First World War Diary of Harry Drinkwater* ed. Jon Cooksey and David Griffiths (2013), cf p.253n.10 above; Robert Graves *Goodbye to All That* (1960, paperback edn,), pp. 158-9; The National Archives WO 339/42787 (Callaway's personal file); M. Hardy, *Hardy VC: An Appreciation* [1920], p. 44; and see also William Purcell, *Woodbine Willie: An Anglican Incident, Being Some Account of the Life and Times of Geoffrey Anketell Studdert Kennedy, Poet, Prophet, Seeker after Truth, 1883-1929* (1962), p. 117-19; C.E. Montague, *Disenchantment* (1922), p. 78 – pp. 66-79 of this book are a discussion of the ineffectiveness of wartime army chaplains; Captain S. McCance *History of the Royal Munster Fusiliers* (2 vols., privately printed, 1927), passim; The National Archives, WO 95/1279, war diary 2nd Battalion Royal Munster Fusiliers. VC stands of course for Victoria Cross, the most prestigious award for outstanding courage in action in the British armed services, DSO stands for Distinguished Service Order, MC for Military Cross.

20. Robert Graves, 'Postscript to *Goodbye to All That*', in *But Still It Goes On; An Accumulation* (1930), pp. 13-56, at pp. 13-14; Thomas F. Schneider, *Erich Maria Remarque: In Westen Nichts Neues, Bibliographie der Drucke* (Bramsche, 1992), pp. 6, 9, 39; Cyril Falls, *War Books: A Critical Guide* (1930), p. x; Charles Yale Harrison, *Generals Die in Bed* (1930), pp. 150-165, 187-8, 210-7, 237; Helen Zenna Smith, *Not So Quiet … Stepdaughters of War* (1987 edn.), pp. 59, 200, 229-31, and see also pp. 30-31 and 173: Helen Zenna Smith was in fact romantic novelist Evadne Price, who may have been too young to take any part in the war – the date of her birth is uncertain – and almost certainly never drove an ambulance at or near the front. See also Sassoon, *Memoirs of an Infantry Officer*, pp. 152-3, for 'David Cromlech's' (i.e. Robert Graves's) second-hand information regarding 'the ubiquity of

certain establishments in France' and his correspondence with Graves on the subject in Paul O'Prey, ed., *Robert Graves; In Broken Images, Selected Correspondence, 1914-46* (New York, 1988), pp. 201-5, Febuary-March 1930, and Charles Carrington, *Soldier from the Wars Returning* (1965), pp. 162-7. A German work inspired – or provoked – by Remarque's novel was *Im Osten Nichts Neues: Das Buch des Krieges wie es eigentlich war* (Nuremberg, 1920) by Carl A. G. Otto. Despite the title of Charles Yale Harrison's novel, it might be noted that two British lieutenant general, eight British major generals, two from Australia and one from Canada were killed in action or fatally wounded while commanding divisions on the Western Front; more than forty brigadier generals – the rank had no French or German counterpart and ceased to be designated as a general officer's grade after the war – were killed commanding brigades; Frank Davies and Graham Maddocks, *Bloody Red Tabs: General Officer Casualties of the Great War 1914-1918* (1995).

21. *Times Literary Supplement*, 18 June 1931, p. 485c-d; ibid., 25 June 1931, p. 508c. Despite being advertised in *The Times Literary Supplement* it is of course possible that *War, Wine and Women* had a different readership from, e.g., *Memoirs of an Infantry Officer*, but there is no way of establishing this, cf. A.D. Harvey *Literature into History* (Basingstoke, 1988), p. 92 foll.

22. Photographs of physical mutilations were originally published in medical treatises such as Harold Gillies's *Plastic Surgery of the Face* (1920); an example of their use as anti-war propaganda is Ernst Friedrich's *Krieg dem Kriege,* published in 1924 with German, French, English and Dutch captions. Page references are to the 1st edition of *War, Wine and Women:* subsequent printings seem to be identical.

23. E.C. Beasley's version has 'however much the surface may be raging' rather than 'however violently the surface may rage' but in other respects the two versions are identical. The unlikelihood of this being a coincidence, given the style of the original German, will be seen from a comparison with the other available English translations of *Laokoon.* Beasley's rendering was originally published in 1853.

24. *Cul-de-jatte* may be literally translated as 'basin-arse' and is a customary vulgarism in France for a legless cripple. There is of course no Honours School of Philosophy at Cambridge: only the Moral Sciences Tripos. *The Newnham College Register* (2 vols, Cambridge [1965]) suggests two possible originals for the emancipated Daphne. Gladys Todd was at Newnham 1910-1913, reading Moral Sciences and later Medieval and Modern languages: when *War, Wine and Women* was published she was buyer for *The Times'* Book Club. Marjorie Gabain read Moral Sciences at Newnham, 1911-1914, and became an actress: no details survive of her career after leaving Newnham, and this may suggest a Bohemianism that fits in with Saint-Mandé's description. Neither woman is recorded as having married; but as will be seen there are other reasons for doubting Saint-Mandé's account.

25. Wilfred Saint-Mande, *No Repentance* (London, 1935), Foreword. Note that the accent on the final 'e' of the author's name is not used in this, his last publication. Amongst the more notable First World War memoirs that were published pseudonymously are *A Subaltern's War* (1929) by Charles

Carrington, originally published under the name 'Charles Edmonds'; *Fighter Pilot* (1936) by R.J. MacLanachan, published under the name 'McScotch'; and *Flying Minnows* (1936) by Vivian Voss, published under the name 'Roger Vee'. The 1977 edition of *Flying Minnows* gives a key to the names altered in the text.

26. 'Wilfred Saint-Mandé' is identified as H.P. Lamont, 'Formerly lecturer in French in the University of Pretoria', in E.R. Seary, *A Biographical and Bibliographical Record of South African Literature* (Grahamstown, 1938), p. 33. His full name is given in Prifysgol Cymru, *The Guild of Graduates* ([Cardiff], 1975). Further information was kindly provided by Rosemarie Dillon of the Registrar's Department, University College Cardiff, in a letter of 3 August 1989. See further biographical details in A.D. Harvey "Oh, What a Literary War!" An Alternative Version', *London Magazine,* 33, no. 9 & 10 (December/January 1993-4), pp. 43-57, at pp. 51-3. His period in the RAF is deducible from an entry in a register of RAF officers in The National Archives, AIR 76/285/14, though he was never actually commissioned. Lamont may have noticed the name Saint-Mandé while on a train in the environs of Paris but he most probably took it from the location of the palace of Fouquet the financier during the reign of Louis XIV, as it is mentioned several times in a book he had almost certainly read, Alexandre Dumas's *The Man in the Iron Mask.*

27. *Times Literary Supplement,* 18 April 1929, p. 314c; Wilfred Saint-Mandé, *Halcyon Days in Africa* (1934), p. 240; Wilfred Saint-Mande, *No Repentance* (1935), foreword.

28. Charles Carrington ('Charles Edmonds'), *A Subaltern's War* (1929), p. 17.

29. For Crozier's reputation as the best brigade commander in the British army, see *The Times,* 4 September 1937, p. 12c.

30. For Haig's Order of the Day, see James E. Edmonds, *Military Operations: France and Belgium, 1918,* ii (1937), pp. 249 and 512.

31. F.P. Crozier, *A Brass Hat in no Man's Land* (1930), pp. 201, 204; The National Archives, FO 395/447/P1059: Sir Francis Lindley PC, KCMG (1872-1950) was ambassador at Lisbon 1929-31 and at Tokyo 1931-4; Fernando Augusto Branco (1880-1940), Portuguese Foreign Minister 1930-32, had commanded the Portuguese submarine flotilla during the First World War and had been naval attaché in London, 1919-24. Though Lindley's letter was dated 3 May, it was stamped on arrival at the Foreign Office only on 12 May, and both Duff's and Gallop's minutes are dated 15 May. Charles Duff (1894-1966), author of *A Handbook on Hanging* (1928) and numerous other books, had been awarded the *Medalha de Valor Militar* for his work as an interpreter with the Portuguese during the war. R.A. Gallop (1901-48) was in Lisbon as Second Secretary, 1931-5, and published editions of Portuguese folk songs.

32. The National Archives, WO 374/16997 – Crozier's army personal file: in fact it is a heavy box, and the two documents cited are in a file in the box labelled 'Br. Gen. F.P. Crozier C.B.C M.G. D.S.O. Birth Enquiry', minute dated '24.4.30' by Major General G.S. Clive and letter from Sir Clive Wigram, the King's Secretary, to Sir Herbert Creedy, Permanent Under-Secretary of State at the War Office, 30 April 1930; F.P. Crozier, *The Men I Killed* (1937), p. 49; The National Archives, FO 371/21269/W16242, and cf. *The Times,*

1 September 1937, p. 14d. Sir George Mounsey KCMG (1892-1986) was Assistant Under-Secretary of State at the Foreign Office, 1929-39. Stephen Gaselee (1882-1943) was Librarian at the Foreign Office, 1920-43: his views on James Joyce are in FO 395/209/128688 and there are no doubt other literary appraisals by him to be found elsewhere in FO 371 and FO 395. Major General Clive's minute of 24 April 1930 states that Crozier had resigned his original commission in the Manchester Regiment in June 1908 following the recurrence of a problem with bouncing cheques dating back to 1902, and after a year as an officer in the Loyal North Lancashire Regiment had to resign again for the same reason, compounded by bankruptcy; when he requested employment at the outbreak of war 'it was not discovered that this was the Captain Crozier who had to resign his commission.'

33. Crozier, *The Men I Killed,* p. 54: a GSO2 was a grade 2 general staff officer, a CRE a headquarters officer responsible for Royal Engineers: they were presumably from 40th Division HQ but The National Archives, WO 95/2597/2, war diary of the 40th Division's CRE, gives no indication that the CRE spent any part of the day driving around in a staff car: see especially Appendix II to April 1918 War Diary; The National Archives, WO 95/2601 (the war diary of 40th Battalion Machine Gun Corps – attached to 40th Division, of which Crozier's brigade formed part), WO 95/2605 (119th Infantry Brigade), WO 95/2606 (13th East Surrey and 21st Middlesex), WO 95/2607 (18th Welch). Denis Winter, *Haig's Command: A Reassessment* (1991), p.309-10, claims that what The National Archives have is for the most part not the war diaries themselves but sanitized summaries by Charles Atkinson, Director of the Historical Section of the Committee of Imperial Defence from 1915 to 1918, but the war diaries cited here are undoubtedly the originals, in some cases partly comprising jottings in blue pencil on squared sheets of paper from a note pad.

34. Imperial War Museum, Papers of David Starrett, TS entitled 'Batman', p. 112.

35. The National Archives, WO 95/2605, Crozier to Edmonds 24 September 1927, pasted into 119th Infantry Brigade war diary for April 1918. In spite of his hints about Sir John Du Cane, his corps commander, Crozier had presumably not forgotten that the Portuguese 2ª *Divisão* was part of the *neighbouring* corps, commanded by Sir Richard Haking.

36. The National Archives, WO 32/5100, report dated 6 May 1918; Crozier, *The Men I Killed,* p. 54.

37. The National Archives, WO 32/5100, report dated 6 May 1918; The National Archives, CAB 45/122, J.K. Dick Cunynghame to Edmonds, 8 July 1931; F. Haydn Hornsey, *Hell on Earth* (1930), pp. 90-91; cf. p. 16 (where he states he was in the 34th Division: The National Archives's file index of awards of campaign medals has a Frank H. Hornsey in the Suffolk Regiment, of which the 11th Battalion was in the 34th Division) and p. 100. Arthur Stephenson DSO, MC, commanding the 16th Royal Scots, which had been part of the corps reserve of Du Cane's Corps and was sent to reinforce Crozier's brigade during the course of the day, wrote to Edmonds of 'having seen them [the Portuguese] running like hares (and, incidentally, having seen them shot down like the same hares by my own men, on my orders, to try

and stop the rot)': The National Archives CAB 45/125, letter dated 4 January 1932. This too is not quite plausible as the Royal Scots only came into action hours after the Portuguese broke.

38. Manuel de Oliveira Gomes da Costa, *O corpo de exercito português na Grande Guerra: a batalha do Lys, 9 de Abril de 1918* (Porto, 1920), p. 169. The memoirs of Eugenio Mardel Ferreira, *A brigada do Minho na Flandres,* have proved impossible to track down. Mardel was complimented by the general commanding the German division that defeated him, and decorated by the Portuguese, French, Italian, Belgian and Spanish governments: but not by the British.

5 *Technique*

1. Guillaume Apollinaire, 'Merveille de la guerre', in *Oeuvres poétiques* (Paris, 1965), p. 271, originally published in *Calligrammes: poèmes de la paix et de la guerre* (Paris, 1918): Berenice's Hair is the name of a constellation near the tail of Leo; Paul Éluard, *Oeuvres complètes* (2 vols. Paris, 1968), i, p. 14, originally published in *Le devoir* (Paris, 1916); ibid., i, p. 26, 'Notre mort II', originally published in *Le devoir et l'inquiétude, poèmes suivis de Le rire d'un autre* (Paris, 1917); Apollinaire, 'Cote 146' ('Poèmes à Madeleine' version, *not* 'Poèmes à Lou' version), *Oeuvres poétiques*, p. 613; Blaise Cendrars, 'J'ai tué', *Oeuvres* (8 vols. Paris, 1960-65), iv, p. 150, dated 3 February 1918: the word 'chuintements' in Cendrars's text, here rendered as 'slurrings' refers to the pronunciation of 's' as 'sh': a more precise but less familiar English word for this is 'sigmatism'.

2. Carroll Carstairs, *A Generation Missing* (1930), pp. 88, 103; Sassoon, *Memoirs of an Infantry Officer*, p. 114; Sherard Vines, *The Dark Way* [1919], p. 141; Martin Middlebrook, *The Kaiser's Battle, 21 March 1918: The First Day of the German Spring Offensive* (1978), p. 147, quoting *Leutnant* Rudolf Hoffmann; S.W. Beeman, 'The Artillery', in Harry Golding, ed., *The Wonder Book of Soldiers for Boys and Girls* (4th edn. 1916), pp. 178-83, at p. 182, Ford Madox Ford, *A Man Could Stand Up –* (1926), p. 157; Jan Bernaerts, Hendrik Hayman, eds., *Oorlogspoëzie: verschenen in 1914 en 1915 en onuitgegeven gedichten* ([Port Villez], 1916), pp. 129-30. Adolf Hitler, a gifted mimic, impressed Ernst Hanfstengel at Christmas 1924 with his imitation of the sound of artillery at the Battle of the Somme, supplemented with the 'Tacktack' of machine guns: Ernst Hanfstaengel, *Zwischen Weissen und Braunen Haus: Memoiren eines politischen Ausserseiters* (Munich, 1970), p. 165.

3. Robert Southey, 'The Cataract of Lodore'; Isaac Rosenberg. 'Dead Man's Dump', in Ian Parsons, ed., *The Collected Works of Isaac Rosenberg* (1979), p. 109, lines 12-13; Johan De Maegt, 'De Smeden', in Bernaerts and Heyman eds., *Oorlogspoëzie*, p. 30; Nikolai Gumilev, 'Voina', in *Sobranye Sochynenyi* (4 vols., Regensburg, 1947), ii, p. 69, first published in *Kolchan* (1915); August Stramm, 'Granaten', in Stramm, *Das Werk* (Wiesbaden, 1963), p. 94, first published in *Der Sturm*, Jahrgang 6, no. 11/12 (September 1915).

4. Leo Tolstoy, *War and Peace,* x, chapter 30 (World's Classics, 1933 edn., ii, p. 506); F.T. Marinetti, *Zang Tumb Tuum: Adrianopoli Ottobre 1912: Parola in Libertà* (Milan, 1914), p. 145; Henry Williamson, *The Patriot's Progress*

(1930), pp. 97, 99-100. Neither Allyson Booth, *Postcards from the Trenches: Negotiating the Space Between Modernism and the First World War* (New York, 1996) nor Vincent Sherry, *The Great War and the Language of Modernism* (Oxford, 2004), show much awareness of the full range of modernist writing and, for instance, do not mention Henry Williamson, who was evidently not Modernist enough for their purpose. For Sherry the key modernists influenced by the war were Virginia Woolf, T.S. Eliot and Ezra Pound.

5. Robert Graves, *Goodbye to All That* (1960, Penguin edn.), p. 82; J.D. Strange, *The Price of Victory* (1930), p. 119; Cecil Lewis, *Sagittarius Rising* (1942 edn.), p. 111; Richard Aldington, *Death of a Hero* (1965 edn.), p. 296; Adams, *Nothing of Importance*, p. 28; ibid., p. 24; Ford Madox Ford, *A Man Could Stand Up*, p. 93; Hugh Dalton, *With British Guns in Italy: A Tribute to Italian Achievement* (1919), p. 241; Aldington, *Death of a Hero*, p. 276; Ford Madox Hueffer, 'Clair de Lune', in *On Heaven and Poems Written on Active Service* (1918), p. 43-4. Hueffer changed his surname to Ford in 1919.

6. J.F. Snook, *Gun Fodder* (1930), p. 221; Richard M. Ludwig ed., *Letters of Ford Madox Ford* (Princeton, 1965), p. 73, Ford Madox Hueffer (as he then was) to Joseph Conrad 6 September 1916; *The Letters of Charles Sorley: With a Chapter of Biography* (Cambridge, 1919), p. 287, Charles Sorley to Prof. W.R. Sorley, his father, 15 July 1915; Wilfrid Ewart, *Scots Guard* (1934), p. 56; Aldington, *Death of a Hero*, p. 321; Wilfred Owen, 'The Last Laugh' and 'Anthem for Doomed Youth'. See also Rolf Greifelt, *Der Slang des englischen Soldaten im Weltkrieg, 1914-1918* (Marburg, 1937), p. 12-13. By 1956, with another world war to write up, these exercises in onomatopoeia had become something of a cliché – see for example Raleigh Trevelyan, *The Fortress: a Diary of Anzio and After* (1956), p. 15.

7. Paul Lintier, *My Seventy-Five: Journal of a French Gunner (August-September 1914)* (1929) p. 55 – first published as *Ma pièce: souvenirs d'un cannonier, 1914 (avec une batterie de .75)* (Paris, 1916); Henri Barbusse, *Lettres de Henri Barbusse à sa femme, 1914-1917* (Paris, 1937), p. 47; Jean Galtier-Boissière, *En rase campagne 1914: un hiver à Souchez, 1915-1916* (Paris, 1917), pp. 42-3; André Charpentier, *Feuilles bleu horizon, 1914-1918* (Paris, 1935), p. 302; Diogo de Carmo Reis, 'Pum!', in Rogério de Almeida Russo ed. *Arquivio Poético da Grande Guerra* (Porto, [1924]), not paginated, section V; Eugene Rogan, *The Fall of the Ottomans: the Great War in the Middle East, 1914-1920* (2015), p. 77, quoting Ali Riza Eti, *Bir Onbaşının doğu cephesi günlüğü* (Istanbul, 2009); Otto Riebicke, *Ringen an der Somme und im Herzen* (Magdeburg, 1917), p. 31; J. Knight Bostock, *Some Well-Known German War Novels, 1914-1930* (Oxford, 1931), p. 16; Ludwig Renn, *Krieg* (Frankfurt, [1929]) pp. 129, 198, 216, 253, 261, 266, 289, 296; Werner Beumelburg, *Die Gruppe Bosemüller* (Oldenburg, 1930), pp. 14, 15, 103, 279: see also Adam Scharrer, *Vaterlandlose Gesellen: das erste Kriegsbuch eines Arbeiters* (Vienna, 1930), pp. 83, 94, and Thor Goote [pseudonym of Werner Schultze von Langsdorf], *Wir fahren den Tod* (Gutersloh, [1930]), pp. 246, 268, 379; Robert Musil, *Diaries 1899-1941* (New York, 1998), p.195 and, in the Greek army, Statis Myrvilis, *Life in the Tomb* (1987, originally *Hé zōē en taphō*, 1923-4), p. 130.

8. Thomas Dinesen, *No Man's Land: en Dansker med Canadierne ved Vestfronten* (Copenhagen, 1965 edn.), p. 85, cf. the English translation, *Merry Hell: A Dane with the Canadians* [1930], p. 113. The Danish text was first published in 1929. Thomas Dinesen's other books include a biography of his father, Wilhelm Dinesen, who fought in the Danish army against the Prussians and Austrians in 1864, in the French army against the Prussians in 1870 and in the Turkish army against the Russians in 1877: *Boganis. Min Fader hans slægt, hans liv og hans tid*, ([Copenhagen] 1972). Another Thomas Dinesen, a Schleswig Dane, fought in the German army on the Russian front: see Thomas Dinesen, *Pligtens Tunge Bud: en sønderjyder erindringer fra verdenskrigen, 1914-18* ([Esbjerg], 1978).

9. *Some Imagist Poets: An Anthology* (1915), pp. vi-vii (Preface by Richard Aldington); Richard Aldington, 'Concert', in *Collected Poems* (1929), p. 95.

10. For Owen's rhymes, see Dennis Welland, *Wilfred Owen: A Critical Study* (1978 edn.), pp. 104-24; Wilfred Owen 'Strange Meeting'; T.S. Eliot, introduction to 1961 paperback edition of David Jones, *In Parenthesis*, pp. vii-viii, at p. viii.

11. Valerie Eliot, ed., *Letters of T.S. Eliot, i, 1898-1922* (1988), p. 205, Eliot to Eleanor Hinkley, 31 October 1917; T.S. Eliot, 'The Metaphysical Poets', in T.S. Eliot, *Selected Essays* (1951 edn.), pp. 281-9, at pp. 287-9: first published *Times Literary Supplement*, 20 Oct. 1921, pp. 669-70. W.B Yeats also seems to have had a problem with the war poets, excluding all poems written about the war during the war itself from the anthology of contemporary verse he edited for Oxford University Press on the grounds that 'passive suffering is not a theme for poetry': *The Oxford Book of Modern Verse, 1892-1935* (Oxford, 1936) p. xxxiv.

12. Wilfred Owen, *Poems* (1920), Preface; Ewart Alan Mackintosh, 'Ghosts of War (Sent from France in October 1917)', in *War the Liberator and Other Pieces* (1918), pp. 38-39: Mackintosh won the MC in May 1916 was invalided home with septic scratches from German barbed wire – like Osbert Sitwell – but unlike Sitwell returned to the front and was killed at Cambrai in 1917, cf. The National Archives WO 374/44805 for his army personal file and WO 339/9308 for Osbert Sitwell's. Mackintosh's poem is printed here without the first and last stanzas.

13. John MacCrae's 'In Flanders Fields' was first published in *Punch*, 8 December 1915; he served as a lieutenant-colonel in the Royal Army Medical Corps, attached to the Canadian Expeditionary Force, and died of pneumonia on 28 January 1918; William Jerdan ed., *Letters from the Earl of Perth ... to his Sister, the Countess of Erroll* (1845, reprinted 1968), p. 28: the Battle of Landen, or Neerwinden, was in 1693.

14. Phillip Bainbrigge's poem was printed, apparently for the first time, in Nevil Shute, *Slide Rule* (1954), p. 29: soon after writing this poem Bainbrigge was killed in action; see also Jean Findlay, *Chasing Lost Time: the Life of C.K. Scott Moncrieff: Soldier, Spy, Translator* (2014), pp. 62-3 for Bainbrigge's gay friend. Findlay gives the poem quoted on p. 158 but follows the 1956 Readers Union edition of Shute's *Slide Rule*, p. 28 in printing 'shrieks' for 'shirks': 'shrieks' is a less interesting word, not what was printed in the original 1954 edition of *Slide Rule* or the 1968 paperback, and probably not the word Bainbrigge used.

15. Geoffrey Dearmer, 'Keats before Action', in *Poems* (1918), p. 41 – see also the sonnet 'Keats' in the same collection; untitled poem by W.S.S. Lyon in *Easter at Ypres, 1915, and Other Poems* (Glasgow, 1916), pp. 12-13: these verses are printed with the note 'Written in the trenches by "Glencorse Wood" 19-20th April 1915': Lyon, a young Edinburgh lawyer and sub-warden of the Edinburgh University Settlement, was killed less than three weeks later, cf Wilfred Owen's 'Strange Meeting'; Gilbert Frankau 'The Voice of the Guns', in *The Guns* (1916), p. 34: Frankau's army personal file in the National Archives, WO 339/11211 shows however that though in the Royal Artillery he probably never served with a battery, not having had artillery training; he was adjutant of an artillery brigade for just over a year and later took charge of British cinema propaganda in Italy; A.P. Herbert, 'Beaucourt Revisited', in *The Bomber Gipsey and Other Poems* (1918), p. 29 – originally published in *The Mudhook: Journal of the 63rd (RN) Division,* 1 September 1917; Charles Hamilton Sorley, *Marlborough and Other Poems* (Cambridge, 1922), p. 78; Parsons, ed., *Collected Works of Isaac Rosenberg,* p. 267, Rosenberg to Joseph Leftwich, 8 December 1917, and p. 198, Rosenberg to Winifreda Seaton, December 1912-January 1913, and cf. p. 102, 'In the Trenches', and p. 103, 'Break of Day in the Trenches'.

16. John Brophy and Eric Partridge, *Songs and Slang of the British Soldier, 1914-1918* (1930), p. 49, establishes the link between 'Parley-voo' and 'Der Wirthin Töchterlein'.

17. W. Somerset Maugham, *Ashenden* (1928), Preface. Maugham is about the only author whose short stories based on wartime experiences are much read today. There are at least half a dozen anthologies of First World War short stories but a recent critic has suggested that because First World War stories are 'in competition... with a plethora of other texts with a higher claim to truthfulness and authenticity' and fail to be 'what a "good" modern(ist) short story ought to be', they tend to be overlooked: Ann-Marie Einhaus, *The Short Story of the First World War* (New York, 2013), pp. 29 and 37. This seems to be merely a polite way of acknowledging that these stories are not very good.

18. Stephen Graham, *Life and Last Words of Wilfrid Ewart* (1924), p. 147; *Times Literary Supplement,* 24 November 1921, p. 769a; ibid., 5 February 1920, p. 85a-b.

19. *Cambridge Review,* 51, p. 61 (25 October 1929), review by F.R. Leavis; *Great Soviet Encyclopedia* (32 vols, New York, 1973-1983), xiii, p. 483.

20. The passage quoted is from Henry Williamson. *The Patriot's Progress* (1930), pp. 169-71. John Galsworthy, in his preface to R.H. Mottram's *The Spanish Farm* (1924), which depicts phases of the British army's sojourn in France from the point of view of a young French woman on a farm behind the lines, claimed that Mottram's book 'exhibits a new form, distinct even in this experimental epoch ... not precisely a novel ... not altogether a chronicle' (pp. ix-x), but most readers would suppose it was simply a rather loosely structured novel.

21. Thomas Mann, *Death in Venice: and Other Stories* (1998 pbk. edit.) p. xv, Introduction by David Luke; for Barbusse's war service, see *Lettres de Henri*

Barbusse à sa femme, 1914-1917, p. 22, 26 December 1914, and p. 148, 20 June 1915; Jean Vic, *La littérature de la guerre*, iii, p. 257.

22. Siegfried Sassoon, *Memoirs of a Fox-Hunting Man* (1928), p. 346; C.E. Montague, *Disenchantment* (1922), p. 35.

23. Ernst Johannsen *Four Infantrymen on the Western Front* (1930), p. 11. Later contributions to the 'group-experience' war novel were Hubert E. Gilbert's *Drei Krieger* (Oldenburg, 1934) and Erich Hoinkis's *Er und seine Kompanie* (Berlin, 1936).

24. Roland Dorgelès, *Souvenirs sur les croix de bois* (Paris 1929), pp. 25, 33-34; Erich Maria Remarque, *All Quiet on the Western Front* (1930), pp. 235, 238-9, 242, 245, 247.

25. Charles Carrington ('Charles Edmonds'), *A Subaltern's War* (1929), p. 17.

26. Wilhelm von Sternburg, *'Um Deutschland geht es uns': Arnold Zweig: die Biographie* (Berlin, 1998), p. 103.

27. Jaroslav Hašek, *The Red Commissar* (1981), p. 192, 'Introduction' by Sir Cecil Parrott to the section comprising the five pre-war Šveik stories.

6 Heroes

1. Wilfred Owen, 'Insensibility', stanza 2.

2. Ernest Raymond, *Tell England* (1953 edn.), pp. 168: first published 1922; Edwin Campion Vaughan, *Some Desperate Glory: The Diary of a Young Officer, 1917* (1981), p. 107, 1 May 1917: this diary seems to be almost too good to be true, with its painstaking account of the disengagement and general uselessness of the writer, but it is undoubtedly genuine, even though Vaughan, still aged only nineteen, was in fact sufficiently effective as an officer to be promoted acting captain a few weeks after the diary's conclusion, and was later awarded the Military Cross: see his army personal file, The National Archives, WO 374/70492; Chaz Bowyer, *Albert Ball VC* (1977), pp. 50, 54-55, 63, 83, quoting his letters home and the reminiscences of Air Vice-Marshal Stanley Vincent. 'Pill' is early twentieth-century slang for 'bore'. See above p. 262n.19 for explanation of abbreviations VC, DSO, MC.

3. John Bell, ed., *Wilfred Owen: Selected Letters* (Oxford, 1985), p.210,Owen to Susan Owen, 7 January 1917; Siegfried Sassoon, *Memoirs of a Fox-Hunting Man* (1928), p. 330; Rupert Hart-Davis, *Siegfried Sassoon: Diaries, 1920-1922* (1981), p. 30, 10 January 1921; T.E. Lawrence, *Seven Pillars of Wisdom: A Triumph* (1976, paperback edn.), pp. 8-9: first printed for private circulation 1926; Ernest Raymond, *The Story of My Days: an Autobiography, 1888-1922* (1968), pp. 180-81: the witty Irishman's tasteless joke refers of course to the fact that male homosexual practices were illegal till 1967, though two rather than five years was the normal gaol sentence. The homoeroticism of *Tell England* is in fact mainly in the part dealing with school, written 1906-7 and obviously modelled on Horace Annesley Vachell's *The Hill* (1905), in which the war that provides a kind of off-stage resolution to the novel is the Boer War. In Ernest Raymond's novel Edgar Doe, then aged thirteen, has a crush on a prefect and confesses, 'I simply love being whacked by him.' The prefect's feelings about the matter are not indicated. See also Adrian Caesar, *Taking It Like a Man: Suffering and Sexuality and the War Poets Brooke, Sassoon, Owen, Graves* (Manchester, 1993), p. 225.

4. Charles Doyle, *Richard Aldington: A Biography* (Basingstoke, 1989), pp. 1, 3, 9-11, 53, of Aldington's army personal file, The National Archives, WO 374/726; Verna Coleman, *The Last Exquisite: A Portrait of Frederic Manning* (Melbourne, 1990), p. 118, quoting Aldington to Harriet Monroe, 7 August 1914; Hans Peter Des Coudres and Horst Muhleisen, *Bibliographie der Werke Ernst Jüngers* (Stuttgart, 1985), p. 197.

5. For Lettow-Vorbeck, see his *My Reminiscences of East Africa* [1920], and Edwin P. Hoyt, *Guerilla: Colonel von Lettow-Vorbeck and Germany's East African Empire* (New York, 1981), especially p. 206; Ivo Elliott, *The Balliol College Register: Third Edition, 1900-1950* (Oxford, 1953), pp. 203, 205.

6. Robin Maugham, *Escape from the Shadows* (1972), p. 39; Hart-Davis, ed., *Siegfried Sassoon: Diaries, 1920-1922*, pp. 73,30 June 1921; [Cyril McNeile], *Bull-Dog Drummond* [1920], p. 25, and cf. p. 24; A.D. Harvey, 'Who Were the Auxiliaries?', *Historical Journal*, 35 (1992), pp. 655-9; The National Archives, WO 374/9054 (Brighten's army personal file); Sir Henry Birkin, *Full Throttle* [1932], pp. 25-6.

7. For Norwest, see *Canada in the Great War: An Authentic Account of the Military History of Canada from the Earliest Days to the Close of the War of Nations* (6 vols, Toronto, 1917-21), iii, p. 312-3: like the other leading snipers of the Canadian Expeditionary Force, Ballendine (fifty 'kills'), Philip McDonald (forty) and Riel (thirty-eight), Norwest was a Native American; Ernst Jünger *Copse 125: A Chronicle from the Trench Warfare of 1918* (1930), translation of *Das Wäldchen 125: eine Chronik aus dem Grabenkämpfen 1918* (Berlin, 1926), p. 253. Martin Pegler, in *Out of Nowhere: a History of the Military Sniper* (Oxford, 2004), p. 139 attributes 376 sniping kills on the Western Front to another native American in the Canadian Army, Francis Pegahmagabow, but it is slightly odd that Pegahmagabow's success was not known to the compilers of *Canada in the Great War*. In the Second World War according to Andy Dougan, *The Hunting of Man: a History of the Sniper* (2004), p. 235 the Russian sniper Fyodor Okhlopkov was credited with 456 'kills. During the Russo-Finnish 'Winter War' of 1939-1940 Simo Häyhä of the Finnish army is said to have killed over five hundred Soviet personnel within the space of a hundred days using a relatively short-barrelled carbine without telescopic sights, but according to some sources he disposed of up to half of his victims with a submachine gun.

8. Wilhelm von Schramm, 'Schöpferische Kritik des Krieges', in Ernst Jünger, ed., *Krieg und Krieger* (Berlin, 1930), pp. 33-49, at p. 33.

9. Jack Lindsay, *The Writing on the Wall: an Account of Pompeii in its Last Days* (1960), p. 63: Robert Knapp, *Invisible Romans: Prostitutes, outlaws, slaves, gladiators, ordinary men and women... the Romans that history forgot* (2011), p. 277 suggests that one gladiatorial contest in ten, perhaps only one in twenty, ended in a death; Stephen R. Turnbull, *The Book of the Samurai: the Warrior Class of Japan* (1982), pp. 31-3;

10. Paul Meyer, ed., *L'histoire de Guillaume le Maréchal ... poéme français* (3 vols. Paris, 1891-1901), ii, p. 305, lines 18483-85, and cf. iii, p. xl; J.W. Fortescue, *A History of the British Army* (13 vols. 1899-1930), xi, p. 129, cf. Eric Wakeham, *The Bravest Soldier: Sir Rollo Gillespie, 1766-1814. A Historical Military Sketch* (1937), passim.

11. Carl Bock, *The Head-Hunters of Borneo: A Narrative of Travel up the Mahakkam and down the Barito* (1881), pp. 216, 219; Michael J. Harner, *The Jívaro: People of the Sacred Waterfall* (1973), pp. 115-6, 183; Fortescue, *A History of the British Army*, xiii, pp. 395-6 n. 2. Christopher Hibbert ed., *The Recollections of Rifleman Harris* (1985 edit.), p. 58-9 refers to Rifleman Mayberry having killed seven men with his bayonet at Badajoz during the Peninsular War, and Rifleman Jackman having killed eleven French gunners while sniping from a fox-hole at Flushing in the same period, but recorded 'scores' if this kind are not usual for the Napoleonic War era, were little attended to by officers and were not reliably confirmed by witnesses: no-one takes notes in a bayonet charge, and in those days riflemen in fox-holes were not accompanied by observers with binoculars.

12. *Annual Register* (1803), p. 9 *; *Authentic Memoirs of George Robert Fitzgerald* (1786) and Patrick Faulkner, *The Career of George Robert Fitzgerald* (Dublin, 1893); for J.P. Curran and the O'Gorman Mahon, see the *Dictionary of National Biography* (22 vol. Oxford edition), xii. pp. 778-9 at p. 779: the new *Oxford Dictionary of National Biography* (60 vols. Oxford 2004), xxxvi, pp. 158-9 of p.159 does not mention the two notches but suggest the total number of the O'Gorman Mahon's duels may have been eighteen. For McIver, see W.D. L'Estrange, *Under Fourteen Flags: Being the Life and Adventures of Brigadier-General McIver, a Soldier of Fortune* (2 vols, 1884).

13. For Hickok's guns see Joseph G. Rosa, *They Called Him Wild Bill: The Life and Adventures of James Butler Hickok* (Norman, Oklahoma, 1974 edn.), p. 7; Robert G. McCubbin, ed., *The Life of John Wesley Hardin: As Written by Himself* (Norman, Oklahoma, 1961), pp. 13-14: Billy O'Neal, *Encyclopaedia of Western Gun Fighters* (Norman, Oklahoma, 1979), credits Hardin with killing only eleven or twelve men in nineteen shoot-outs, but conditions in the western territories of the United States in the period 1868-77 were hardly conducive to accurate and comprehensive reporting of homicide. The important point is that Hardin killed more men than most academics, even if it was not perhaps quite as many as forty-four.

14. Burton P. Turkus and Sid Feder, *Murder, Inc.* (1957, paperback edn.), p. 201; *Financial Times*, 16 August 1994, p. 16d; Robert J. Schoenberg. *Mr Capone* (1993), pp. 185-86; Turkus and Feder, *Murder. Inc.*, p. 6; *The Times*, 11 February 1994, p. 1b: McGlinchey's conviction was later quashed on appeal.

15. David Armstrong, *At Close Quarters: SOE Close Combat Pistol Instructor Colonel Hector Grant-Taylor* (2013), pp. 28-30, 104 and see also The National Archives HS 9/1446/8 and www.gutterfighting.org.

16. A French classic on the same theme was Jules Gérard, *La chasse de lion* (Paris, 1854).

17. Selous, incidentally, was commissioned in the army in 1915, was awarded the Distinguished Service Order, and was killed in action in Tanganyika on 4 January 1917, being then aged 65: see The National Archives WO 339/24672. One of a slightly younger generation who knew Selous's writings was Robert Pigot who rose to the command of a brigade by the end of the

First World War and went on to write a book entitled *Twenty-Five Years Big Game Hunting.*

18. Manfred von Richthofen, *Der rote Kampfflieger* (Berlin, 1917), p. 178; W.A. Bishop, *Winged Warfare* (New York, 1981 edn), p. 141: first published 1918: and see also, James Thomas Byford McCudden, *Five Years in the Royal Flying Corps* [1919], pp. 286, 311, 325; W.M. Fry, *Air of Battle* (1974), p. 79. There is now a wealth of evidence to suggest that Bishop's record of 72 German aircraft shot down was grossly exaggerated; see especially William Mays Fry, 'The Bishop Affair', *Cross & Cockade International Journal*, 32 no.1 (Spring 2001) pp. 38-45, and Ian Mackersey, *No Empty Chairs: the Short and Heroic Lives of the Young Aviators Who Fought and Died in the First World War* (2012), p.212 - 222. Great War fighter pilots, contrary to what Bishop implies, aimed – or were assumed to be aiming – directly at the enemy pilot, perhaps disposing first of a rear-gunner if attacking a two-seater aircraft. For this reason they used only ball ammunition, and if loaded with explosive and/or incendiary rounds for use against enemy observation balloons were warned not to fire on enemy aircraft as the use of such ammunition against people would be a violation of the Geneva Convention.

19. The National Archives, AIR 1/2392/228/11/169; *Australian Dictionary of Biography* (14 vols. so far published, Melbourne 1966–), x, p. 120-21; Cecil Lewis, *Sagittarius Rising* (1966 edn.), p. 173, 174: first published 1936.

20. Richard Meinertzhagen, *Army Diary, 1899-1926* (Edinburgh, 1960), p. 242; Alvin C. York, *Sergeant York: His Own Life Story and War Diary,* ed. Tom Skeyhill, (Garden City, 1928), p. 228.

21. A.D. Harvey, 'Revolver VCs', *Guns Review,* 32, no. 11 (November 1992) p. 858-9, and cf. Joseph Maxwell, *Hell's Bells and Mademoiselles* (Sydney, 1932), pp. xiii-xiv, Foreword by Lieutenant Colonel G.F. Murphy.

22. A.D. Harvey, 'The Hand Grenade in the First World War', *RUSI Journal,* 138, no. 1 (February 1993), pp. 44-47.

23. H.J. Cupper, *Hints on Grenade Work (Tactical)* (1917), p. 5: the author was Chief Instructor VII Corps Bombing and Trench Mortar School; 'Egyptforce', *Street Fighting: For Junior Officers* [1919], pp. 40-41; O'Moore Creagh and E.M. Humphris, *The VC and DSO: A Complete Record ... with Many Biographical and Other Details* (3 vols. 1924), i, p. 224, account by Lance-Sergeant Fred McNess of the Scots Guards of his exploits at Ginchy in September 1916.

24. John Buchan, *Mr Standfast* (1919), p. 24; *Days on the Wing: Being the War Memoirs of Major the Chevalier Willy Coppens de Houthulst* (1934), p. v, Foreword by Marshal of the Royal Air Force Sir John Salmond; Bishop, *Winged Warfare,* p. 248; Johannes Werner, *Knight of Germany: Oswald Boelcke, German Ace* (1933), p. 164. I have substituted my own, more literal rendering of the German verses, as given in Johannes Werner, *Boelcke der Mensch, der Flieger, der Führer der deutschen Jagdfliegerei* (Leipzig, 1932), p. 151, for Claud W. Sykes's rhyming version in the English edition of 1933.

25. Robert Wohl, *A Passion for Wings: Aviation and the Western Imagination, 1908-1918* (New Haven, 1994), pp. 233-5; Philippe Ochsé, *Les avions de Guynemer* (Rennes, [1985]), p. 24. The statue to Albert Ball was erected in the grounds of Nottingham Castle.

26. Christopher Shores, Norman Franks, Russell Guest, *Above the Trenches: A Complete Record of the Fighter Aces and Units of the British Empire Air Forces, 1915-1920* (1990), pp. 106 (W.G. Claxton), 115 (Raymond Collishaw), 368 (J.L. Trollope), 390 (H.W. Woollett); René Fonck, *Mes combats* (Paris, [1920]), pp. 231-46.

27. Werner, *Knight of Germany*, p. 212; A.D. Harvey, *Collision of Empires: Britain in Three World Wars, 1793-1945* (1992), p. 388-89; *Hansard: House of Commons*, 98, col, 1247, 29 October 1917; The National Archives, AIR 1/1589/204/82/74; Bruce Robertson, ed., *Air Aces of the 1914-18 War* (Letchworth, 1959), p. 29, photo caption: Frigyes Hefty, a Hungarian pilot flying on the Italian Front in the same period, is known to have scratched details of his victories on the windscreen of his Albatros D.III: see photo in Martin O'Connor, *Air-Aces of the Austro-Hungarian Empire, 1914-1918* (Mesa, 1986), p. 180: one notes however that Lieutenant Commander Max Horton flew a Jolly Roger with a bar for each German ship sunk when entering harbour in his submarine as early as the winter of 1914-15: Richard Compton Hall, *The Underwater War, 1939-45* (Poole, 1982), p. 62. Incidentally only some of Richthofen's planes were painted red all over: see Alex Imrie, *The Fokker Triplane* (1992), p. 79. There is also a possibility that the Nieuport Jean Navarre flew at Verdun was not painted red all over but red, white and blue: A.D. Harvey, 'Why Was the Red Baron's Fokker Painted Red? Decoding the way Aeroplanes were Painted in the First World War', *War in History*, 8 (2001), pp. 323-40, at p, 334.

28. For the snide remark about Lumsden dancing about in No Man's Land see H.M. Davson, *Memoirs of the Great War* (Aldershot, 1964), p. 76: Davson, though claiming to have been frequently recommended for awards, only received the DSO once. Proportionately fewer medals were awarded in the British army to Other Ranks than to officers: in the 1914-18 war 9002 officers received the Distinguished Service Order (counting first awards only) and 37,104 the Military Cross but though in the front line there were about thirty Other Ranks for every officer, only 24,620 Distinguished Conduct Medals and 115,589 Military Medals were awarded to Other Ranks; 472 first bars to the DCM were awarded as compared to 708 first bars to the DSO: P.E. Abbott, J.M.A. Tamplin, *British Gallantry Awards* (1981) pp. 82, 126, 220, 226. The DCM was regarded as 'the best all-round medal of the Army': Tom Bridges *Alarms and Excursions: Reminiscences of a Soldier* (1938), p. 155. Mannock was awarded the VC, DSO and two bars, MC and bar, Barker the VC, DSO and bar MC and two bars, and McCudden (promoted from the ranks) the VC, DSO and bar, MC and bar and MM; seven other pilots received five British gallantry awards: apart from Lumsden, who was killed in action, and Coltman, the only members of the British ground forces to be decorated five times were Lord Gort, VC, DSO and two bars, MC, Frank Naden DSO and two bars, MC and bar, James Frederick Plunkett, DSO and two bars, MC, DCM, William Biddle, MC, DCM and bar, MM and bar, and Stephen Forbes DCM and bar, MM and two bars, though of course ground troops vastly outnumbered aviators. In Italy, Luigi Rizzo was awarded two gold and four silver medals for military valour, as compared to their top air ace Franco Baracca's one gold and three silver medals. Rizzo's feats included

the sinking of *two* Austro-Hungarian battleships, the pre-dreadnought *Wien* and the more modern *Szent István.*

29. In October 1940, an Italian submarine named after Enrico Toti sank the British submarine *HMS Rainbow* in a gun battle on the surface – the only instance of an Italian submarine sinking a British one.

30. *Leamington and District Morning News,* 22 December 1977, p. 1b-e: obituary of Henry Tandey VC; David Johnson, *The Man Who Didn't Shoot Hitler: The Story of Henry Tandey VC and Adolf Hitler, 1918* (Stroud, 2014), p.110; *Burton Observer and Chronicle,* 4 July 1974, p. 3c-f: obituary of W.H. Coltman VC; Sir Ian Hamilton, 'The End of War', *Life and Letters,* 3 (November 1929), p. 403; Wilfred Saint-Mandé, *The Devouring Flame* (1935), Author's Foreword.

31. 'Broken Soldiers', *Eugenics Review,* 7 (October 1915), p. 202, quoted in Seth Koven, 'Remembering and Dismemberment: Crippled Children, Wounded Soldiers and the Great War in Britain', *American Historical Review,* 99 (1994), pp. 1167-1202, at p. 1189.

7   Lessons

1. Walter Flex, *Der Wanderer zwischen beiden Welten* (Munich, 1924 edn.), p. 12; ibid., p. 100 (Afterword by Martin Flex); ibid., p. 36.

2. Ernst Jünger, *The Storm of Steel: From the Diary of a German Storm-Troop Officer on the Western Front* (1929), p. 1. The 'ideals of '70' refers to the ideals supposedly involved in German unification and the establishment of the Empire in the aftermath of the Franco-Prussian (or more accurately Franco-German) War of 1870.

3. Jünger, *Storm of Steel,* pp. 109-10; Otto Riebicke *Ringen an der Somme und im Herzen* (Magdeburg, 1917), p. 27; Jünger, *Storm of Steel,* p. 109; Riebicke, *Ringen an der Somme,* p. 136. Some of the not-so hidden agendas of Jünger's writings about the war are analysed in Bernd Weisbrod, 'Military Violence and Male Fundamentalism in Ernst Jünger's Contribution to the Conservative Revolution', *History Workshop Journal* no. 49 (Spring 2000), pp. 69-94. The literal meaning of Jünger's title *In Stahlgewittern,* incidentally, is not 'The Storm of Steel' but 'In Steel-Storms'.

4. E.P. [Ezra Pound], *Hugh Selwyn Mauberley* (1920), p. 13, 'Ode pour l'élection de son sépulchre', part V; Jünger, *Storm of Steel,* pp.316-7. I have altered the last word, given as *resolve* in the 1929 translation: the German is 'Und jeder der Unzähligen, die wir auf unserem Sturmgänge verloren, ist nicht umsonst gefallen, er hat seinen Sinn erfüllt.' *Sinn* means 'sense', 'meaning', 'significance', 'tendency' – something more intrinsic, instinctive and innate, less self-conscious than 'resolve'.

5. Ralf Georg Reuth, ed., *Joseph Goebbels: Tagebücher, 1924-1945* (5 vols. Munich 1992), i, p. 221, 13 January 1926. The 63-67,000th copies of the Zurich edition of *Das Feuer* (i.e. *Le feu*) were printed in 1929 and the 68-82,000th in 1930. The 22-25,000th copies of *In Stahlgewittern* were printed in 1927, the 116-125,000th in 1935.

6. Werner Beumelburg, *Sperrfeuer um Deutschland,* (Oldenburg, 1929), Vorwort; Erwin Zindler, *Auf Biegen und Brechen* (Leipzig, 1929), p. 256; Ulrich Sander, *Das feldgraue Herz* (Jena, 1934), p. 12; Franz Schauwecker, *Aufbruch der Nation* (Berlin, 1930), p. 410. Two excellent books on the

Weimar Republic are Theo Balderston, *The Origin and Course of the German Economic Crisis: November 1923 to November 1932* (Berlin, 1993); and Richard Bessel, *Germany after the First World War* (Oxford, 1993).

7. Herbert Cysarz, *Zur Geistesgeschichte des Weltkriegs: die Dichterischen Wandlungen des deutschen Kriegsbilds, 1910-1930* (Halle, 1931) p. 84n.; for the confiscation of Zweig's manuscript see W.K. Pfeiler, *War and the German Mind: The Testimony of Men of Fiction at the Front* (New York, 1941), p. 137. Another war book that seems to have been officially sponsored was Hans Zöberlein's *Der Glaube an Deutschland* ('Belief in Germany,') first published in 1931 in an 890-page edition, with a resounding preface by Adolf Hitler: by 1943 it was in its forty-third edition, and there had also been four editions of an abridged version, presumably for children. After the war Zöberlein, an *SA-Brigadeführer* and leader of the *Freikorps* Adolf Hitler, was sentenced to death for organizing the summary execution of eight 'disloyal' Germans at Penzberg, and served ten years in prison. The publishing history of *Reichsminister* Dr Joseph Goebbels's novel *Michael: ein deutsches Schicksal* illustrates the commercial advantage enjoyed by literary works that were seen to be in tune with the regime. It was first published in 1929, and had a second edition in 1931, both editions comprising issues in two formats, one of 158 pages, the other of 243. That would probably have satisfied ordinary demand: but in the ten years that followed Goebbels's appointment as propaganda minister there were *fifteen* more editions.

8. Heinz Grothe, *Das Fronterlebnis: eine Analyse, gestaltet aus dem Nachleben* (Berlin, 1932), p. 32; Herbert Weyand, *Der Englische Kriegsroman (Strukturprobleme)* (Bonn, 1933), p. 42; ibid., p. 18-19; Hermann Pongs, *Krieg als Volksschicksal im deutsche Schrifttum* (Stuttgart, 1934), p. 25; Walther Linden, 'Volkhafte Dichtung von Weltkrieg und Nachkriegszeit', *Zeitschrift für Deutschkunde, Jahrgang* 48 (1934), p. 1-22, at pp. 3, 9; ibid., pp. 6-7; ibid., pp. 19-20.

9. Ernst Volkmann, *Deutsche Dichtung im Weltkrieg. 1914-1918* (Leipzig, 1934), p. 25, cf *Führertum und Geführte* (Leader and Led) in Kurt Hesse's proto-Nazi *Der Feldherr Psychologos: ein Suche nach dem Führer der deutschen Zukunft* (Berlin, 1922), p. 192. Weyand, *Der Englische Kriegsroman* p. 42 uses Führer and Geführte as a sub-heading but does not elaborate.

10. Pongs, *Krieg als Volksschicksal*, p. 27.

11. For the word *duce*, see *Enciclopedia italiana di scienze, lettere ed arti* (35 vol:. Milan, 1929-37), xiii, p. 247; for Udet see report reproduced between p. 104 and p. 105 of his *Mein Fliegerleben* (Berlin, 1935): *Oberlt d. R.* means senior lieutenant of the Reserve. For Hitler's First World War career – mostly behind the firing line – see Thomas Weber, *Hitler's First World War: Adolf Hitler, the Men of the List Regiment, and the First World War* (Oxford, 2010), p.95-6, 99-100 and The National Archives WO 208/4475, MI3b report date-stamped 20 January 1936.

12. Fritz Baur, *Vom Sterben ..., 1914-1918* (Vienna, 1930), p. 60; Erhard Wittek *Durchbruch anno achtzehn* (Stuttgart. [1935]), pp. 189-90, end note; Otto Paust, *Volk im Feuer* (Dresden, 1935), p. 31; ibid., p. 39; ibid., p. 153. One of the peculiarities of English is that we use a relatively bland term, 'the country,' 'my country' where our neighbours use a much more evocative,

resonant word, *la patrie, la patria, das Vaterland* – though to be fair they don't use these words very often in normal conversation.

13. Sigmund Graff, *Unvergesslicher Krieg: ein Buch vom deutschen Schicksal* (Leipzig, 1936), pp. 125-26; Jürgen Hahn-Butry, *Die Mannschaft: Frontsoldaten erzählen vom Front-Alltag* (4 vols. Berlin, 1936-38), i, p. 7.

14. Günther Lutz. *Die Front-Gemeinschaft: das Gemeinschaftserlebnis in der Kriegsliteratur* (Greifswald, 1936), section 3 and also p. 54; ibid., p. 90; ibid., p. 92. See Weber, *Hitler's First World War*, p.290-6 for the central role in Nazi propaganda of Hitler's career (or alleged career) as a *Frontsoldat*.

15. Lutz, *Front-Gemeinschaft*, pp. 62-63; ibid., p. 64; *Dichtung und Volkstum*, 39 (1938), pp.247-9. Another academic treatise was *Der Soldat in der deutschen Dichtung* (Stuttgart 1938) by Arno Mulot, 'Dozent an der Hochschule für Lehrerbildung in Darmstadt'. Mulot's *Die deutsche Dichtung unserer Zeit (*2nd enlarged edition Stuttgart 1944*)* includes chapters headed 'Der Frontsoldat als Führer und Kamerad' and 'Frontsoldatentum und Volksschicksal.' By 1944 Mulot had been serving on the Eastern Front for more than two years.

16. Till Kalkschmidt, *Der deutsche Frontsoldat; Mythos und Gestalt* (Berlin, 1938), pp. 48-49; Ernst Jünger, *Copse 125: A Chronicle from the Trench Warfare of 1918* (1930). pp. 20-21 – originally published as *Das Wäldchen 125: eine Chronik aus dem Grabenkämpfen, 1918* (Berlin, 1925); Jünger, *Storm of Steel*, p. xii; Joseph Goebbels, *Michael: ein deutsches Schicksal* (168-page edition Munich 1929), p. 41. The distinction between the comradeliness of Beumelburg and the leaderishness of Jünger is somewhat spurious. Jünger does not become a company commander till halfway through the war; Beumelburg's protagonist Bosemüller is a corporal commanding a squad or section (*Gruppe*), promoted to sergeant (*Vizefeldwebel*) at the end of the book so that, though not commissioned, he is also a leader of other men.

17. Günther Lutz, 'Europas Kriegserlebnis: ein Überblick über das ausserdeutsche Kriegsschrifttum', *Dichtung und Volkstum*, 38 (1938), pp. 133-68, at pp. 141-5; ibid., pp. 148-151; ibid., pp. 161-2. The Italian authors he cited were Mussolini, the Fascist intellectual Marciapati and Gino Cornali, author of the insipid frontline memoir *Un fante lassù*: the appropriateness of the last two authors was demonstrated by the fact that their war books had been translated into German since Hitler's accession to power.

18. Emilio Lussu, *Un anno sull'Altipiano* (Paris, 1938), Preface (dated from a Swiss sanatorium, April 1937: Lussu had contracted a lung complaint in one of Mussolini's gaols); Francesco Formigari, *La letteratura della guerra in Italia, 1915-1935* (Rome, 1935), p. 51: this book was published by the Istituto Nazionale Fascista di Cultura; Michele Campana, *Perchè ho ucciso?* (Florence, [1918]), p. 137; Enrico Corradini, 'Commemorazione' [18 December 1918], in Gualtiero Castellini, *Tre anni di guerra* (Milan, 1919), p. xviii: the word translated here as 'race' is *stirpe*, which has the sense of lineage or stock. Lucio Valent, 'Experience, Images and Political Reflections on the First World War in Italian Interwar Literature,' *History* vol.102 (2017), pp.92-110, which deals mainly with writing published before

1922,refers pp.109-110 to the Fascist regime 'downgrading' the significance of the war: it was after all a war only recently won by the regime which Mussolini had overthrown.

19. Michael Moynihan, ed., *A Place Called Armageddon: Letters from the Great War* (1975), p. 128, letter by Lieutenant Robert Charles Case, July 1916; Cyril McNeile, *Sapper's War Stories: Collected in One Volume* [1930], p. 10, Foreword: cf. A.D. Harvey, *Collision of Empires: Britain in Three World Wars, 1793-1945* (1992), p. 633.

20. Henri Barbusse, *Under Fire* (1917), p. 16.

21. Patrick MacGill, *Red Horizon* (1916), pp. 86-87; The National Archives, FO 395/222/46969, draft by Robert Nichols; Liam O'Flaherty, *Return of the Brute* (1929), pp. 47-53; John W Thomason Jr., *Fix Bayonets! With the US Marine Corps in France, 1917-1918* (1925). pp. ix-x.

22. *Fernand Léger, 1881-1955* (Catalogue of Exhibition at Palais de Beaux-Arts, Brussels October-November 1956), p. 30; Stephane Audoin-Rouzeau, *Men at War, 1914-1918; National Sentiment and Trench Journalism in France during the First World War* (Providence, Rhode Island, 1992), p. 49, quoting *L'horizon,* November 1917.

23. Richard Aldington, *Death of a Hero* (1965 edn.), p. 253; Frederic Manning, *Her Privates We* (1930), p. 203.

24. Thomas Dinesen, *Merry Hell! A Dane with the Canadians* (1930), pp.238-9: the jeer 'Here you are, Fritzie boy, damn you!' isn't in the Danish text; ibid., p. 216; Thomas Dinesen, *No Man's Land; en Dansker med Canadierne ved Vestfronten* (Copenhagen, 1965 edn), pp. 160-61. Dinesen explained *(Merry Hell!,* pp. 13-14) that he attempted to enter France and Britain to enlist and finally went to Canada to join up not out of 'hatred of the Prussians ... enthusiasm for the cause of Liberty in danger; nor indignation at the sight of justice outraged ... [but because] Everything at home seemed insufferably void, trivial and insignificant: Ypres, Gallipoli, Verdun; those were the names that stood for life and reality!' Other gung-ho writers in the armies of the British Empire include A.O. Pollard VC, MC and Bar, DCM, author of *Memoirs of a Fire-Eater* (1932), and Joseph Maxwell VC, MC and Bar, DCM, author of *Hell's Bells and Mademoiselles.* For other Danish volunteers see J. Ravn-Jonsen, ed., *Danske Frivillige I Verdenskrigen: Soldaterbreve fra Fronterne* (Copenhagen, [1917]).

25. Jünger, *Copse 125,* p. ix; ibid., p. 3.

26. Jünger, *Storm of Steel* (1930 edn.), p. vi; Richard Devonald-Lewis, ed., *From the Somme to the Armistice; The Memoirs of Captain Stormont Gibbs MC* (1986), p. 68; Llewelyn Wyn Griffith, *Up to Mametz* (1931), pp. 149-50. After the war Stormont Gibbs ran a preparatory school. A rather different type of school-master, an officer who was indeed one of the war's real heroes, rising from lieutenant to acting lieutenant colonel in two years and winning the Victoria Cross, is depicted in Thomas Hope Floyd, *At Ypres with Best-Dunkley* (1920). George Brighten, the future Stock Exchange shyster, also features in this book – as the intimidating Best-Dunkley's agreeable second-in-command. As for Gibbs's remark about athletes, former public-school boy Arnold Strode Jackson, awarded the Distinguished Service Order four times, had won the 1500 metres in the 1912 Stockholm Olympics

while still an undergraduate at Oxford. Cambridge blues who distinguished themselves on the Western Front included the Rev. Bernard Vann, VC, MC and bar and John Brenchley Rosher DSO and bar, MC, both of whom, like Strode Jackson, rose to command battalions.

27. Georges Duhamel, *Vie des martyres* (1966 edn), pp. 187-8 first published 1917; Pierre Drieu la Rochelle, 'Chante de guerre des hommes d'aujourd'hui', in *Interrogation: poèmes* (Paris, 1917), pp. 169-71.

28. For Mannock as a public speaker, see Ira Jones, *King of Air Fighters; Biography of Major 'Mick' Mannock VC, DSO, MC* (1934), pp. 101-2, 160, 165, 203, 205. For an amplification of some of the ideas in this paragraph see A.D. Harvey, *Literature into History* (Basingstoke, 1988), pp. 69, 76-84.

29. Recently published Turkish memoirs and diaries of the First World War include Emin Çöl, *Çanakkale-Sina Savaşları: Bir Erin Anıları* (Istanbul, 2000), Abidin Ege, *Harp Günlükleri* (Istanbul, 2010), Ali Riza Eti, *Bir Onbaşının doğu cephesi günlüğü* (Istanbul, 2009), I. Hakki Sunata, *Gelibolu'dan kafkaslara: Birinci Dünya Savaşı anılarım* (Istanbul, 2003) and İsmet Üzen *I. Dünya Harbinde Sina Cephesi ve Çöl Hatıraları* (Istanbul, 2007). Mehmet Fasih, *Kanlısırt günlüğü: Mehmet Fasıh Bey'in Çannakale anıları* (Istanbul, 1997) has appeared in English translation as *Gallipoli 1915: Bloody Ridge (Lone Pine) Diary of Lt. Mehmet Fasih* ed. Hasan Basri Danışman (Istanbul, 2001). For Kraus's exemption from military service, see Heinrich Fischer, Michael Lazarus, eds., *Karl Kraus: Briefe an Sidonie Nadherny von Borutin, 1913-1936* (2 vols, Munich 1974), i, p. 204, letter 302, 24 September 1915, and ii, p. 161 and 175, notes to letters 235 and 290. For Wittlin see Walter Jens, ed., *Kindlers Neues Literatur Lexikon* (20 vols, Munich, 1988-92), xvii, p, 765; *Österreich-Ungarns letzer Krieg, 1914-18* (5 vols. only, published Vienna 1930-34), i, p. v, 'Zum Geleite'.

30. Another Hungarian novel about the First World War – published in Russian translation in 1937 but in Hungarian not till 1947 – was *Doberdo* by Máté Zalka (real name Béla Frankl, but best known, in the final stages of his career, as General Lukács). *Doberdo* describes how an enthusiastic, politically liberal officer in a Hungarian unit is converted to communism and pacifism by his experiences on the Italian front. Frankl, having been taken prisoner by the Russians, distinguished himself as a Red Army officer in the Crimea during the Russian Civil War, served in the *Cheka* and was killed in action, aged forty-one, while commanding the XIIth International Brigade in Spain in 1937; Vieth von Golssenau ('Ludwig Renn') commanded a battalion under him. Lajos Zilahy also published *A szökevény* (Budapest, 1930 translated as *The Deserter*, 1932) in which the protagonist deserts at the battle of Piave. Amongst other novels about camp life in Siberia by Austro-Hungarian prisoners of war perhaps the most notable is *Prameny* ('Rivulets') (1934), by the Czech writer Jaroslav Kratochvíl, who died in a German concentration camp in 1945.

31. For Radnóti see Introduction note 4.

32. For fatalities amongst Hungarian-speaking combatants see Wilhelm Winkler, *Die Totenverluste der ost.-ung. Monarchie nach Nationalitäten* (Vienna, 1919), p. 16: my calculation is from figures quoted of 47.5 and 46.1 per thousand of total population. Most of the memoirs of captivity of British Prisoners of War are included in the bibliography of John Lewis-Stempel, *The*

War Behind the Wire: the Life, Death and Glory of British Prisoners of War 1914-18 (2014).

33. Marlis G. Steinert, *Hitlers Krieg und die Deutschen; Stimmung und Haltung der deutschen Bevölkerung im zweiten Weltkrieg* (Dusseldorf, 1970), pp. 91foll.; Arthur Bryant, *The Turn of the Tide, 1939-1943: A Study Based on the Diaries and Autobiographical Notes of Field Marshal the Viscount Alanbrooke* (1957), p. 71: though printed with parts of Brooke's diary for 5 November 1939 the passage quoted was in fact written after the Second World War, and does not appear in his diary entry for 5 November 1939 in the definitive edition of his *War Diaries: 1939-1945* edited by Alex Danchev and Dan Todman (Berkeley, 2001); R.H.S. Stolfi, 'Equipment for Victory in France in 1940', *History*, 55 (1970), pp. 1-20; A.D. Harvey, 'The French Armée de l'Air in May-June 1940: A Failure of Conception', *Journal of Contemporary History*, 25 (1990), pp. 447-65; MacGregor Knox, *Mussolini Unleashed, 1939-1941: Politics and Strategy in Fascist Italy's Last War* (Cambridge, 1982), especially pp. 232-72, and Stephen Harvey, 'The Italian War Effort and the Strategic Bombing of Italy', *History*, 70 (1985), pp. 32-45

34. See A.D Harvey, *A Muse of Fire* (1998), pp. 285-90 for the influence of the literature on the First World War on the literature of the Second World War.

Conclusion

1. 'Shakespeare our Contemporary' is of course the title of the English translation of Jan Kott's *Szekspir Współczesny* first published in English in 1964, in Polish 1965, which does in fact work rather well as a reading of a classic text in the light of current preoccupations.

2. For more of my ideas on this theme see 'Connections not Causes', *Critical Quarterly*, 52, no.3 (October 2010), pp.47-54 and for my suggestions regarding the possibility of a scientific history, 'Can History be a Science?', *Oxford Magazine*, no.237 (Ninth Week, Trinity Term 2005), pp.7-10.

3. *Parliamentary Debates* n.s.7 col.1663, 16 July 1822, speech by the Earl of Liverpool, prime minister 1812-27. While this book was being prepared for press an English translation of a monograph by the Belgian poet-professor Geert Buelens was published under the title *Everything to Nothing: the Poetry of the Great War, Revolution and the Transformation of Europe*, proclaiming the transformational effect of the First World War, with poetry again having a key role: the question of *how* poetry transforms and, if it transforms anything, *what* specifically it transforms is not explored.

4. The quotation is from Siegfried Sassoon, *Memoirs of an Infantry Officer* (1930), p. 216-7.

INDEX OF NAMES